THIS INSCRUTABLE ENGLISHMAN

'A story full of romance and violence, trust and deceit. By looking at the historical record from both sides, the authors give readers a wonderfully human view of people caught in an earnest and deadly political game.'

Professor Richard Bailey, University of Michigan

'At once a work of art which, while showing the authors' astonishing literary powers, courage and independent judgement, retains the accuracy of a genuine historical work, and one of the supreme examples of the art of biography, combining entertainment with instruction in the most natural manner.'

Professor Lorna Dewaraja, formerly of the University of Ceylon

'The real strength of the book lies in its depth of sympathy with both the character of D'Oyly and his complex position within his own society and within the colonized society with which he interacted. The account is detailed but never loses sight of the bigger picture, that is of the ideologies underlying the positions adopted by individuals.'

Professor Gareth Griffiths, University of Western Australia

'A most accomplished work in the demanding and difficult genre of biography. Bringing together the disparate worlds of nineteenth-century Britain and Sri Lanka through the personality and career of their enigmatic subject, the authors join the ranks of the best in this field: Robert Blake, Roy Jenkins, Anthony Howard and Michael Holroyd.'

Professor A. J. Wilson,
formerly of the University of New Brunswick

Lengthy discussions with the principal chiefs

'John D'Oyly, Ehelepola Adikaram, and the Adigars Molligoda and Kapuwatte in conference'. The only extant portrait of John D'Oyly, reproduced from Brendon Gooneratne, *From Governor's Residence to President's House* (1981), p. 16.

THIS INSCRUTABLE ENGLISHMAN

Sir John D'Oyly, Baronet, 1774–1824

Brendon Gooneratne and
Yasmine Gooneratne

CASSELL
London and New York

Dedicated to

Channa and Devika

joyful results of an earlier collaboration

CASSELL

Wellington House, 125 Strand, London WC2R 0BB, England
370 Lexington Avenue, New York, NY 10017–6550

First published 1999

British Library Cataloguing-in-Publication Data

A catalogue record for this book is available from the British Library.
ISBN   0 304 70094 0 Hardback
0 304 70095 9 Paperback

Library of Congress Cataloging-in-Publication Data

Gooneratne, Brendon.
This inscrutable Englishman: Sir John D'Oyly, Baronet, 1774–1824
/Brendon Wilhelm Gooneratne; Yasmine Gooneratne.
p. cm.
Includes bibliographical references and index.
ISBN   0 304 70094 0 (hardcover).—ISBN   0 304 70095 9 (pbk.)
1. D'Oyly, John, Sir, 1774–1824.   2. Great Britain—Foreign relations—
1800–1837.   3. Colonial administrators—Sri Lanka—Biography.
4. Great Britain—Foreign relations—Sri Lanka.   5. Sri Lanka— Foreign
relations—Great Britain   6. Diplomats—Great Britain— Biography.
7. Kandy (Sri Lanka)— History
I. Gooneratne, Yasmine, 1935–   II. Title.
DA506.D69G66   1999
941.07'3'092—dc21
[B]   99–10212 CIP

Designed and typeset by Ben Cracknell Studios
Printed and bound in Great Britain by Biddles Ltd, Guildford and King's Lynn

CONTENTS

CONTENTS

PLATES

FIGURES

ACKNOWLEDGEMENTS

We would like to express our obligations to the Rockefeller Foundation, the Australian Research Council, and Macquarie University, who financed the far-flung research that provided the basis for this book.

Among the institutions, and among colleagues and friends who encouraged and assisted us in our search for the elusive Mr D'Oyly, we owe special thanks to Diana Kurkjiaan, who helped trace the location of the D'Oyly family papers; Roger Davey, County Archivist of the East Sussex County Council; the East Sussex Record Office, Lewes; the European Parliament UK Office, London; Mrs J. Goddard, of the Sussex Family History Society; the Lewes Town Council; Mr Peter Norman of the Suffolk Family History Society; Mrs P. Webb of the Eastbourne & District Family History Society; the State Library of New South Wales, Sydney; and the Mitchell Library, Sydney.

To Lakshmi de Silva, for her translations of the verses of Dona Isabella Cornelia Perumal (Gajaman Nona), and her personal interest in tracking their linguistic strengths and subtleties; Dr J.J. Nicholls, for his translation of John D'Oyly's 'Commercii Laus'; Peter Roberts, who shared with us his interest and researches into the life and career of Brian Houghton Hodgson; R.J. (Julian) Roberts, Deputy Librarian and Paul Hamlyn Keeper of Printed Books at the Bodleian Library, Oxford; Mohini Pandita-Gunewardene, for assistance with source material on Gajaman Nona; Mr L.S.J. Medis, for information supplied regarding the poet's ancestry and her descendants; Pauline Gunawardena and Lakshman Marasinghe who discussed with us possible interpretations of Gajaman's relationship with John D'Oyly; Captain Elmo Jayawardene, who shared his researches on Ehelepola Maha Nilame; Jim Potts of the British Council, Sydney, who assisted in tracing information on D'Oyly's family; Marea Mitchell and Vivien Wilson, who helped us explore D'Oyly's Sussex background; and Sonia Hall, Jamie Scott and Anthony Vanderwall, who provided several and diverse readings of John D'Oyly's motto, *Omni Solum Forti Patria*. To Devika Brendon and Richard Bailey, for editorial suggestions; Lorna Dewaraja, Gareth Griffiths, A. Jeyaratnam Wilson and Denis Wright for suggestions relating to both style and content; Rosemary Dermody and David Fitzpatrick, who share our interest in the cultural history of the British Raj; Effy Alexakis, Nemone Boteju, Mr Decker of 'Studio Times', and the late Mr Gunamuni Godamunne of Kandy, for assistance with the illustrations; and Janet Joyce, Director (Academic) at Cassell, whose interest in our research has been a constant source of encouragement and support throughout the preparation of this book.

B.G.
Y.G.

ABBREVIATIONS

Writings of John D'Oyly and his Family

D'Oyly, CD	Cambridge Diary. Diary kept by John D'Oyly as a student of Bene't College, Cambridge University, 1792–1796, as extracted in the Introduction to P.E. Pieris (ed.) *Letters to Ceylon 1814–1824*, Cambridge 1938, pp. 1–13.
D'Oyly, CL	John D'Oyly, 'Commercii Laus', Latin ode, awarded the Sir William Browne's Medal at Cambridge University in 1795. Published as Appendix 2 of this book, with an English translation by Professor J.J. Nicholls.
D'Oyly, Constitution	John D'Oyly, *A Sketch of the Constitution of the Kandyan Kingdom* (1832) and other relevant papers, collated under the orders of government, ed. L.J.B. Turner, 1929; second edition ed. S.D. Saparamadu, Tisara Prakasakayo, Dehiwela 1975.
D'Oyly, Family Letters	George, Henry, Mary and Thomas D'Oyly. Letters written from England to John D'Oyly, as printed in P.E. Pieris (ed.) *Letters to Ceylon 1814–1824*, Cambridge 1938.
D'Oyly, SKP	John D'Oyly, 'Official Declaration of the Settlement of the Kandyan Provinces', dated Kandy, 3 March 1815, contained in an Official Bulletin issued from British Headquarters, Kandy, 2 March 1815, signed by James Sutherland, Deputy Secretary 'By His Excellency (Robert Brownrigg)'s command', published as Appendix 1 in John Davy, *Account of the Interior of Ceylon* (1821), 1969, pp. 369–75
D'Oyly, SLD	H.W. Codrington (ed.) *Diary of Sir John D'Oyly, First Commissioner of the British Government in the Kandyan Provinces (1810–1815)*, Colombo 1917.

Writings of Dona Isabella Cornelia Perumal (Gajaman Nona)

Dona Isabella Cornelia Perumal. Poems as published in Lakshmi de Silva (trans.) Dayananda Gunawardena, *The Gajaman Story (Gajaman Puwatha)*, 1991.

—— Additional poems. Cited as published in journals, pamphlets and newspaper articles (see Bibliography).

Other frequently quoted sources

Davy	John Davy, *An Account of the Interior of Ceylon* (1821) 2nd edn, Dehiwela 1969.
D'Oyly Family Letters	Sir Paul E. Pieris (ed.) *Letters to Ceylon 1814–1824*, being correspondence addressed to Sir John D'Oyly, Cambridge 1938.
Epic Struggle	Brendon Gooneratne, *The Epic Struggle of the Kingdom of Kandy and its Relevance to Modern Indo-Sri Lankan Relations*, London 1995.
Hulugalle	H.A.J. Hulugalle, *British Governors of Ceylon*, Colombo 1963.
Ludowyk	E.F.C. Ludowyk, *The Story of Ceylon*, London 1962.
Patriots	Sir Paul E. Pieris, *Sinhale and the Patriots 1815–1818*, Colombo 1980.
President's House	Brendon Gooneratne, *From Governor's Residence to President's House*, Colombo 1981.
Skinner	Thomas Skinner, *Fifty Years in Ceylon*, ed. A. Skinner, 1891.
Travellers	H.A.J. Hulugalle, *Ceylon of the Early Travellers*, Colombo 1969.
Tri Sinhala	Sir Paul E. Pieris, *Tri Sinhala: The Last Phase 1796–1815*, Colombo 1939, 2nd edn 1945.

INTRODUCTION

THE GAPS THAT EXIST in historical accounts have led readers of our own times to doubt – even question – the truth of the historical record. Where does fiction end and fact begin? This question, once routinely applied to historical fiction, is now applied to history itself; and among all branches of history, particularly to biography.

> The question that arises with every biography is, how close to the truth it really is. Does it really tell us of the man within? If we all have different faces for different occasions, 'who can paint the chameleon?' as Keynes had asked of Lloyd George. And much the same question can be asked of many others whose inner lives are shrouded in mystery or half-truths and myths that are impossible to verify.[1]

'D'Oyly of Kandy', as the subject of this book is styled in Burke's *Extinct and Dormant Baronetcies of England, Ireland, and Scotland* (1841), has consistently posed precisely such questions as Ravi Vyas's to those who, in writing of the early years of British colonial rule in Sri Lanka, have encountered his curiously elusive personality.

Mystery, compounded partly of fact, partly of legend, still surrounds the life and personality of Sir John D'Oyly, imperial agent *par excellence.* An important part of the attraction that writing D'Oyly's life had for us was the wish to penetrate and, if possible, solve, that mystery. In the background to a personal fascination, however, loom larger issues.

As scholars interested in the history and literature of the British in Asia, we are very much aware, to begin with, that in the fifty years since 1947 assumptions which lay behind much imperial writing have been called into question in our postcolonial age.

To view John D'Oyly in the context of empire, it must be recognized, first of all, that the times with which this book engages are those of Regency England and not – or not yet – those of Queen Victoria. The shape of the British empire was, in D'Oyly's lifetime, still evolving through a judicious alternation of military force and shrewd diplomacy. The civil servants employed in bringing that evolution about were not yet the empire-builders they became in the mid-Victorian days of *kachcheri* and *durbar*, tiger-shoots and safaris undertaken on elephant-back. The lines that were later to separate the rulers from the ruled had not yet been rigidly laid down, and there seems to have been sufficient space between them still for individuals to follow their interests and express themselves freely without attracting moral condemnation or disciplinary 'punishment'.

Within that context of early and comparative freedom, were there limits beyond which the prudent civil servant did not go? And if so, what were they? Were the interests of the region he ruled always overridden by the mother country's interests? Was commercial profit the goal for which British colonial governments sacrificed everything else? Interaction with the natives was obviously conducive to cordial relations between ruler and ruled, but did such interaction include friendship? Or even love? Or were such attachments the point at which prudence called a halt? For beyond that point it might well be that a Briton's cultural and moral superiority were in danger of erosion.

In this context, we have been intrigued by the way the events and circumstances of D'Oyly's career appear to contradict, and even undermine, its beginnings. His life had all the elements of the medieval quest-romance of chivalry – all, that is, except the last. Historical records supply plenty of information about the preparation of a youthful, brilliant hero for a career dedicated to high and glorious ideals. They tell us of his departure for exotic lands, and his victories over moral temptations and foreign despots. They even provide evidence for the epiphanic experience which changes the hero's life. But when, to complete the cycle, D'Oyly should have returned to England in triumph, ready to pass on his knowledge and wisdom to those who were to come after, all that the historical records give us (masked by the outward decoration of a baronetcy) are details of his defeat, disillusionment and premature death. The eager agent of imperialism lived long enough to see his ideals soured, and his life-enhancing discoveries pushed aside as irrelevant to a new age. The story of John D'Oyly moves, in short, from the genre of quest-romance to the realism of postcolonial tragedy.

Next, we are conscious that a book such as this inevitably places itself at the centre of an ongoing twentieth-century debate on the nature and scope of historiography. Our account of D'Oyly's life draws substantially, like most historical accounts of nineteenth-century events and individuals, on written documents preserved in government archives, record offices and similar institutions. It is natural, indeed inevitable, that it should do so since, as Geoffrey Powell regretfully notes in connection with lacunae in his own history of the Kandyan wars,

> The British story is well-documented; there is no lack of official documents or private memoirs . . . [while] the Kandyans left little or nothing in the way of written records of their misfortunes.[2]

The absence of detailed or reliable information about the inner lives of the 'other', non-British personalities in our story became especially obvious when we came to consider the experiences of the women in it. Gajaman Nona, the eminent Sinhala poet of the Southern Province; Mary D'Oyly, mother of our subject; Venkatta Rengammal, the lovely and tragic young Tamil Queen of Kandy; Ehelepola Kumarihamy and Dingiri Menike, Kandyan women at opposite ends of the Sinhalese social scale who remained steadfastly loyal to the men who deserted them – these are five very distinctive personalities with something of importance to contribute to the colonial story, each of whom deserves study in her own right and on her own terms. Instead, three of them are held captive by 'his/story': the queen in a portrait executed by a European hand and in the self-important and highly suspect narrative of Herbert Caunter, Ehelepola Kumarihamy in propaganda devised by Governor Brownrigg to justify a British invasion,

Dingiri Menike shrinking to a mere footnote in her 'kind' protector
George Calladine's account of his own heroic doings in Kandy. We have
attempted to indicate and outline in our own retelling the ways in which
the politics of orientalism, colonialism and masculine indifference
shaped the 'historical' accounts which entrap these three female figures,
accounts from which it is to be hoped that historians of the future will
strive to release them. Only two of the five resist such reduction, and
speak to us in their own voices: Mary D'Oyly through her letters to her
son, Gajaman through her poetry.

Gajaman Nona is a subject of special interest because, in addition
to contributing to literary developments of her times, she also secured
a place for herself in Sri Lanka's traditionary lore. No serious
biographer of John D'Oyly can ignore the resources of oral history,
since legend, literature and official documents unite unexpectedly to
link the young civil servant with this remarkable woman. Brought
together by the chance that established D'Oyly as British Agent of
Revenue in Matara at the same time that Gajaman Nona's family had
found itself in acute financial distress, a popular tale of a romantic
attachment between the two has been fuelled by a set of complimentary
verses in which she is said to have petitioned him for assistance,
and by the widespread belief that D'Oyly made an outright gift to
Gajaman and her heirs, on behalf of the Crown, of a substantial grant
of land.

In recording the historical 'facts' without ignoring the traditional
legends, in engaging with oral historical sources as well as with archival
documents while doing our best to sift historical fact from speculation,
we are hopeful that we have penetrated in some small way to the
complexity of D'Oyly's character without generating 'the three or four
hundred pages of compromise, evasion, understatement, overstatement,
irrelevance and downright falsehood' which, according to Virginia Woolf,
the twentieth century calls biography.[3]

Closely connected with the problems posed by contemporary
historiography and biography is a third area of enquiry, which relates
to the field of cultural studies. If John D'Oyly was representative of the
finest ideals of his age and nation, Gajaman Nona represented through
her writings the full flowering of a distinctive Sri Lankan poetics. Despite
her marginalized position in her own time as a colonial subject, she
attained fame in cultural circles in her lifetime that survives to the

present day. Dr Lakshmi de Silva has pointed out that Gajaman's poetry and her fame 'survived unsilenced not only because of her talent but because the native tradition was hospitable to such skills, and acknowledged them, irrespective of gender'. Forty years after her death Gajaman was still being acclaimed by knowledgeable critics for the 'exquisite beauty' of her poetry. Citing the Venerable Maedauyangoda Vimalakirti, who in 1953 praised Gajaman's skill in the erotic and satiric vein, as well as the correctness of her language, Dr de Silva makes an interesting point:

> Here we see that unlike Western writers who in the 1950s still combined prudishness with prurience in their attitude to sex, it remained possible for a monk in Sri Lanka to publish a study of literature which showed a relaxed acceptance of feminine sexuality which, as in the days of Knox, was considered a fact rather than a threat or a vice.[4]

In deliberately placing near the centre of our biographical study of a 'representative' Englishman, John D'Oyly, such a hitherto marginalized subject as the life and literary productions of his female Sri Lankan contemporary, we have attempted to redress the 'balance of power' between these two interesting individuals.

It seems likely that among the translations of Sinhala verses D'Oyly is said to have sent home to his family in England[5] was his own translation of Gajaman's verse petition, a poem remarkable for its combination of elegant verbal harmonies with formidable erudition, to say nothing of its powerful appeal to a patron's compassion and sense of chivalry (as well, of course, as his vanity).

> Like Eros himself, handsome above all others, are you
>   O noble John D'Oyly, Lord of this District,
> Like the Moon itself, you light up a whole city with the
>   gentle radiance of your virtues,
> Like Lord Ganeshvara himself in the range and depth of
>   your wit, you grasp the intricate meanings of poets'
>   linked verses and phrases,
> And like the Divine Tree itself your shining right hand
>   rewards with gifts their hopes and desires.[6]

5

As D'Oyly knew, Sinhala poets of the time routinely addressed their patrons in terms of elaborate compliment, but he would also have been well aware that Gajaman's specific reference to his skill in grasping the intricate metaphorical meanings of poets' linked verses and phrases, coming from a poet of her social standing and acknowledged erudition, amounted to a substantial acknowledgment of his literary accomplishment. It was as valuable a prize, in its own way, as the Sir William Browne's Medal, which he had won while at Cambridge for his composition of a Latin ode.

Would D'Oyly's family at Buxted have appreciated this fact? It is much more likely that they regarded the petition as quaint and amusing, an oriental oddity. In any event, D'Oyly's translations do not appear to have survived, although the Sinhala original is still extant, and was published many years after the poet's death. We have addressed the interesting subject of D'Oyly's relationship with Gajaman Nona in Chapter 5. Through analyses in Chapters 1 and 5 of their several literary productions (given in translation in Appendices 2 and 4), we have sought to provide truthful accounts of D'Oyly and Gajaman that resist the tendency among commentators either to privilege D'Oyly at the expense of Gajaman, or to overlook her altogether. In this matter as in several others, it is our conviction that a *Life* of D'Oyly has profound implications for the cultural historian as well as for the biographer.

Moving to another area of our interest in undertaking this biography: as individuals whom circumstance has brought into personal touch with the psychology of exile and expatriation, and as writers concerned for the language to be used in discussing such matters, we are interested in correcting, from historical bases, contemporary misinterpretations and misreadings of such terms as 'colonial', 'native', 'postcolonial', 'oriental' and 'orientalism'.

Edward Said's theories of 'orientalism' impute to European activities east of Suez the joint construction of 'an elaborate European imaginative creation which sustained a myth of western superiority'.[7] This is true enough, as anyone born and brought up in an Asian colony can testify from personal experience. Students of colonial and imperial history cannot avoid noticing how the historical expansion of Europe into Asia, and the concentration of political power in European hands, gradually bring about a situation in which, as Said rightly asserts, knowledge of the Orient, because generated out of strength, in a sense *creates* the Orient, the Oriental, and his world ... The Oriental is depicted as something one judges (as in a court of law), something one studies and depicts (as in a curriculum), something one disciplines (as in a school or prison), something one illustrates (as in a zoological manual). The point is that in each of these cases the Oriental is *contained* and *represented* by dominating frameworks.[8]

These statements can be amply illustrated from Sri Lanka's nineteenth-century experience. In 1816 the system of customary law operative in the newly annexed Kandyan kingdom was *judged* and found wanting, so a committee (headed by John D'Oyly) was appointed to codify it.[9] Sri Lanka's religions and philosophies were *studied* by European civil servants, and *depicted* by them in texts prepared for use by teachers in the island's schools, as demonstrably inferior to the scientific progress accomplished in Europe.[10] The island's people, already subjected in the eighteenth century to a legal system based on Roman-Dutch law, were further *disciplined* by the establishment of British-style schools which superseded the temple schools of tradition.[11] They were *categorized* and *classified* by caste, religion and occupation[12] and, of course, endlessly painted and photographed, the products of such activities fetching high prices from European collectors of the exotic and the picturesque.

Even the island's original name, which derives its sound from a Sanskrit root, *alankara,* meaning 'light', and its (moral) significance from the fact that the Buddhist enlightenment found a second home there in pre-European times, underwent multiple changes in maps and histories constructed by Europeans. In the course of such changes the regional and cultural associations of the name were gradually covered over and the island was firmly situated within the 'dominating framework' of imperialism by such terms as 'Pearl of the East', 'Jewel of the Orient' and 'the finest jewel in the Imperial Crown'. In Queen Victoria's jubilee year, a handsome publication by John Ferguson paid glowing tribute to this 'most important of her Majesty's Crown Colonies', and asserted that the island had 'long been "Confess'd the best and brightest gem / In Britain's orient diadem"'.[13]

What seems *not* to be true is the construction that is all too frequently placed on Said's theories, suggesting that the 'myth of western superiority' he discerns was created deliberately or intentionally by Europeans, as some kind of sinister conspiracy. On the contrary, an unbiased study of the lives and careers of numerous so-called 'empire-builders' such as John D'Oyly, whom circumstance placed at the centre of a particularly interesting process of historical and political transition in Sri Lanka, does much to support the view that 'orientalism' as we know it today was brought into existence by political expedients. These were necessitated by, and frequently arose from, historical events which were unexpected and entirely unplanned. Such political expedients sometimes ran contrary, not only to the corporate ideals that inspired the Colonial Service, but to the explicit agendas of the Colonial Office itself.

As examples of the above we may briefly point to the stereotyped depiction, generally accepted as accurate by the end of the nineteenth century, of Sri Lanka's last ruler as a 'cruel monster', a 'tyrant king . . . hated by his own chiefs and people',[14] which resulted from the determination of a governor of Ceylon to bring the Kingdom of Kandy under British control despite explicit orders from the Colonial Office in London that peaceful trade, not war, was to be Britain's policy in regard to Kandy. Or, equally striking, the stereotyped depiction of Kandyans as 'treacherous' and requiring strict discipline, a direct result of Britain's overreaction to the unexpected outbreak of the Kandyan War of 1818 and the need to justify it.

The context (see Chapter 8) makes it abundantly clear, in addition, that when Sir James Mackintosh wrote of John D'Oyly in 1810 that, 'like many Orientalists, [he had] almost become a native in his habits of life', he was using the word 'native' in a manner quite innocent of malicious or denigrative intent. In 1810, when the British were still tentatively feeling their way as a colonial power, the word 'native' did not carry the derogatory associations that were to become its burden a century later, when the British had grown arrogant regarding their imperial role in Asia. As is well known, E.M. Forster captured the insolence and arrogance of British India in his novel *A Passage to India*, but that was published a hundred years after D'Oyly's death, in 1924.

Similarly, when Mackintosh used the word 'orientalists', he did so with reference to Europeans who had dedicated themselves so whole-heartedly to the study of oriental languages and literatures that they had adopted the frugal diet and reclusive habits of the Asian teacher or guru. There were many such, as Mackintosh well knew, and he must have felt (perhaps with dismay) that D'Oyly seemed to be well on the way to joining their number. Mackintosh was *not* referring (in the sense in which the word 'orientalist' has been constantly misused by Edward Said and others in our own times) to Europeans intent on stereotyping Asians as backward and inferior.

While Europe stereotyped Asia and Asians, the reality of both remained elusive and slippery. Early responses, especially from missionaries, repeatedly show Europeans bewildered by an unexpected disparity between what they had been led to expect in 'the East' and what they actually found there. 'I am fully persuaded if I had been sensible of the qualifications necessary for an Eastern Indian Missionary I could not have been prevailed upon to have left my native Shore,' wrote Benjamin Clough in 1814.[15] Fifty years later, Clough's fellow Methodist Robert Spence Hardy was still demanding a change in policy as regards the training of recruits for overseas service:

> The glorified spirits of Wesley, Fletcher, Benson, and Watson, must smile at the thought that their works alone are regarded as sufficient for the missionary who will have to grapple with the most specious arguments ever presented by man against the word and work of God.[16]

'What happens,' asks Kateryna Longley, 'if something slips out from under the heavy apparatus of the dominating knowledge machine, defying representation and refusing to be contained?'[17] For a brief period, Sri Lanka – and possibly D'Oyly himself – did just that. Our story is a record of 'what happened', and how it happened in an Asian colony between 1802 and 1824, and of the means by which the imperial machine successfully brought matters back into containment, and under control. So efficiently was this done that by 1887 it could be confidently stated that 'the spirit of the Highland chiefs of Ceylon . . . [had been] effectually broken',

> and although the military garrison of Ceylon has gone down from about 6,000 troops to 1,000, and, indeed, although for months together the island has been left with not more than a couple of hundred of artillerymen, no serious trouble has been given for nearly

seventy years by the previously warlike Kandyans or the Ceylonese generally.[18]

When John D'Oyly (1774–1824) entered the pages of history, he was 28 years old, one of an elite group of young men hand-picked by Frederick North, first British Governor of Ceylon (as Sri Lanka was then known), to help him administer the new Crown Colony. It was an appropriate, even an obvious choice: D'Oyly's ancestors and kinsmen had served church and state with distinction in the past, and had in addition a well-documented record of civil and military experience in British India. Following an unusually brilliant career at Cambridge University, the young man was recognized as gifted with particular skills in languages. He enjoyed the advantage, in addition, of the patronage of his father's personal friend the Earl of Liverpool, Secretary of State for the Colonies at the time and a future Prime Minister.

D'Oyly sometimes figures in modern accounts of his times as representative 'in origin, in upbringing, and in education' of the best type of Englishman appointed to the Ceylon Civil Service in those early years:[19]

Administrative authority, it was believed, could with propriety be entrusted only to those whose social status was such that its exercise would be instinctive with them.[20]

When D'Oyly worked in Colombo and Matara as Agent of Revenue between 1802 and 1815, therefore, and functioned thereafter as the first British Resident of Kandy from 1816 to 1824, the values of Regency England that he represented and, in a sense, embodied were being brought into contact, first, with an Asian society that had already been exposed for three centuries to European rule along the island's coastal fringe; and later, with a feudal kingdom in the interior that was still virtually untouched by Western influences of any kind.

Other commentators, however, identify D'Oyly as 'unusual' rather than representative:[21] the criterion applied here being that his 22 years of unremitting service, the expertise he achieved in the Sinhala language, and the respect and sympathy he evinced for the culture and customs of the people he was appointed in 1816 to govern, were so rare in his time as to be unique. 'Neither the Governor nor his military advisors shared . . . the genuine interest in the life of the people' shown by this 'English intellectual who stepped into the shoes of a Sinhalese Adigar and, by his actions and writings, secured for himself a niche in the history of Ceylon'.[22]

Among the few British civil servants whose careers are comparable at some points with D'Oyly's was his near-contemporary Brian Houghton Hodgson (1800–1894). A descendant of prosperous country gentry, Hodgson was educated in the classics up to the age of sixteen, and was a keen cricketer, huntsman and rider. In 1816 he obtained entry to the Indian Civil Service (ICS) through the influence of James Pattison, a family friend and a director of the East India Company. Having successfully passed out from Haileybury in 1817, gaining prizes for Bengali and classics, Hodgson sailed for India in 1818. Arduous study of Sanskrit, Bengali and Persian at the Fort William College in Calcutta helped break down his health. He received medical advice to go home to Britain or get a hill-country appointment. In 1819 he was appointed Assistant Commissioner of Kumaon, and in 1820 became Assistant Commissioner in Kathmandu. He attributed his successes in Nepal to the example of William Traill, under whom he had served in Kumaon, travelling through the province, visiting every village and hamlet, and gaining an intimate knowledge of its land and people.

Hodgson's pioneer studies of Nepalese Hindu law helped him build up a widespread intelligence network which detected anti-British manoeuvres almost before they started, steadily moving towards actual intervention in the complex world of Nepalese politics. Resigning from the ICS in 1843, he settled in Darjeeling, and between 1844 and 1853 lived there as a scholarly recluse before returning to England, where he lived until his death in 1894. Hodgson is remembered by orientalists mainly as the co-discoverer, with Csoma de Koros, of Mahayana Buddhism, and as the first collector of Sanskrit Buddhist manuscripts.[23]

The interest of historians in issues relating to the historical or political development of South Asia and Sri Lanka has kept D'Oyly's name in the history books. In most accounts of the British colonial period he is regularly listed among those present on the crowded and spectacular stage upon which, at that time, Europe and Asia confronted each other in Ceylon, but he is seldom given much particular or detailed attention. Modest by nature, discreet by habit and apparently self-effacing in manner, D'Oyly becomes almost invisible among the colourful major players in those crucial events in Sri Lanka's early British colonial history which led, first, to the peaceful acquisition by the British government of the Kandyan kingdom of Sri Lanka in 1815, and, three years later, to the suppression by force of a war of rebellion in which some leaders of the Kandyan provinces attempted to regain the kingdom's lost sovereignty.

And yet, D'Oyly's contribution to the negotiations surrounding Britain's annexation of Sri Lanka's Kandyan kingdom in 1815 was rewarded by King George IV with a baronetcy in 1821. Historical research has not yet revealed in just what that contribution consisted. Extracts from a diary D'Oyly kept as a Cambridge undergraduate were published in 1938 by Sir Paul Pieris in his introduction to a collection of letters addressed to their empire-building relative by his family in England, and the minutely detailed diaries D'Oyly kept during his period of service in Sri Lanka were published in 1917. Yet, more than a century after his death in 1824, history, as E.F.C. Ludowyk noted in 1962, had yet to determine the share of 'this inscrutable Englishman who had learned Sinhalese and could speak and write it, in encompassing the ruin of the Kandyan kingdom':

> On the surface he appears to have been . . . nothing more than the conscientious official engrossed in his duties and interested in Kandyan institutions. He had gained the goodwill of some of the Kandyan chieftains and one of them entrusted his family to his care. He was assiduous in his letter-writing – to the chiefs, and to the Governor – but hardly anywhere does he betray anything more than the feelings of the good Civil Servant.[24]

Ludowyk evidently believed that there was more to John D'Oyly than the written records, the official letters and diaries, and, eventually, the obituaries, reveal. The present writers share his view.

Since D'Oyly arrived in Sri Lanka in 1802 and worked there until his death in 1824 without once returning to Britain, making no impact on the world outside the island, it is not surprising that no biography has yet been written of this remarkable man. The most significant years of D'Oyly's life were passed in a colony far removed from the imperial 'centre' of Britain. William Cobbett would refer to London in 1822 as 'the monster, called . . . "the metropolis of the empire",'[25] but history that was made outside that metropolis hardly merited the name.

British contemporaries of D'Oyly who left records of the two major historical events in which he figured include Sir Robert Brownrigg, who presided as British governor over them both, and conducted a regular correspondence about them with the Secretary of State in London; and two physicians, Dr John Davy and Dr Henry Marshall, who published, after leaving the island, accounts of their experiences during those turbulent times. Brownrigg's successor as Governor of Ceylon, Sir Edward Barnes, wrote D'Oyly's obituary. As the reader of this book will discover, their several accounts of John D'Oyly and the events in which he played a part differ in interesting ways which reflect not only their personal viewpoints, but the changing attitudes of imperial Britain towards her colonies and the men who served in them.

The authors of historical studies of nineteenth-century Sri Lanka that have provided a background for this book are listed separately in the bibliography. Most, significantly, are Sri Lankan. For, although Sri Lanka attained its freedom from Britain in 1948 and has now enjoyed complete political independence for fifty years, the fall of the Kandyan kingdom in 1815 and the Kandyan War of 1818 are two events of such crucial significance to the nation's development that they have consistently attracted attention from its scholars and writers.

Like Governor Brownrigg, John D'Oyly was a loyal servant of the empire. He has been viewed, however, with a greater degree of sympathy than Brownrigg by Sri Lanka's historians, partly because of his dedicated study of the Sinhala language and his documented identification with Buddhist custom and ritual. Brought into close contact with the Kandyan nobility and the Buddhist *sangha* by his duties as Resident, and by having being commissioned by the British government to record the customs and constitution of the Kingdom of Kandy, D'Oyly appears to have developed a deep respect and fascination for the social structure of this ancient Sinhala kingdom. Although frequently misunderstood by his fellow Britishers, especially the missionaries, D'Oyly's expression of such feelings quite naturally strike a responsive chord in the assessments made of him by Sri Lankan commentators.

References to D'Oyly, by even the most nationalistic among the latter, are often half-admiring even when hostile. In his introduction to the second (1975) edition of D'Oyly's *Sketch of the Constitution of the Kandyan Kingdom*, S.D. Saparamadu characterizes D'Oyly as 'a super espionage agent for the British over the Kingdom of Kandy' who 'set out deliberately to subvert the chiefs of the country against their legitimate king'.[26] Similarly, Tennekoon Vimalananda, one of D'Oyly's most trenchant critics, renders prickly praise to the civil servant's 'craft and cunning', taking the view that

Sir Robert Brownrigg was singularly fortunate in having the services of John D'Oyly. The swashbuckling Brownrigg . . . could not easily reconcile himself to the ignominy suffered by the might of British arms, and came [to Sri Lanka] resolved to succeed, if possible by craft and guile, where the show of valour had so signally failed. In this design he found available on the spot, ready to hand, a most able, faithful and conscientious assistant in John D'Oyly, prototype of the later and more widely publicised Lawrence of Arabia . . .

It would be no exaggeration to say that the thoroughness of D'Oyly's work more than any other single factor made it possible for the British Governor Brownrigg to cause the Sinhalese nation which had remained free for two thousand, three hundred and fifty years, to lose its independence and become a subject territory of the British. Where the Portuguese and Dutch had failed in their efforts to subjugate the Kingdom of Kandy, D'Oyly's astuteness, cunning and efficiency succeeded in securing for the British the possession of this ancient Kingdom without a single shot being fired and without loss of any soldiers.[27]

The same writer refers to D'Oyly's 'skill, courage and perseverance'[28] while L.S. Dewaraja notes that

Among the early British administrators whose writings have come down to us, pride of place must be given to John D'Oyly (1774–1824) who, during his period of service in the Island, mastered the Sinhalese language and acquired a . . . thorough knowledge of the details of the Kandyan administrative system which had frequently baffled other foreigners.

She adds that 'no student of Kandyan institutions could afford to ignore the importance of this work, since in many matters it remains the sole authority'.[29]

British scholars who have taken an interest in D'Oyly include J.P. Lewis, whose *List of Inscriptions on Tombstones and Monuments in Ceylon* (1913) provides some factual details of D'Oyly's family background and career, and Geoffrey Powell, whose admirably balanced account of *The Kandyan Wars* (1973) goes beyond the details of D'Oyly's work as negotiator, head of British intelligence, and military adviser to the forces in the field, to look perceptively, if briefly, at such non-military matters as his sympathy for the people whose affairs he administered as Britain's first Resident in Kandy.

When we look back at the nineteenth century from the last decade of the twentieth, the early days of British colonization appear to us only as the distant past. Of the Sussex countryside D'Oyly knew as a boy, little now remains to ignite a biographer's imagination or increase the slender knowledge we have of him. The downs still rise above the county town of Lewes in East Sussex where D'Oyly's father, Archdeacon Matthias D'Oyly, was rector, and the River Ouse runs through it. But much of the deep forest, rich in beauty and legend, through which (far away in Sri Lanka) he remembered walking in search of game, has been replaced by a countryside of farms and villages, orchards, gardens and, inevitably, the pseudo-Elizabethan half-timbered mansions of stockbrokers commuting between their toy farms and the City. Lewes is today a flourishing centre for tourists, offering the remains of a Norman castle, streets that retain their medieval character, and many fine Georgian houses and public buildings. The history of the D'Oyly family, no longer extant in the form of an ancestral house, must be traced with the help of the kindly curators of the East Sussex Record Office.

Sometimes, however, by some trick of chance or coincidence, the past makes contact with the present. In 1992, while searching H.A.I. Goonetileke's monumental *Bibliography of Ceylon* for something entirely different, we came upon a bibliographical citation[30] which led us, through various byways (including the writing of a novel by one of us), to working together on this book. The citation referred to an auction sale that had taken place in London in 1820. We have since located a copy of the sale catalogue, printed as an Appendix to Sir Paul Pieris's historical study, *Tri Sinhala: The Last Phase 1796–1815* (1939), which we reproduce below:

Regalia of the King of Kandy.

A CATALOGUE

of

A Splendid and Valuable Collection of Jewellery forming the Regalia of the King of Kandy,

The whole of the purest massive Gold comprising the Crown, a complete Suit of Embossed Armour, a great variety of armlets, bracelets, breast ornaments (*called Paddakums*), plumes of jewels for the head, chains for the neck, particularly one 23½ feet in length, a magnificent dagger, and various other costly articles of regal decoration, all of them of elaborate workmanship and richly studded with diamonds, emeralds, rubies, sapphires, pearls, etc., many of which are of an extraordinary size and beauty; a cat's eye of matchless grandeur, an immense mass of ruby in the rough, etc. Presented by His Majesty to the captors for whose benefit they will be sold without the slightest reservation by Mr King, at his great room, 38, King Street, Covent Garden, on Tuesday, the 13th day of June, 1820, very punctually at one o'clock.

May be viewed on Monday, 5th June, till within two days preceding the sale in their present state, after which they will be unset and lotted out. Catalogues, price *2s.6d*, without which no person will be admitted may be had at the Auction Room.

PRINTED BY W. SMITH, KING STREET, SEVEN DIALS (1820) 14 P.

Our attention was caught by the Covent Garden address of the auctioneer. Number 38 King Street is an address well known to us both, since it is the home of the British publishing enterprise which had in 1986 published Yasmine Gooneratne's memoir of the Bandaranaike family of Sri Lanka, *Relative Merits*. Enquiry established that the building had indeed been formerly the 'Great Room' of a London auctioneer named Thomas King, and that Mr King had sold on 13 June 1820 'without the slightest reservation' to the highest bidder for each lot, the royal regalia of the Kingdom of Kandy.

Since historical research by past scholars has indicated that the various parts of the royal regalia had been yielded up by the King of Kandy and some of his nobles between 1815 and 1816 to the British government on the strict understanding that these were sacred objects which were not to be sold nor even exposed to unworthy eyes,[31] their unwarranted appearance in a London auction room in 1820 presents a problem with fascinating historical, political and ethical implications. The British official who had given that promise on the Crown's behalf, who had taken charge of the jewels in Kandy, catalogued them with Civil Service precision, and dispatched them to the British Governor in the capital, Colombo, became the focus of our interest. His name was John D'Oyly, and he has become the subject of this book.

The incident that we have just described, relating to our own indirect and coincidental connection with the royal regalia of Kandy, brings forward a second problem: what, ideally, should be a biographer's relationship to subject and text? How, especially, is a subject's character to be evoked and convincingly established? James Boswell, writing his classic *Life* of Dr Samuel Johnson that is based on intimate acquaintance with his mentor and friend, inscribed himself into the text without a second thought. As a result, the Johnson the reader meets in that *Life* is Boswell's Johnson, captured for the most part through incidents which Boswell witnessed, and conversations Boswell heard, initiated, or in some cases had deliberately provoked as potential material for his own book. Writing, as we do, 170 years after John D'Oyly's death, we lack the advantage of personal acquaintance with our subject.

We have found Roger W. Oliver's observations on '*L'umorismo* and the Theater' (1979), therefore, very relevant to the genre of biography which, like history with which it is so closely linked, resembles the theatre in serving as 'mirror of reality, as re-creator of life's actions and people'.

The whole process by which character is created and past events retold, for the biographer as much as for the historian and the actor, is an act of construction. Biographers and historians begin with the foundation of events, words, ideas and actions (which the actor draws from the playwright). Imagination, intelligence and knowledge of a particular period and background must then assist in building up a composite vision. Not only are biographers and historians committed to show the events of the past, but they must attempt, by every means at their disposal, to convey the temper of the time, and to demonstrate its relevance today.

As an actor cannot construct his character in a vacuum, a biographer must take into consideration what a subject's contemporaries were doing at any particular time, and how his individual life fitted into the overall design of the period in which he lived as conceived in his own age and in ours. Finally, and essentially, a biographer must bring to a project a personal sense of the various ways in which chance, likelihood, and human nature operate in the 'theatre' of an individual life.[32]

The failure to survive of many letters or any private journals written by D'Oyly during the period 1802–1815, when he was active in gathering intelligence on behalf of the British government, or during the period 1816–1824, years which saw the Kandyan War and its terrible aftermath, is a circumstance that has led us, naturally, to enquire why this should have been so. Sir Paul Pieris's introduction to the D'Oyly family letters shows that D'Oyly had been, in his Cambridge years, a compulsive diarist. He kept detailed daily records of his official transactions up to 23 April 1815. One would have expected him to maintain his Cambridge practice of keeping personal records during the whole period of his service in Ceylon, but even if pressure of work prevented this, it is curious that no official diary or log-book survives to document the period 1816–1824. The damp, termites and white ants of the tropics are famously destructive of papers and documents, and one or all of them might certainly have been responsible for the absence of primary evidence. But could there be another more complicated reason for that absence? Might such journals and letters have contained details relating either to D'Oyly's private life or to his politics that the British government in Colombo preferred to edit out of the official record of an otherwise exemplary public servant?[33]

The 'creative' editing of historical records is not as rare an occurrence as one might like to think. A recent instance of such editing came to our notice during a visit to the Nehru Memorial Museum in Delhi in 1997, when we perceived that not a single photograph or text relating to the presence in India in 1947 of Lord Louis Mountbatten and Lady Edwina Mountbatten is to be seen on the walls and in the display cabinets of the museum. In view of the crucial part played by the last British viceroy in the run-up to India's independence – surely a matter of greater importance than the gossip that links the name of Lady Mountbatten romantically to that of Pandit Jawarharlal Nehru – such a gap in the official record would seem to require an urgent explanation. But as long as no one notices the existence of a gap, no explanation will be forthcoming.

In the absence of substantial personal records on which we could base an impression of John D'Oyly's character and personality, we have been obliged to resort to other evidence. This includes letters sent to him by others, official documents in which he is mentioned, and his presence in (or, in one case, his conspicuous absence from!) the memoirs or letters of his contemporaries. The letters that were written to D'Oyly by members of his family in England between 1805 and 1824 reveal that he kept in regular touch with them, and in particular with his elder brother Thomas D'Oyly, serjeant-at-law. D'Oyly's relatives, especially his mother Mrs Mary D'Oyly, express their feelings with vivid immediacy in their letters. The question of a probable date for his return was frequently canvassed by them, but D'Oyly, it would seem, made no promises. A dutiful son to his widowed mother, and a large-hearted benefactor to his nephews (the sons of his brothers Thomas and George D'Oyly), we learn of his thoughtful arrangements on their behalf only because members of his family write from time to time to thank him for his generosity.

We had hoped that good fortune might turn up a cache of letters or a private journal in which D'Oyly revealed something of himself, and of his thoughts about the people he ruled as well as about those with whom he had had professional dealings for 22 years. Exhaustive library searches have yielded nothing. If such materials exist, they will brighten the task of future biographers. We have, for our part, refrained from building more on the extant evidence than probability and common sense together would support.

However, as the Chinese proverb has it, 'He that runneth too fast after the horse of history frequently gets kicked in the teeth.' Following one's subject at a respectable distance may have some advantages. The same 170 years that have denied us personal acquaintance with our subject have certainly bestowed on our efforts an historical perspective that was denied to Boswell. The official diaries and log-books kept by government agents who succeeded D'Oyly, working as he did in the Southern and Central Provinces of the island, help to build up a reliable picture of the indigenous societies with which D'Oyly came in contact, rural communities which changed very slowly if at all in the intervening years. (In the case of Leonard Woolf, who worked as a government agent in both provinces a century later, we have not only diaries on which to draw, but letters describing in the frankest possible terms to correspondents such as Lytton Strachey in England, a colonial officer's day-to-day experiences in an 'out-station', in the *kachcheri*, and on circuit.)

We have tried to make the most of that perspective, making use, especially, of one very significant way in which D'Oyly himself has assisted us. It was his habit to note meticulously on each letter as it came to him, exactly where he was when he received it, the precise date on which it arrived and, in many cases, the name of its carrier (e.g. 'By Mr Gisborne', 'By the Eclipse', 'Via Madras'). It has thus occasionally become possible to deduce by working backwards, even after a lapse of 170 years, something of the mixed emotions with which D'Oyly, who was dealing from day to day with political events and intrigues of a complexity almost unimaginable by his relations in rural Sussex, must have read some particular passages in his family's letters: his elder brother Thomas's descriptions of the newly established Travellers' Club in London, for example, his younger brother George's complaints against his country parishioners, or his mother's petulant appeals that he should return forthwith to England, marry and settle down.

Aware that our subject was a poet and translator whom a Sri Lankan poet had compared with Lord Ganeshvara, the Hindu God of Wisdom who was also the chosen scribe of the epic poem *Mahabharata*, our reading of D'Oyly's written texts has been attentive and consciously analytical. This approach, which has directed our scrutiny of even the most cryptic among John D'Oyly's diary entries and the scrupulously factual notes he left at his death on the constitution of the Kandyan kingdom, has been directed by our interest, not in a particular political agenda, but in what D'Oyly's writings might reveal of his deepest feelings about the kingdom he had won for his country.

Was D'Oyly merely the Crown's 'obedient servant', constructing a blueprint for British imperial domination? Or had he permitted himself to dream a romantic dream? For many years D'Oyly was the only member of the British administration in Ceylon capable of under-standing the people of the island through their own language. Did he consider it possible for the British government, having dethroned and exiled Kandy's tyrannical king, to preserve the complex social organization of the kingdom intact, unaltered in every way except for the substitution of the benevolent (and conveniently distant) King George III for the ancient line of Sinhala royalty?

In effect, were his voluminous notes and writings, which documented the ancient codes according to which the kingdom had been governed in pre-British times, motivated by a desire to preserve the kingdom or merely to control it?

Our studies have a very close relationship with concerns that today engage academics worldwide. In teaching and research conducted in the Postcolonial Literature units offered by Macquarie University, as well as in its Postcolonial Literatures and Language Research Centre, many of the issues we have taken up in this book are constantly being explored and discussed. In pursuing the present study we have benefited from the constant support and encouragement of friends and scholars – in particular Meenakshi and Sujit Mukherjee, Lakshmi de Silva, Richard W. Bailey, A. Jeyaratnam Wilson and S.C. Harrex. It gives us great satisfaction to thank them here.

In introducing 'D'Oyly of Kandy' and his contemporaries, both British and Sri Lankan, to a wider circle of readers than they might have encountered before this time, we hope that the present study will take further a subject that has had exposure in a series of regional contexts: the cultural implications of the colonial experience for a feudal Asian state catapulted by colonization into a nineteenth century dominated by Eurocentric concepts of 'morality' and by utilitarian notions of 'civilization'.

Linked with that subject, however, is another: a major area of contest among new historicists is the extent to which an individual, despite being subjected to the play of power and ideology within the discourse of a particular era, may be able to retain some scope for individual initiative. In a context such as the imperial system, which came in time to rely to a very great extent on corporate conformity, we have attempted to discover how much scope there was for individualism, how much 'space' was permitted, in particular, for the pursuit by a man such as John D'Oyly of individual interests and personal ideals.

During the months that followed the ruthless suppression of the 1818 rebellion and the reorganization of Britain's administration of the Kandyan provinces, D'Oyly was, according to that perceptive scholar of the British period in Ceylon, H.A.J. Hulugalle,

> the only official who preserved his calmness of judgment and exercised some compassion. He continued for three more years in service, but his heart was not in it.[34]

To his parents and siblings, living quiet lives in Sussex and London, D'Oyly always remained, despite his successes at Cambridge and the key role he played in dramatic events in Ceylon, their own familiar 'Jack'. To a woman poet on the other side of the world, however, the young civil servant appeared in 1810 as a divine *avatar*, rivalling in beauty, omniscience and generosity the deities of East and West. What did 'Jack D'Oyly' himself think of the oriental world in which he figured in such exotic splendour? He sent his translation of the poem home to England, but what he thought of the poem itself, or of its author, we may never know with any certainty.

A modern historian of Sri Lanka, E.F.C. Ludowyk, has described D'Oyly as 'sphinx-like' in his discretion, and 'ambiguous as the Delphic oracle': an 'inscrutable Englishman'.[35] We are aware of the presence in our own account of D'Oyly of what must seem, to the reader unacquainted with the process of decolonization, a constantly changing point of view. Do you, such a reader might justifiably enquire of us, come to bury D'Oyly or to praise him?

Our answer to such a question is, of course, 'Neither.' D'Oyly was a man of his time, and we have striven throughout this study to see and present him as such. The issues involved in the early days of British colonial rule are too complex, the experience of a sensitive individual caught up, as D'Oyly was, in the process and aftermath of empire too profound, to be resolved with ease or simplicity. Postcolonial writers who hope to explore them objectively are inevitably involved in the struggle that is an indispensable part of the postcolonial condition: the struggle to achieve, and sustain, a balanced point of view.

This being so, we are hopeful that our attempt to unravel in this book the seemingly inscrutable personality and apparently contradictory motives of the enigmatic D'Oyly will help in the better understanding of the psychological implications of colonial rule, not only for the colonized subject, but for the colonizer and those who write about him.

BRENDON GOONERATNE · YASMINE GOONERATNE

Sydney 1999

CHAPTER ONE

'CULTURED GENERATIONS'

Sir Jellaby Jingle and Admiral Sneeze
Have each got a son in Ceylon.
If I stand you five thousand, you can, if you please,
Make a fortune. Come, say are you on?

Stewart Fasson, *'John Folingsby, Bart.'*

THE SHORES OF SUSSEX AND KENT in south-east England inherit an ancient history of war and successive invasion. The Romans under Aulus Plautius made landfall there in AD 43, and left behind them the closest concentration of Roman shore-castles in Britain. The Anglo-Saxons under Hengist and Horsa landed on this coast, and later the Cinque Ports were created to stave off Danish intruders. The Normans landed there too, and set up a ring of massive fortresses such as those at Rochester, Dover and Canterbury.

'The people match the land,' says a contemporary guide book of the rolling countryside and the 'wooded, dim blue goodness' of south-east England. 'They have a rich, soft dialect, a ruddy English look and a character which is as tenacious as Wealden clay.' The writer, evidently Sussex-born, informs us that Sussex folk, 'like their lovable land, are English to the backbone.'[1]

Like many old English families of the region, the family of Sir John D'Oyly, Baronet (1774–1824) was French before it became English. Sir John was descended from Seigneur de Oyly of Oyly, near Lisieux in Normandy, whose three sons (Robert, Nigel and Gilbert) all accompanied William the Conqueror to England in 1066. In 1067

Robert de Oyly received the city and barony of Oxford, and built a castle there. Having no male issue, he was succeeded by his brother Nigel de Oyly, whose great-grandson Sir Foulk de Oyly, the crusader, shared the captivity of his master and friend King Richard I.

In more recent times, the D'Oyly family served with distinction on European battlefields. It had multiple connections with India, one of which may be recognized in Sir John Hadley D'Oyly, sixth Baronet, who was a friend and loyal supporter of Warren Hastings, the first Governor-General of Bengal. When Hastings, titled 'Saviour of India' by the English East India Trading Company, was impeached in 1785 and tried at Westminster Hall on the grounds of corruption and cruelty in his administration of Bengal, Sir John Hadley D'Oyly contributed generously to his friend's defence, and the baronet's young kinsman John D'Oyly (then an undergraduate at Bene't College, Cambridge) was among the spectators.[2]

The Indian connection was continued by the sixth Baronet's four successors in the title. Maurice Shellim, writing of Charles Walters D'Oyly as the painter of a dashing watercolour of Government House, Calcutta, signed and dated 1855, refers to the artist as 'the ninth Baronet of that distinguished family long associated with India'.[3] Shellim adds that 'five generations continued to serve in India, in one capacity or another, and the men and women of this family were more often in the East than in England'.[4]

John D'Oyly, second son of Mathias D'Oyly, Archdeacon of Lewes and Rector of Buxted, was born on 11 June 1774. He was called 'Jack' by his siblings, of whom there were five: Thomas D'Oyly, John's senior by two years; Francis, George, Henry and Henrietta. The D'Oyly children grew up in the red-brick rectory attached to a thirteenth-century church, St Margaret's at Buxted. Within a ten-mile radius of Buxted stands Lewes Castle, symbol of the Norman Conquest, whose thirteenth-century towers give commanding views to the sea. With Ashdown Forest in close proximity, not to mention such rivers beloved of anglers as the Arun, the Adur, the Cuckmere and the Ouse, it need not surprise us that shooting, fishing and rowing were among the favourite sports of the younger D'Oylys.

The river valleys of Sussex still flood in winter, forming long lakes alive with widgeon and teal, snipe and wild duck. The surrounding woodlands, which were very deep in D'Oyly's boyhood, mysterious, and rich in legend, also yielded plenty of pheasant, partridge and many other varieties of birds. The rector's brood enjoyed the friendship and hospitality of several land-owning families in the countryside around, and John and his brothers had many opportunities to indulge their liking for active country sports. As a young man D'Oyly gloried in his marksmanship. Writing to his brother Thomas on 18 June 1809, he recalled with some nostalgia the carefree days when he had been accustomed 'to wander through the Sussex Woods, in quest of Game'.[5]

John was educated at Westminster School and at Cambridge University. He was elected captain of the school in 1791, but was not allowed to present himself for election in 1792 on account of his conduct as Captain during a sudden 'insurrection' of the School, when all the boys, leaving their forms and their masters, played truant from school to watch an open-air prize-fight (bloody, bare-knuckled and definitely illegal), refusing to return until it was finished.[6] Such schoolboy pranks apart, it was obvious from the beginning that John's inclination was towards study (unlike that of his younger brothers Francis and Henry, both of whom became military men). On 9 November 1792 he entered Bene't College (later Corpus Christi), where his father and his elder brother had been before him.

John's interest in sport went hand in hand with extraordinary academic gifts, and his university career was punctuated with scholarships, prizes and other awards. He competed for and won two scholarships in his very first year at Cambridge, and in 1795 added to these the Mawson Scholarship. At his first examination John had won a third prize. In his next two years he made up for this by competing for and winning first prizes. He was awarded a silver cup for speeches delivered in Hall, and two more silver cups for declamations in Chapel, as well as three Opponencies in the Schools. On 1 June 1795, he crowned this glittering record by winning the Sir William Browne's Medal for a Latin ode.

Traditionally a ceremonious poem composed on an occasion of public or private importance, in which personal feeling and general meditation are united, the ode (as English literature inherited and developed it from Greek drama and Horatian *carmina*) had become by the early eighteenth century a genre that was very much a part of the period's conscious emulation of Rome's Augustan Age. In its English version, it was essentially a poem of praise, and it was in this form that England's scholars and poets composed their occasional odes.

According to an academic friend of D'Oyly's contemporary Robert Southey, Cambridge University prided itself at this time on producing 'verses both Greek and Latin which are worthy of gold medals, and English ones also after the newest and most approved receipt for verse-making'.[7] And since the annual Birthday Ode written by the current Poet Laureate in praise of the reigning British monarch was, of course, pre-eminent among the English odes in public importance, it would have been natural for D'Oyly to look to the Laureate for 'the newest and most approved' recipe for this kind of literary confection.

The efforts of Henry James Pye (1745–1813), a country squire whom Pitt appointed Laureate at the time John D'Oyly was at Cambridge, did not, however, provide models that an intelligent young poet in his right mind would have wanted to adopt. In his delightful book, *The Joy of Bad Verse*, Nicholas T. Parsons provides numerous examples of 'limping Laureate' verse, including Pye's. No doubt the form itself was against the unfortunate Pye: the composition and presentation of the Birthday Ode was an institution designed simultaneously to celebrate the achievements of the Hanoverian dynasty and to demonstrate what the British public at any particular historical moment recognized as, and expected of, poetry. Whatever its design might have been, its effect was – almost inevitably – failure, since most of the effusions written, as it were, to order by the Poets Laureate, fail dismally as poetry. 'The nature of the job', writes Parsons,

> made absurdities inevitable – thoroughly unpleasant or even lunatic kings had to be praised to the heavens, English military victories presented as a boon to all mankind, and political controversies systematically misrepresented.

A Laureate's talent for versifying was, according to Parsons, 'one of the least important considerations for those who selected him'.[8]

The elevated diction and declamatory tone that came to be associated with the ode proper held out, of course, an open invitation to satirists: Byron's satire *A Vision of Judgment* (1822), which is set outside the celestial gates of heaven, has Southey reciting his verse to the heavenly throng. The recently deceased George III 'suddenly jerked into wakefulness [and] imagining himself to be the victim of a poetical performance by the dreaded Pye', exclaims:

> What! What!
> *Pye* come again? No more – no more of that!

At its inception, in the hands of such a poet as John Dryden (1631–1700), the first to be appointed to the Laureateship, literary quality in the Birthday Ode had managed to survive the destructive workings of politics and self-interest. But Pye's attempts to soar were, writes Parsons, embarrassingly obsequious and 'spectacularly inept'. He was respected among the country gentry, but was as much an object of ridicule among the *literati* as Thomas Shadwell and Colley Cibber before and Alfred Austin after him.[9]

And yet, while literary critics and his fellow poets might have found the verse of Laureate (later magistrate) Pye stupefyingly dull or unintentionally comic, few conservative Englishmen innocent of literary skills or pretensions would have objected to Pye's favourable comparison of Britain to southern Europe:

> No purple vintage though she boast,
> No olive shade her ruder coast;
> Yet here immortal Freedom reigns,
> And law protects what labour gains;
> And as her manly sons behold
> The cultur'd farm, the teeming fold . . .[10]

The Laureate's patriotic sentiments were well known and, like his background of country gentility, were probably approved of in 1796 (especially in rectories like Revd Mathias D'Oyly's in Buxted, and by the hunting, shooting, fishing squirearchy all over England with which they were so closely connected). Indeed, whatever his failings as a poet of skill, the similarity of parts of H.J. Pye's 'epic poem' about the achievements of King Alfred the Great to some verses in D'Oyly's 1796 ode appear to demonstrate that despite their difference in quality, the two writers shared the period's popular belief in the value of commerce to Britain's standing in the world. We might compare, for example, Pye:

> 'Tis from the rustic swain's diurnal toil,
> That Commerce draws, with powerful grasp, the stores
> Of every clime from Earth's remotest shores,
> That navies o'er the obedient billow ride ...

with stanza 20 of D'Oyly's 'Commercii Laus' as given in Appendix 2.

The question of form once settled, what about theme and subject? D'Oyly's intellectual and sporting interests would have ensured that, at the very least, he was not short of acceptable subjects for the composition of occasional verse.[11]

But in choosing a subject for a university ode, D'Oyly needed to be very sure what he did *not* want to write about. The madness of King George III and the profligacy of his sons, prominent features of the English political scene during D'Oyly's undergraduate years, were hardly tempting topics for budding writers. In his search for a suitable subject for poetic praise, D'Oyly (unlike Laureate Pye) rejected the 'achievements' of contemporary kings and statesmen, and looked instead to the past for his inspiration. Basing his view of the ancient world on the writings of Ovid and other Latin poets, he offered his university an original work on an unusual theme: the praise of commerce.

John D'Oyly's choice of subject might, at first sight, surprise the modern reader. Aware of the snobbish prejudice against 'trading connections' that was a feature of eighteenth-century social life in Britain, observant of the fact that none of John D'Oyly's forebears seems to have evinced any kind of open commercial interest, we might query the source of the young man's unexpected interest in such a subject. The established concerns of the D'Oyly family had traditionally been focused on service to church and state, in which areas they had distinguished themselves in the past, and continued to do so in D'Oyly's generation. John's younger brother Francis, later Sir Francis D'Oyly, KCB, a lieutenant-colonel in the 1st Guards, met his death in 1815 at Brussels, soon after the English victory at Waterloo. George D'Oyly followed his father the archdeacon into the Church, becoming in time a Doctor of Divinity, and serving as Rector of Lambeth and of Sundridge. Henry, like Francis, joined the army and served as a captain in his elder brother's regiment. Nowhere in the D'Oyly family records can there be found any overt mention of commerce or of trade.[12]

In the two centuries prior to John D'Oyly's writing of his ode, however, British interests in India had undergone a noticeable change. Established originally as an entirely commercial enterprise, the English East India Company had been formed for the promotion of trade with the Far East and India, incorporated by royal charter in December 1600. Starting its career as a monopolistic trading body, 'John Company' (as it was affectionately known in its heyday) became involved in politics and acted as an agent of British imperialism in India from the early eighteenth century to the mid-nineteenth century.

When the company acquired control of Bengal in 1757, British policy with regard to India was influenced for a period of some sixteen years by the views of its shareholders: votes could, it is said, be bought by the purchase of shares. This unsatisfactory state of affairs led to government intervention. The Regulating Act (1773) and William Pitt's India Act (1784) put Indian affairs on a different footing altogether: for the future, political policy would be put into effect through a Board of Control responsible to Parliament, rather than to the company.[13]

The D'Oylys' 'Indian connection' begins to assume, in this altered context, a notable significance. Over two hundred years, service in the East under the British flag had inevitably come to involve the making of commercial decisions and the promotion of British trading interests. It was a situation that had been created by circumstance, and that situation continued to exist until 1813, when the commercial monopoly of the English East India Company was officially ended. As a result, the D'Oylys who had served in India had served in a country governed by commercial rule. The high regard in which the family was held in Sussex might perhaps, in this respect, be attributed in some degree to the consequence enjoyed by English 'nabobs' and 'West India merchants' of the eighteenth century whose wealth (displayed in England in the form of opulently furnished town houses, and expensively landscaped estates and gardens in the country) was founded on profits wrung by extortion or force in India, and by the exploitation of African slaves labouring on sugar plantations in the West Indies.

Commerce, then, at least by 1795 when John D'Oyly composed his ode, if not yet quite respectable, did not necessarily degrade. English society, traditionally stratified by class, had always understood the value of money, and many families that had enriched themselves through trade in the mid-eighteenth century found themselves (possibly after some initial rebuffs and snobbish hesitations) accommodated comfortably enough in English society at the start of the nineteenth. The D'Oylys, an old country family with aristocratic connections, did not, of course, belong in that category. Those members of the clan who went to India 'in one capacity or another' were most unlikely to have considered themselves as lowering themselves socially by dabbling in 'trade': on the contrary, they probably saw themselves, and were seen by others, as extending to a new theatre – the Orient – the duty they had traditionally and loyally fulfilled at home in England in the service of their king and country. Commerce had proved its worth as an agent for the expansion of British political and financial power. By the end of the eighteenth century it was beginning to be regarded as an agent of civilization.

This is the attitude towards commerce adopted by John D'Oyly in his prize-winning poem, 'Commercii Laus', the original text of which, together with a literal English translation by J.J. Nicholls, is given as Appendix 2 of this book.[14] An attentive reading of D'Oyly's ode reveals how closely and uncompromisingly the ideas of commercial prosperity and intellectual progress had come to be knitted together in the mind of its youthful author.

D'Oyly asserted in verses 6–10 that it was by virtue of the daring of the seamen of the ancient world, and the heroic efforts they expended on behalf of all mankind, that the discovery of gold was made possible, together with the wealth and prosperity which flowed from that discovery. Such prosperity, he suggested, offered a welcome change from the past times he had described in verses 1–5, times in which war, savagery and brutish ignorance had marked the lot of humanity and prevented the establishment of 'a common bond of Peace'. The birth of intellectual and civilized life, he continued in verses 11–14, was an integral part of a new order of things.

It is interesting to note, particularly in view of the D'Oyly family's Indian connections and the career path he was himself destined to take, that (in verse 12) D'Oyly first located this auspicious event in 'distant India', offering 'Egypt's land' as a second alternative.

Sidon, Tyre and Carthage having been severally cited next (in verses 15–18) as examples of commercially successful, culturally brilliant, and politically powerful cities which had tragically misused their advantages and been brought, as a result, to destruction, the poet celebrated in verse 19 the success of Rome and the glory of its civilization which,

> by uniting the nations, gathered the diverse blessings of the earth into one embrace, lording it over the whole world with a powerful, but unjust sway.

The involvement of his family in Britain's imperial enterprise might conceivably have added some nuance to verse 19, since the achievements D'Oyly celebrated there as specific to Rome – of 'uniting the nations and gathering the diverse blessings of the earth into one embrace' – are, significantly, imperial achievements.

Eighteenth-century England had been regarding itself for some time, of course, as the 'new Augusta', one of the prime inheritors in Europe of the Roman legacy. It is evident from what follows (verse 20) that D'Oyly shared the assumptions common in his age and nation.

> But we, why are we reluctant to enjoy the many good things which a better age has produced? For to us the Sea Sisters and the West Winds bring into harbours of our choice whatever merchandise Pergamene and Cypriote offer for mankind's use, all the spices that both Indies produce beneath their kindly skies.

In the closing verses (20–28) of his ode, D'Oyly related what had gone before to Britain in general, and to Cambridge University in particular. He had suggested (verse 19) that the civilization of Rome, though undoubtedly glorious, had been a civilization tragically flawed by injustice. Concluding by this example that hidden dangers have historically attended the accession of any nation to absolute power, he warned that Britain, now succeeding to dominance and international influence comparable with that wielded by Rome in the ancient world (verses 20–21), should learn from Rome's example and avoid the errors she had made.

Moving into the final verses of his ode, D'Oyly claimed confidently that he and his contemporaries in Britain were entering upon a golden age free of 'the madness of war', an era happier and better than any the world had known. By virtue of her sea-driven commercial success (verses 20–21, 25) Britain now commanded, he declared, the 'harbours of our choice', enjoying by right not only the products of the known world but what was virtually a monopoly on learning. Implying that commercial prosperity is invariably accompanied by peace and the spread of freedom and knowledge, the poet looked forward to a future symbolically filled with light and resonant with music, celebrating the part that would be played in that glowing future by his own university. Cambridge, he wrote, while providing a new theatre for the humanizing and civilizing activities of art and science, would not take second place even to 'the ancient grove of the Muses' in its sacred power to inspire and educate the coming generations.

The metre D'Oyly had chosen was the Alcaic metre of the Roman poet Horace, and he employed it skilfully to express a boundless confidence in the future of his country. D'Oyly's faith in his own poetic powers was, incidentally (and rather endearingly), not quite so firm as were his convictions regarding Britain's present and future glory. His Cambridge diary, as published by P.E. Pieris in *Letters to Ceylon*, tells us a great deal about the young undergraduate's extreme nervousness regarding his performance in the competition for the medal, and his reliance upon his friends for their moral support at moments both of crisis and of celebration:

Tuesd. 7th – Commencement Day – Took a walk early with Strachey & B. Allen – came home, wrote over my Ode & dressed – heard from home – breakfasted at Ainslie's at 10 – adjourned to the Senate-house – took a walk with Strachey to refresh ourselves – came, in a hurry, spoke my Ode & received the Medal – Strachey his Epigrams – formidable Audience – Wrote to my Brother Francis, Warley Camp – Walked with Ainslie, afterwards with him & Strachey & B. Allen – Had company to dinner Strachey, Ainslie, Bayley & B. Allen –[15]

While D'Oyly's views as expressed in his Ode were representative of the thinking at this time of most English people of his class and background, it should be remembered, however, that there were some notable voices raised in dissent. Among these were the voices of Coleridge and Sheridan. The very year after D'Oyly composed his ode, Coleridge delivered a forceful public lecture on 9 or 12 June 1796, at the Assembly Coffeehouse on the Quay, in Bristol, in the course of which he discussed the link between sin, death and Britain's trade in the East Indies and mentioned, in that sinister context, a personality with close connections to D'Oyly's family:

> Now can a conscientious man make himself the Instrument of upholding and increasing those Enormities, which make the World a contradistinction to the kingdom of God? If he be a Commercial Man . . . let him look around his shop? Does nothing in it come from the desolate plains of Indostan? From what motives did Lord Clive murder his million and justify it to all but his own conscience? From what motives did the late rice-contracting Governor famish a million and gain from the Company the Title of Saviour of India? Was it not that wicked as they were they increased and preserved the commercial Intercourse?

The 'rice-contracting Governor' whom Coleridge here accused of murdering Britain's Indian subjects was none other than Warren Hastings, President of the company since 1772 and from 1774 to 1785 the first governor-general of all the British territories in India. Hastings was a close friend of John D'Oyly's relative Sir John Hadley D'Oyly, who had helped pay Hastings's legal costs in the seven long years during which he had faced impeachment proceedings.

In his thirteen years of rule Hastings had transferred the government of Bengal from the nawab's court to Calcutta, remodelled the administration and subjected it completely to British control. He was opposed by determined Indian forces from the Marathas in central India, menacing Bombay, and from Hyder Ali of Mysore, challenging in the south. To meet these challenges, Hastings had demanded subsidy from subject or client princes, and requisitioned their treasure. Where persuasion failed, he had employed force, notably against Raja Chait Singh of Benares, and against the dowager princesses of Oudh. His enemies accused him of securing the judicial murder of Nandakumar, a Bengali official who had accused him of embezzlement.

Coleridge quoted facts and figures, claiming that Britain's 'commercial Intercourse with the East Indies' had cost eight million lives, in return for which most foul and heart in-slaving [*sic*] Guilt we receive gold, diamonds, silks, muslins & callicoes [*sic*] for fine Ladies and Prostitutes. Tea to make a pernicious Beverage, Porcelain to drink it from, and salt-petre for the making of gunpowder with which we may murder the poor Inhabitants who supply all these things.[16]

For 170 years before D'Oyly composed his ode or Coleridge delivered his lecture, the affairs of 'British' India had been run by the East India Trading Company, operating under royal charter. Vast profits were being made by the company's employees and officers, so that the luckier or more unscrupulous of them returned as 'nabobs' (nawabs or princes) to England, laden with riches, much as Sheridan's character Sir Oliver Surface does in *The School for Scandal* (1777). By 1784 even George III was writing to Pitt of 'shocking enormitties [*sic*]' perpetrated by the British in India 'that disgrace human nature'.

Ten years earlier, a Commons committee led by Sheridan's friend 'Gentleman Johnny' Burgoyne had unsuccessfully tried to bring to book the greatest of the nabobs, Robert Clive. On that occasion the Commons, while voting that all the company's territorial acquisitions ought to belong to the nation, decided to condone Clive's fortune-hunting since, like Othello, he had 'done the state some service'. (He had come home with close on a quarter of a million pounds, astonished, as he said, at his own moderation.)

Burke's intended victim was Clive's successor-but-two, Warren Hastings. Burke was determined that Hastings should be impeached, that is, prosecuted by the House of Commons in the House of Lords. Sheridan had entered with gusto into the spirit of the battle on behalf of the princesses of Oudh. John D'Oyly may have been too young in February 1787 to hear the whole of the great speech, lasting 5 hours and 40 minutes, with which Sheridan assailed Hastings, using every oratorical device he had learned in a lifetime of work in the theatre.[17] But he knew of his family's connection with Hastings, who had, like himself, been educated at Westminster School. He knew that Hastings was generally considered to have been one of the ablest statesmen Britain sent to India. He was not too young to have heard, while at Westminster, a good deal about Sheridan's dramatic doings, and during his last undergraduate year at Cambridge, he went up to London to attend the impeachment proceedings.[18]

Despite the emotions universally aroused by Sheridan's eloquence, Hastings's trial, which had begun in 1788, ended in his acquittal before the House of Lords on 23 April 1795. In the year following, which was D'Oyly's last at Cambridge, the young man competed for the Chancellor's Medal, translating Thucydides, Horace and Demosthenes, writing verses and prose composition, and rendering Cromwell's *Character* from Clarendon into Latin prose. (He was awarded the second medal.) Launching out at about the same time on what was evidently a course of self-education, he proceeded to store his mind. His reading at this period included, in addition to Locke and Paley, Hume's *History of England* (he finished it in July 1799), Tully's *Offices*, Voltaire's *Peter the Czar* and *Charles XII*, de Lolme (then the chief authority on the English Constitution), Robertson's *Charles V*, Watson's *Philip II* and *Philip III*, together with Goldsmith's *History of England*, Watson's *Chemical Essays* and Adam Smith's *Wealth of Nations* (which he found, according to a diary entry for 1797, 'an highly instructive & entertaining Book').

The emphasis his reading list placed on history prompts the question as to whether or not D'Oyly had taken as his guide Niccolo Machiavelli's advice that

> as exercise for the mind, [the prince] ought to read history and study the actions of eminent men, see how they acted in warfare, [and] examine the causes of their victories and defeats in order to imitate the former and avoid the latter.[19]

Hastings's career, however, provided D'Oyly with a nearer, more immediate, and more strikingly dramatic illustration of the victories and defeats attending the actions of 'eminent men' than any of Machiavelli's. D'Oyly's career would resemble that of Hastings to the extent that his interest in languages, literature and constitutional law would also take an orientalist direction during his years in the East. Hastings, who had established a *madrasa* in Calcutta for Muslim traditional education, was one of the founders of the Asiatic Society of Bengal and the initiator of an Arabic college, besides being himself a student of Arabic, Persian and Sanskrit, which he wished to master in order to ascertain the nature of Indian law. D'Oyly, appointed very early in his Civil Service career as Chief Translator to the British

Government of the Maritime Provinces of Ceylon, later applied his knowledge of the Sinhala language to the preparation of a code of Kandyan customary law.

But, as D'Oyly had had occasion to observe at first hand, Hastings was impeached in 1787 on 23 counts as a moneymaker and oppressor. Eight long and painful years, during which he lost most of his fortune, had passed before he was acquitted. If D'Oyly's Latin ode gives us some insight into the young man's view of the world at the close of his university career (he graduated on 22 January 1796), his personal observation at Westminster Hall of the last part of the trial of Warren Hastings was another event of 1795 which might well have prompted the meticulous care with which he later kept detailed records of all diplomatic transactions he made on behalf of the Crown during his years in Ceylon.

Meanwhile, the future beckoned, requiring of D'Oyly, then 22 years old, that he put off no longer the making of certain important choices. Possibly considering a legal career (which had been the choice of his elder brother Thomas), he observed judicial procedure at the Cambridge Assizes. Presumably planning a post-university tour of Europe of the kind taken at the time by many young Englishmen of his age, education and station in life, he also learned Italian. Then, on 12 February 1798, he was elected to a fellowship at Bene't College.

Despite the glorious future he had prophesied in his ode for British influence overseas, and his probable hope that he might have an opportunity to help make that promise a reality, the receipt of such an honour must have given D'Oyly pause. His mind and talents (and his ecclesiastical family background, too, perhaps) undoubtedly fitted him for an academic career at one of the universities. On the other hand, it seemed that there was now room (to say nothing of good financial prospects) in Britain's overseas service, not only for daring sailors and swashbuckling soldiers, but for scholars and intellectuals.

For quite some time there had been a determined and growing effort by the East India Company and many of its leading servants to create 'an empire of knowledge', as well as of commerce, in the Orient. In 1801 the company's directors founded Haileybury, a college for training new arrivals ('griffins') before they were posted out to the districts. The company established its library and museum in London. According to Paul Johnson, who documents this interesting development in his study

The Birth of the Modern: World Society 1815–1830 (1991), the new policy had many manifestations besides the offer of a formal training at Haileybury. They included research in botany, the assembling of menageries and the collection of geological specimens, plants, coins, books, maps and prints.[20]

They also included the shipping of statuary home to England through the Admiralty. The Elgin Marbles, sections of the Acropolis, were removed by Lord Thomas Elgin between 1801 and 1803, and shipped 'home' in this manner. A first shipment was lost at sea. The rest were sold to the British Museum in 1816.

For such initiatives as the establishment of an 'empire of knowledge' in the Orient, John D'Oyly, with his proven interest in languages and literature and his 'Indian connections', must have seemed an ideal recruit. His employers recognized his potential, and it is quite probable that he might also have seen himself in the same light. 'The East' offered hope of a promising career to active and scholarly young men – even if a young recruit were aware, by any chance, that in Calcutta at this time, presumably as a result of Warren Hastings's recent and notorious fall from grace, 'it was no longer fashionable in Government House circles to profess interest in Persian poetry or Indian metaphysics'. Such matters, states S.C. Welch in *Room for Wonder*, 'were now left to academics and eccentrics'.[21]

D'Oyly's destination, although (like a later recruit to the Indian Civil Service, Leonard Woolf) he probably did not aim specifically for it, was to be the tropical island of Ceylon, whose maritime provinces, lately wrested by British arms from the Dutch, were about to be formally declared a Crown Colony.

A map of Ceylon drawn in 1802 by Major A. Allan, Quartermaster-General on the expedition commanded by Major-General James Stuart that captured the Fort of Colombo from the Dutch, shows very clearly how matters stood between Britain and the Kingdom of Kandy at the beginning of British rule in the island. Areas coloured red denote the Maritime Provinces, territory formerly belonging to the Dutch East India Company that were ceded to the British by the Treaty of Amiens, while areas coloured orange mark 'Territory belonging to the King of Candia' (see Plate 1). Allan based his work on an original map that had been drawn in 1789 from surveys made by order of William Jacob Van de Graaff, a Dutch governor of the Maritime Provinces, and dedicated it to the Right Honourable Lord Hobart, 'one of His Majesty's Principal Secretaries of State'.

John D'Oyly duly secured a cadetship in the Ceylon Civil Service, his father's friendship with the Earl of Liverpool, Secretary of State for the Colonies, doubtless facilitating the appointment. As Disraeli was to remark in his novel *Tancred* some 45 years later, the East had become a career.[22]

CHAPTER TWO

1801–1805: 'HARBOURS OF OUR CHOICE'

It is with nations as with men –
One must be first, we are the mightiest,
The heirs of Rome.

John Davidson

WITH THE ESTABLISHMENT OF EMPIRE, the image (which had been general in British literature throughout the sixteenth, seventeenth and eighteenth centuries) of Asia as a source of mystery, beauty, dignity and unparalleled wealth, the source of mathematical knowledge, religious philosophy and the most delicate (or, alternatively, the most sensual) art, gave way to an image that justified the British imperial presence in the East.

The new image represented Asians as childlike, in need of moral education and political guidance, and above all in need of *control*. Book after book published in the nineteenth century, especially in Britain, took up this point of view as an established fact; popular culture in the form of song and story popularized it. Against such a background of ideas, it was hardly possible for the British in Ceylon to be objective or unbiased observers of the 'native' scene. And they were not, affirms Elizabeth J. Harris, in *The Gaze of the Coloniser* (1994):

[The British] were conditioned by the conviction of cultural superiority and the power relationships of their imperial adventure. What they wrote as colonial rulers in the nineteenth century reflects the concerns of . . . Britain as much as it describes Sri Lanka . . . The British . . . stepped into the island to rule, convert, educate, make money or discover 'the Orient'.

In her analysis of attitudes adopted by the British towards the 'oriental' society they encountered in nineteenth-century Ceylon, Harris overlooks or ignores one very important factor: that among those who came to Ceylon 'to rule, convert, educate, make money [and] discover "the Orient"', there were some, especially in the colony's early years, who came out to serve. Part of the twentieth century's postcolonial reaction against imperialism has been a reluctance to acknowledge the evidence that an ideal of corporate service existed in colonialism's early stages, and that it inspired a small but significant section among the English people who came out 'East'. That section included a number of government officials, of whom John D'Oyly, the subject of this book, is an outstanding example.

Harris emphasizes instead the political base of the attitudes she has identified:

When power is wrested from the Dutch in 1796, the British who visit Sri Lanka see it as a strategically useful possession, potentially rich in resources. Robert Percival, a Captain who served in Sri Lanka between 1797 and 1800, stresses '. . . the vast importance of the island both in a commercial and political view', and Lord Valentia, an aristocratic world traveller, claims that the treasures of the country 'will, I think, render it one of our most valuable possessions'. At this point [in the development of British relations with Sri Lanka] considerations of economic and political expediency are paramount.

However, these are soon combined with a nexus of Empire-justifying attitudes centering on the self-image of the British male and the myth of a civilizing and Christianizing mission. British male [writers] are quick, for instance, to define themselves in contra-distinction to the perceived rapacity and greed of the Portuguese and the Dutch, by laying claim to a greater sense of justice and 'mild' government in line with the stereotype fostered by British public schooling of the morally upright, competitive but fair, well-mannered British gentleman. Important for this study is that this came to be combined with a sense of moral duty and the conviction of cultural superiority. Both were used to justify political domination.

In the development of her argument – and especially in its closing sentences – Harris draws a striking picture of a representative English gentleman whose 'mythical' existence was 'used to justify political domination' of Ceylon by the British.[1]

An extensive literature exists to support such a thesis as Elizabeth Harris's, and there is no doubt that a great deal of the energy of twentieth-century postcolonial literature has been generated by the psychological need of writers born or educated in former British colonies to 'write back' to the empire. By doing so, they retrieve lost national myths and images, and attempt to retrieve lost or suppressed languages and cultures. The 1990s have witnessed the forging by such writers of new literary techniques which incorporate those languages and cultures, and the development by them of ways of writing and looking at the world which have found acceptance in a world that professes to have turned its back on empire and the imperial ideas of the past.

This having been said, it is important in saying it to avoid generalizations, lest we stereotype the British in much the same way that, as Harris claims in her thesis, the British stereotyped the people of colonial Ceylon. The nineteenth century visitors who recorded their responses to the island and its people were certainly, as Harris points out, almost exclusively male, but they emerged from varied backgrounds and cherished different objectives. They included scientists and surgeons like Dr John Davy and Dr Henry Marshall, well-heeled politicians and aristocratic travellers like Charles Wentworth Dilke and Lord Valentia, Anglican clergymen like James Cordiner, Methodist missionaries like George Osborne, Robert Spence Hardy and Benjamin Clough who were convinced that Buddhist monks and Hindu priests were agents of the Prince of Darkness, journalists and writers like William Knighton, army officers like Robert Percival, Captain Arthur Johnston, Thomas Skinner, James Campbell and George Calladine, and civil servants like Sir James Emerson Tennent and John D'Oyly. Can Harris be justified in her claim that, despite such variety of background, most of them were 'conditioned by cultural and class attitudes which placed . . . Britain in the forefront of global progress'?

42

The study of lives such as John D'Oyly's, and of the circumstances in which those lives touched the life of the Orient, might help to disentangle theory from fact and shed some light on the human, and therefore complex, issues which underlie the deceptively simple colonizer/colonized dichotomy of much postcolonial theory.

A sea passage between Europe and the East in 1801, when John D'Oyly made his journey to Ceylon, could take up to eight months. Later in the century, steam-driven ships would reduce the length and tedium of that journey, and deep-water harbours would be artificially constructed to accommodate such vessels. But the natural harbour of Colombo was not deep enough in 1801 to accept passenger ships, and Point-de-Galle, 72 miles south of the capital, was still the point of landing for all large craft when Charles Wentworth Dilke visited the island in 1867. Ships arriving there had to anchor at some distance in the Galle harbour, while passengers with their baggage were transported by rowing-boat from the decks to the shore. D'Oyly's first sight of the country that would be his home for the next 23 years was taken, therefore, from a rowing-boat coming into harbour.

Many European writers have described that first impression of Asia in their travel memoirs and diaries. Joseph Conrad committed his memorably to fiction through his *alter ego*, Marlow, who reflects in the story *Youth* (1898) what his creator's sensations had been on encountering the East for the first time:

> And this is how I see the East. I have seen its secret places and have looked into its very soul; but now I see it always from a small boat, a high outline of mountains, blue and afar in the morning; like faint mist at noon; a jagged wall of purple at sunset. I have the feel of the oar in my hand, the vision of a scorching blue sea in my eyes. And I see a bay, a wide bay, smooth as glass and polished like ice, shimmering in the dark. A red light burns far off upon the gloom of the land, and the night is soft and warm.

Drifting into harbour at night, Marlow experiences 'the East' as 'impalpable and enslaving, like a charm, like a whispered promise of mysterious delight'. He would never forget the scent of a night wind 'laden with strange odours of blossoms, of aromatic wood, [that came] out of the still night – the first sigh of the East on my face'.[2]

This is very much a young man's vision: Conrad's first journey to Indonesia, fictionalized in *Youth*, could have taken place at any time between the ages of 17 and 37. When John D'Oyly made his journey from England to Colombo in 1801, he was 27 years old. We have no record of his sensations and feelings at a similar moment in his life, but he was a young man in his twenties when he sailed from Europe to Asia, and the harbour at Point de Galle into which this first sea journey took him would have been very much like the bay at Java Head that Marlow recalls so vividly in Conrad's tale.

Europeans coming ashore in Galle on a sunny morning experienced 'the East' somewhat differently. First, there would be a vivid visual contrast: a golden shoreline edged with palm trees, in its own way a vision of perfection that for the rest of their lives would probably linger with them as their first impression of the 'mysterious' and 'romantic' Orient (see Plate 2). Charles Wentworth Dilke, arriving in Galle in 1867, found himself at anchor 'in a small bay, surrounded with lofty cocoa palms', and noted how 'in the damp hot air the old tattered union-jacks seemed brilliant crimson, and the dull green of the cocoa palms became a dazzling emerald'.[3] Next, for all Europeans, and in many cases equally lasting in their memory, would come their first view of 'the natives'.

In the September of 1801 John D'Oyly stepped ashore in Galle harbour, and journeyed by coach to Colombo. In the rural southern districts through which he passed, life is leisured and change has always been slow. When Dilke made the same journey in 1867, little in the landscape had altered in 60 years. Dilke found himself driving along

a magnificent road in an avenue of giant cocoa-nut palms, with the sea generally within easy sight, and with a native hut at each few yards. Every two or three miles, the road crossed a lagoon, alive with bathers, and near the bridge was generally a village, bazaar, and Buddhist temple, built pagoda-shape, and filled with worshippers. The road was thronged with gaily dressed Cinghalese; and now and again we would pass a Buddhist priest in saffron-coloured robes, hastening along, his umbrella borne over him by a boy clothed from top to toe in white . . . The Cinghalese farmers we met travelling to their temples in carts drawn by tiny bullocks. Such was the brightness of the air, that the people, down to the very beggars, seemed clad in holiday attire.[4]

To Dilke, 'the natives' are little more than curious and amusing figures in a brightly coloured scene. As beggars, as hotel servants in Galle, and as farmers and priests glimpsed from a moving carriage, they provide an animated picture-show of oriental life. Dilke remarked with some satisfaction in his Preface to *Greater Britain* (1872) that

> the idea which in all the length of my travels has been at once my fellow and my guide – a key wherewith to unlock the hidden things of strange new lands – is a conception, however imperfect, of the grandeur of our race, already girdling the earth, which it is destined, perhaps, eventually to overspread.[5]

In such a privileged traveller as Charles Wentworth Dilke we may recognize, perhaps, the typical 'colonizer' of Harris's theory.

But was Dilke typical of his countrymen and women? And especially of those English people who, like John D'Oyly, Henry Marshall, Thomas Skinner and Captain Arthur Johnston, had come East in order to serve the empire in various capacities? The 'natives' certainly appeared somewhat differently to William Knighton, an Englishman who arrived in Colombo some years after John D'Oyly's death, and made the same journey from ship to shore by rowing-boat that D'Oyly had made before him. Knighton too had been, like D'Oyly – and like Conrad and Dilke some decades later – a young man receiving his first impression of the East. A thoughtful individual of imagination and intelligence, Knighton became fascinated by the island's history and published an account of it in 1845. He described his experiences in Ceylon in *Forest-Life in Ceylon*, a novel published in 1854, and described there in the heightened language of fiction the primary *and* secondary effects upon a British traveller of his time of what is now called 'culture shock':

> To my unsophisticated eyes, the crew of this boat appeared to be tame monkeys. So completely was my conception of humanity mixed up with clothes and white or black skins, that it was, for a time, impossible for me to realize to myself the idea that these gibbering, long-armed, brown, naked animals were fellow-creatures. Even now, after having had many years' experience of the East, I still believe that more unfavourable specimens of the natives of Ceylon could scarcely have been met with than those in the boat. Three of them were old

men, their ribs too distinguishable through their leather-like skin, their arms dry and shrivelled; yet their advanced age was not to be seen at once – their long, bony, and muscular arms, deprived of every particle of fat; their fingers rendered remarkable by the white nails at the tips; the palms of their hands white from constant labour; and the contrast between their brown, shrivelled-up wrinkled skins, and the scanty white or blue cloth which they wore round their loins, all formed a picture so like that which a party of tamed monkeys would present, that it was not without disgust I gazed at them – disgust, mingled with something of indignation, that these animals should be of the same species as myself. Nor did the grizzled beards, and the bare shaggy heads, from which they had removed their straw fishermen's hats, tend to improve the picture, or make them more human-like. My feelings were shared by my companions, and, as we muttered to each other, 'These are the natives', we could not help wondering how humanity could degenerate into such figures; *forgetting that the want of dress and difference of colour were the only real points of contrast between them and similar specimens of our own countrymen.* [Emphasis added.][6]

Unlike Dilke on his whirlwind tour of English-speaking countries, Knighton stayed long enough in Ceylon to study the country, its history and its people, and in the light of such study, to review his first impressions.

No record kept by John D'Oyly of his early years in Ceylon has survived, but there is no reason to think that his own feelings on arrival and his own first impression of 'the natives' would have been very different from Knighton's. It was probably inevitable, as David Fitzpatrick has suggested, that at this particular point in time, 'the division between West and East [should have been] typically seen through imperial eyes as a clash between the civilised and the savage, the godly against the heathen, the intelligent versus the ignorant, the moral over the unmoral, the advanced controlling the primitive'.[7]

It was not that British observers were less sensitive or more insular than other Europeans – than the Polish Conrad, for instance. It would be truer to say that the structure of colonial society did not generally provide opportunities for British people who travelled East to go beyond first impressions to others less distorted by their own insularity and their cultural and political conditioning. The writings of both Knighton[8] and D'Oyly show that when such opportunities presented themselves, both men grasped them with enthusiasm. There is little doubt, admittedly, that both were exceptions to what seems to have been a general rule. But it is important to recognize that such exceptions as D'Oyly, Knighton, George Turnour (who translated the *Mahavamsa*, the island's 'Great Chronicle'), Thomas Skinner (who devoted fifty years of his life to the island) and – in a later generation – Leonard Woolf, did exist, and that they were more influential and effective than is generally recognized.

On arrival in Colombo, D'Oyly simultaneously entered not only the main thoroughfare of the capital of a British colony, but a topographical arrangement which reflected and reinforced the ideological division that marked off West from East in the European mind. Within the walls of the massive fort built in Colombo by the Dutch now stood the barracks of the Crown Colony's British troops. 'Old Government House', formerly the residence of Johan Gerard van Angelbeek, the last Dutch governor of Colombo, was now the bachelor quarters of Major-General Hay Macdowall, commander of the British forces in the Maritime Provinces. (Frederick North, the British governor, who was also a bachelor, had found his first residence in Colombo 'hot and confined', and had moved to a villa at Hulftsdorp.)

As time went on, and the British settled comfortably into their newly acquired colony, these buildings would be enlarged and improved, and others built around them, so that by the 1860s the walls of the fort would extend their protection to most of the island's major public and mercantile offices, several banks, a library, and a Chamber of Commerce, together with an Anglican, a Presbyterian and a Methodist church.

The houses of the European residents who made up 'Colombo society' were scattered along the shores of the picturesque Beira Lake, in the cinnamon gardens which adjoined it, or along the seashore. Outside the walls of the fort, and on the opposite side of the lake was the 'Native Quarter' or Pettah, occupied principally by Burghers, as descendants of the Portuguese and Dutch who had formerly ruled Colombo were called. The Pettah was laid out in the manner of Dutch towns, in streets that ran parallel or at right angles to one another and were lined with *suriya* or 'tulip' trees which cast a pleasant shade. A mixed population inhabited the rest of the town. Social interaction between British ruler and Ceylonese subject was as limited as in other British colonies, 'natives' figuring in the colonial 'world' of Colombo mainly as coachmen, grooms, shopkeepers and vendors of sweetmeats.

The English society of Colombo, as in most British colonies, appears to have faithfully mirrored English society at home in its consciousness of status and class. The youthful D'Oyly, one of the first batch of civil servants sent to Ceylon to staff the administration of the new Crown Colony, was well received at King's House due to the aristocratic connections and 'cultured generations' of the D'Oyly family, and (last, but probably most important of all) the patronage of Lord Liverpool.

Elizabeth Harris's portrait of 'the morally upright, competitive but fair, well-mannered British gentleman' is touched with some strokes of satiric irony, but it is not quite the stereotype she claims it to be. It is evident that Frederick North, third son of the second Earl of Guildford and the colony's first governor, was looking for precisely such qualities, together with unusually high intelligence, in the group of young men he personally chose to surround him in this, Ceylon's first colonial administration.

North had been educated at Eton and at Christ Church, Oxford. He was something of an aesthete besides being an accomplished scholar in the Western classics. He conversed fluently and wittily in German, Spanish, French, Italian and Romany, and he read Russian with ease. Devoted to the arts, some of his initiatives had about them a flavour of eccentricity. The ruins of 'The Doric', a villa that North designed and had built for himself at Arippu on the lines of a Greek temple may still be seen today, its crumbling pillars slipping into the sea on the western coast of the island near Mannar.

North had designed and built his charming 'folly' when he travelled north to personally supervise the pearl fisheries at Mannar. It was somewhat cramped within, but outwardly so elegant and imposing, with a flat roof commanding a fine view of the sea, that James Cordiner refers to it in *A Description of Ceylon* (1807) as 'undoubtedly the most beautiful building in the island' and accompanies the compliment with a pleasing drawing.[9] The foundations of the building proved too fragile to withstand the stresses of sea erosion and climatic variation, and North's attractive fancy soon deteriorated beyond repair. Picturesque even in its ruined state, North's 'Doric' continues to fascinate artists

FIGURE 1 Picturesque even in ruin

Governor Frederick North's 'Doric' folly at Arippu. From James Cordiner,
A Description of Ceylon (1807).

and writers. John Davy's *Account of the Interior of Ceylon* (1821) features
an artist's representation of the building on its last page,[10] and Richard
Boyle is among the contemporary writers who have accorded it an
important place in their accounts of the island's beauties and
curiosities.[11]

The officials who accompanied North to Ceylon included Hugh
Cleghorn, the Chief Secretary (formerly Professor of Civil History at
the University of St Andrews), Antony Bertolacci (North's Corsican
private secretary, and the author some years later of a book on the
island's economy), and H.A. Marshall (nicknamed 'Iniquity Marshall',
to distinguish him from Sir Charles Marshall, a lawyer who was called
'Equity Marshall'). There were also three very young men: Sylvester
Gordon, Robert Barry and George Lusignan, who were expected to
learn the languages of the country and work under the first assistant to
the Chief Secretary until they were considered ready for promotion to
positions of responsibility.[12]

A member of this elite group whom D'Oyly, the possessor of impressive intellectual gifts of his own, is likely to have found congenial during his first years in Colombo, was a talented Frenchman, Joseph de Joinville. A civil servant who had accompanied Governor North to Ceylon in 1798 as a naturalist, and remained in the island until 1805, de Joinville was given responsibility for agriculture and natural history. Promotion seems to have been rapid under North, and by 1800 de Joinville had become Surveyor-General. He was interested in the island's history, in Buddhism and in the Sinhala language. He is said to have made the first translation from Sinhala into English, a translation of the classical 'message' poem *Kokila Sandesaya*, which North sent to England in 1802.

Also among the men who came out to Ceylon with D'Oyly in 1801 was Samuel Tolfrey. Tolfrey was almost immediately appointed Member of the Board of Revenue on a salary of £1,500 a year, becoming subsequently Civil Auditor-General. He shared D'Oyly's interest in languages, and his collection of Sinhalese words was purchased by the Ceylon government, to be later used in the preparation of Benjamin Clough's *Dictionary*.[13]

John D'Oyly and his colleagues, who were members of that first, early administration, seem to have set a pattern for those who followed them. The British civil servant belonged to a corps pledged to support traditional institutions. They were, many of them, trained in oriental languages, which helped those who were interested to maintain a sympathy with local traditional society. A.L. Lowell gives an interesting account in his *Colonial Civil Service* (1900) of the selection and training of Britain's colonial civil servants, including a description of Haileybury by H. Morse Stephens: both writers stress the effectiveness of the system in promoting among the men an intellectual sympathy for oriental culture.[14] The conservative traditions and orientalist training of the service did not attract marked criticism until the 1860s. By that time the authoritarian attitude recommended by James Mill to the rulers of India had combined with early imperial sentiment to promote firmness and efficiency at the expense of an intellectual and sympathetic appreciation of oriental culture.

It was expected that most British civil servants, however sympathetic to the peoples and cultures of the 'Orient', would return at some time or another to Europe. Unless they developed a personal interest in some

FIGURE 2 This pleasant country

'Kandy – Temple of Buddha, Dalada Maligawa'. Plate III in Prince Friedrich Wilhelm Waldemar of Prussia, *Journey of Prince Waldemar of Prussia to India* (1853).

aspect of local life or history, there was nothing to keep them in an Asian colony. Service overseas, writes S.C. Welch, was essentially a temporary affair: 'Visitors in another man's land, few Britishers went to stay.'[15]

Dr John Davy, younger brother of Sir Humphry Davy, was among the visitors who spent time in Sri Lanka, and increased Western knowledge of the island through their wide-ranging interests, their research and their publications. Davy graduated in medicine from Edinburgh in 1814, by which time his elder brother, then 36 years old, had been knighted nearly two years. Davy served in Ceylon between 1817 and 1819 as an army surgeon, and acted as physician to the governor and his wife from 1820. Many aspects of the island aroused his scientific interest, among them the island's geography and geology and the species and habits of Ceylon snakes, all of which receive attention in the volume he published on his return to England, *An Account of the Interior of Ceylon and of its Inhabitants* (1821). His book reflects a scientist's interests, including sections on cobras and leeches,

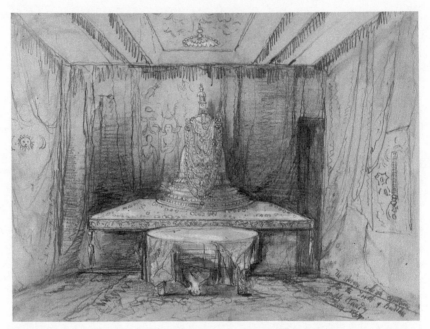

FIGURE 3 A shrine for the most sacred of the relics of the Buddha

'The Shrine which contains the Tooth of Buddhu', pencil drawing by Andrew Nicholl. From J.E. Tennent's manuscript 'Notes and Drawings of Ceylon' (Gooneratne Collection).

but he ignores neither the subject of elephant-hunting nor the island's system of writing on palm-leaf *olas*, though the subjects and style of such writing (which Davy presumably approached through translation and the assistance of local scholars) do not appear to have appealed to him – he thought the prose 'gaudy and obscure' and the poetry 'unsuited to English taste'.

From chapter 4 onward of his *Account*, Davy surveys the social structure of the Kandyan kingdom as he found it in the early nineteenth century. He records with scientific care the forms of administration and ceremony customary to the court, the forms of religious worship existing in the country, information relating to Sinhalese arts and crafts, and the character of the people as revealed by their domestic habits and manners.

In collecting his material, Davy travelled a great deal. The organization of a typical expedition in his time could be very elaborate as regards numbers of servants and quantities of provisions for, as Davy wrote, 'you are under the necessity of carrying with you every thing you want, as in a campaign, or in journeying on the desert'. Most of the journeys he undertook were made on foot, in palanquins or in tomjohns. These were chairs lashed to a pole and carried on the shoulders of two bearers (not unlike the sedan-chairs used in England at the same period) where the road or path could not admit a horse. Carriages were, of course, out of the question.[16]

Nor, until after 1815, did travel into the 'Kandyan country' of any kind, whether in tomjohns or on horse- or elephant-back, become possible for Europeans. Inland from the tranquil lowlands over which the British ruled rose the towering mountains that for three hundred years had guarded the Kingdom of Kandy from European eyes. Many legends about the kingdom circulated in the Maritime Provinces, legends which celebrated the majesty and ferocity of its reigning king, the opulence of its treasure, the tedious punctiliousness of its court life, and the leeches that infested its picturesque rivers. Songs told of the extreme holiness of the Dalada Maligava in the centre of the Kandyan capital, a shrine for the most sacred of the relics of the Buddha. Story upon story related instances of the bravery of Kandy's warriors and the beauty of its women.

D'Oyly's French colleague Joseph de Joinville had covertly observed the young women of the hill country villages of Ceylon, and had found them pleasing. 'The women of the lower orders,' he wrote in 1803,

> wear a petticoat of white cloth which, passing between their legs, is thrown over the right shoulder, and is fastened to the ligature about the waist; it has a very pretty effect. This is the dress in Candy.[17]

The wilderness that characterized the Kandyan country was later to delight lovers of the picturesque, and it is represented in countless attractive 'views' and 'vistas' in the collections of engravings, plates and prints published by nineteenth-century travellers such as Lord Valentia and Prince Friedrich Wilhelm Waldemar of Prussia. But travel beyond the Maritime Provinces in order to see and sketch such marvels as the Rock Fortress at Sigiriya or the caves at Dambulla, or even in observance of military duty, was extremely dangerous in the early years of the nineteenth century. Lieutenant William Lyttleton, several of whose

FIGURE 4 The marvel of Sigiri

'Fortified Rock of Sigiri', pencil drawing by Andrew Nicholl. From J.E. Tennent's manuscript 'Notes and Drawings of Ceylon' (Gooneratne Collection).

coloured aquatints illustrate this book, while in the company of a sergeant of the 73rd Regiment on the march to Kandy in 1815, attacked a wild elephant which pursued the two officers. 'The sergeant', reported the *Asiatic Journal*, 'was torn piecemeal, and the lieutenant found safety in a nearby tree, where he was obliged to remain many hours, closely watched by the elephant.'[18]

All in all, travel for the European unfamiliar with the local terrain could be, and was, extremely uncomfortable until Brownrigg's successor, Governor Edward Barnes, introduced a network of roads that effectively opened up the hill country to Western influence and – very important indeed to British interests – the world of commerce.

CHAPTER THREE

1801–1805: 'ENJOYING THE GOOD THINGS OF THE AGE'

Miss Rebecca asked [Mr Sedley] a great number of questions about India, which gave him an opportunity of narrating many interesting anecdotes about that country and himself. He described the balls at Government House, and the manner in which they kept themselves cool in the hot weather, with punkahs, tatties, and other contrivances; and he was very witty regarding the number of Scotchmen whom Lord Minto, the Governor-General, patronised; and then he described a tiger-hunt; and the manner in which the mahout of his elephant had been pulled off his seat by one of the infuriated animals. How delighted Miss Rebecca was at the Government balls, and how she laughed at the stories of the Scotch aides-de-camp, and called Mr Sedley a wicked satirical creature; and how frightened she was at the story of the elephant! 'For your mother's sake, dear Mr Sedley,' she said, 'for the sake of all your friends, promise *never* to go on one of those horrid expeditions.'

'Pooh, pooh, Miss Sharp,' said he, pulling up his shirt-collars; 'the dangers make the sport only the pleasanter.' He had never been but once at a tiger-hunt, when the accident in question had occurred, and when he was half-killed – not by the tiger, but by the fright.

W.M. Thackeray, *Vanity Fair*

THERE IS NO DOUBT that while they were 'out East', the British made the most of what was on offer, often achieving a close approximation to English life 'at home' – but, as Welch points out, 'with more amenities and servants'.[1] Welch is understating the realities of colonial living. British people who had lived quiet, middle-class lives in England discovered that they could enjoy in a British colony in Asia (and at no great expense) splendour and luxury comparable with nothing that D'Oyly could have seen in any of the English country houses which he and his family were accustomed to visit. 'The rent of the most magnificent mansion at Colombo amounts to only three hundred pounds per annum,' wrote James Cordiner in 1807, 'and a good family-house can be procured for one hundred.' To live comfortably in either Madras or Colombo, an English bachelor required a palanquin and a one-horse chaise, and when travelling in Ceylon at least thirteen palanquin bearers were an absolute necessity. 'No bachelor can keep house at Colombo comfortably for less than £800 a year,' added Cordiner: 'and he may live at Madras for the same sum.'[2]

D'Oyly's bachelor household in Colombo included five servants, and very likely more. When his duties took him out of Colombo, one or several members of this personal staff accompanied him. Fanny Parks, a contemporary of D'Oyly's who visited India and other parts of colonial Asia in the first half of the nineteenth century, recorded in 1850 'A List of Servants in a Private Family' such as she had observed in India. Her list makes interesting reading. A British resident's household in India would, according to Mrs Parks, have been staffed by some or all of the following servants (whose monthly wages are given in parentheses below):

1. A Khansamah, or head man; a Musalman servant who purchases the provisions, makes the confectionary [sic], and superintends the table (Rs. 12)
2. The abdar, or water-cooler; cools the water, ices the wines, and attends with them at table (Rs. 8)
3. The head khidmatgar; he takes charge of the plate-chest, and waits at table (Rs. 7)
4. A second khidmatgar, who waits at table (Rs. 6)
5. A Bawarch, or cook (Rs. 12)
6. Mate bawarchi (Rs. 4)
7. Mashalchi; dish-washer and torch-bearer (Rs. 4)

8. Dhobee, or washerman (Rs. 8)
9. Istree wala, washerman for ironing (Rs. 8)
10. A darzee, or tailor (Rs. 8)
11. A second tailor (Rs. 6)
12. An ayah, or lady's maid (Rs. 10)
13. An under woman (Rs. 6)
14. A doriya; a sweeper, who also attends to the dogs (Rs. 4)
15. Sirdar-bearer, an Hindoo servant; the head of the bearers, and the keeper of the sahib's wardrobe, the keys of which are always carried in his kamarband, the folds of cloth around his waist (Rs. 8)
16. The mate-bearer; assists as valet, and attends to the lamps (Rs. 6)
22. Six bearers to pull the pankhas (ceiling fans), and dust the furniture, etc. (Rs. 24)
23. A gwala, or cowherd (Rs. 4)
24. A bher-i-wala, or shepherd (Rs. 5)
25. A Murgh-i-wala, to take care of the fowls, wild ducks, quail, rabbits, guinea-fowls and pigeons (Rs. 4)
26. A malee, or gardener (Rs. 5)
27. A mate, *do.*
28. Another mate, or a cooly (Rs. 2)
29. A gram-grinder, generally a woman who grinds the chana for the horses (Rs. 2)
30. A coachman (Rs. 10)
38. Eight sa'ises, or grooms, at five rupees each, for eight horses (Rs. 40)
46. Eight grass-cutters, at three rupees each, for the above (Rs. 24)
47. A bhishti, or water-carrier (Rs. 5)
48. A mate bhishti (Rs. 4)
49. A Bar'hai mistree, a carpenter (Rs. 8)
50. Another carpenter (Rs. 7)
52. Two coolies, to throw water on the tatties (*Khus* grass, used to cover windows in hot weather) (Rs 4)
54. Two chaukidars, or watchmen (Rs 8)
55. A durwan, or gate-keeper (Rs. 4)
57. Two chaprassis, or running footmen, to carry notes and be in attendance on the verandah (Rs. 10)

The staff of 57 servants listed by Mrs Parks cost their employers a mere Rs. 290 a month (£290 per annum).[3]

A British household in Colombo would presumably have been conducted on a slightly less opulent scale, but otherwise there would have been few differences. In both countries, for example, it was essential that some way should be found to counter the intense heat of April and May. The hill country of Ceylon being in Kandyan hands, retreat to the mountains during the hot season (as famously celebrated by Kipling and his fellow-writers of the Raj) was not an option for British officers and their families as it was in India. Major-General Hay Macdowall, who had served in India before being appointed to Ceylon, introduced into his large and comfortable house the Indian amenity of the *punkah*, which required half-a-dozen extra bearers called *khelassis*, taking turns, to operate.[4] Most Colombo residents took to the innovation with enthusiasm. They thought the added expense negligible, since it added so much to the comfort of a dining room in the East.[5]

Living in style and splendour such as they could never, for the most part, have enjoyed in England, gentlemen in India and other British colonies – like the *nouveau riche* English landowners of eighteenth-century England, who commissioned artists to paint them in the settings of their palatial residences and landscaped gardens – commissioned local artists to record in paint the details of their local establishments. Stuart Cary Welch provides, in *Room for Wonder*, a fascinating portrait of the British in India, their pavilions and other outbuildings, walled gardens, trees, boats, indoor and outdoor staff, crews, guards, soldiers, palanquins, horses and dogs, all seen through Indian eyes.

All things considered, it can be said with truth that one of the principal amenities British residents enjoyed in the colonies was comparative freedom from taxation. Whereas in Britain the continuing war with France resulted in taxes being imposed on such things as the number of windows in private houses and the number of domestic servants employed, a private citizen in India or Ceylon enjoyed a standard of living quite beyond the reach of his equivalent in Britain. This is amply illustrated in Welch's fascinating study, in the splendour of the mansions the British built for themselves in the East, and the armies of servants and 'bearers' they employed.[6]

The comforts of British colonial life are probably seen in truest perspective if we compare them with conditions in England during the same period. At the mid-eighteenth century, according to Ian Fullerton, there was still a sense that direct taxes on property or wealth were somehow abnormal, to be imposed only in an emergency. (William III's bills imposing direct taxes on individuals invariably explained that money was being raised 'for the purpose of waging a vigorous war with France'.) Following the repeal in 1765 (after vociferous protests from the American colonists) of the notorious Stamp Act passed earlier that year, which had imposed a tax on all colonial commercial and legal papers, newspapers and pamphlets, a trend appears to have developed in Britain of taxing luxuries. The earliest example of this was a tax on persons keeping carriages. In 1777 came a tax on servants, in 1778 a duty was imposed on inhabited houses (in addition to the 'window tax' which survived beyond 1792), and a tax on pleasure horses and racehorses. In 1785 taxes were imposed on female servants and on hair powder (used on footmen's wigs), together with a tax on sporting licences and gamekeepers. Taxes had been imposed on bricks for some time. In 1791 they were extended to other building materials, including glass, tiles, slates, stone and marble.

The need to spend money on war increased the burden of taxation on Englishmen at home. For all but fourteen months of the years 1793 to 1815, Britain was at war with France, a state of affairs that destabilized and drained Europe and had a profound effect on Britain's economy. William Pitt, Prime Minister from 1783 to 1801 and from 1804 to 1806, was responsible for many new taxes on luxuries. In 1795, for example, he imposed a tax on the wearers of wigs, to be paid by the head of the family. In 1796 he imposed a tax on dogs. In 1797 he imposed a tax on clocks and watches which, when it was repealed in the following year because of its disastrous effect on the clock-making industry, he replaced with a tax on armorial bearings. One of the heaviest taxes was that on spirits. Pitt steadily increased the rates, saying in 1796 that 'the consumption is so pernicious that with respect to this article no man could wish there to be any limits to the duty, as far as is consistent with the means of safely collecting it'.

In 1796 Pitt proposed a comprehensive death duty, to be imposed on the executors or administrators of deceased estates, and imposed new taxes on property insured against risk at sea and agricultural horses. By 1797 the costs of the war with France could no longer be funded from the tried and tested sources of revenue. New sources were hard to find, and in an Act of 1798 called the 'Triple Assessment', Pitt doubled, tripled and even quintupled the rates applying to the 'assessed taxes'. Finally, he introduced the first income tax, imposing in 1799 a direct tax at two shillings in the pound (10 per cent) on the total income of the taxpayer from all sources. This included income remitted from property outside Great Britain, and so swept into the country's coffers some part of the profits from individuals' holdings in the colonies, but this was a small price for the nabobs of India to pay for escaping taxation under three other heads that was currently plaguing their contemporaries in Britain.[7]

Despite the comforts that supported a British resident in India and Ceylon, contemporary accounts indicate that everyday life in both countries had its share of irritations and dangers. Thomas Babington Macaulay, like many of his countrymen and women, found the extremes of climate and weather in the tropics difficult to cope with, and grumbled about them continually. Civilization itself (as the British knew it) could be said to be in danger in the tropics, for one 'execrable effect' of the Indian climate, as Macaulay complained, was that it destroyed 'all the works of men':

> Steel rusts; razors lose their edge; thread decays; clothes fall to pieces; books moulder away and drop out of their bindings; plaster cracks; timber rots; matting is in shreds.[8]

The tropics were believed by others to pose serious moral dangers. It was generally believed, wrote Dr John Davy in 1821, that 'a hot climate disposes to voluptuousness'. Davy presumably had in mind Byron's well-known observation in *Don Juan* that 'what men call gallantry, and gods adultery / Is much more common where the climate's sultry'. Davy added, a trifle primly, that his own experience of tropical heat did not incline him to that view.[9]

Maintaining high standards of personal cleanliness presented problems of a different kind. Most British people took considerable time to adapt their clothing to tropical conditions. D'Oyly and his fellow civil servants would have been expected, even in the humid conditions of Colombo, to dress for dinner and to adopt a regulation daytime attire of breeches, a linen shirt, a stock or cravat, tall boots, a waistcoat, a black tail-coat and a top hat. In 'Emperor Akbar Receives the British Resident', a painting *c.* 1811 by an unknown Delhi artist which is reproduced in Welch's *Room for Wonder*, John D'Oyly's contemporary Mr Archibald Seton stands before the Mughal emperor (who is enthroned above him in a chair borne on the shoulders of bearers) in order to present a letter, presumably from Lord Minto in Calcutta. Seton, a tall, thin figure, wears white breeches and patent leather shoes, a black tail-coat and a black top hat.[10] The only portrait in existence of D'Oyly (frontispiece to this book) shows him similarly dressed, deep in conversation with three Kandyan chieftains, his top hat up-ended on the floor beside him.

In Ceylon as in India, established local custom influenced British behaviour, especially in matters relating to status. Observing that no local dignitary would receive visitors or stir abroad on foot without attendants to carry ceremonial fans, and hold umbrellas or leaf parasols over his head, also that it was considered demeaning not to be carried about in a palanquin, the British in the East did likewise (see Plates 3 and 4). Although D'Oyly's physically active and comparatively austere habits of life prevented his putting on an unhealthy degree of weight, many British people in India and Ceylon tended to do so, the result of too much rich food and too little exercise.

As sinister additions to such problems as these, 'Fear of illness and death,' writes Welch, 'was omnipresent, if seldom mentioned. Poisonous snakes and insects might strike suddenly, in one's tent, or hiding in a boot.' Until the days of modern medicines every 'griffin' (as new arrivals in Ceylon, such as John D'Oyly in 1801, were called) paled at stories of predecessors in abundant good health who suddenly expired, moments after drinking a glass of water.[11] Reading the dates in Kandy's Garrison Cemetery, now a neglected wilderness of weather-beaten monuments and obelisks (including one which was erected in D'Oyly's memory by his brothers in England, see Figure 15), the visitor realizes that many British people died within a season or two of 'coming out'.[12] As in the Presidencies of Bengal, Bombay and Madras in the same period, only the hardiest survived.

John D'Oyly's social life in England, both in Sussex and at Cambridge, had been lively and varied. The diaries he kept in his youth yield an attractive picture of the 'full and merry life' John D'Oyly had led as a Cambridge undergraduate. P.E. Pieris's introduction to his *Letters to Ceylon* gives us an engaging picture of young D'Oyly entertaining parties of his friends to supper in his rooms ('A Noisy, rowing, pleasant Evening,' D'Oyly wrote of one such occasion on 20 November 1796), visiting the Rose Coffee House with his boon companions Robert Ainslie, Baugh Allen and George Strachey, playing billiards, bowls, fives and cricket. He enjoyed rowing and fishing, and liked riding and playing both chess and whist – the latter game would occasionally keep him up till two o'clock in the morning. He was also a good, if not brilliant, shot.[13]

Many, if not all, of D'Oyly's sporting interests could be kept up in Ceylon, since the English community in Colombo in the early years of the colony was predominantly male, consisting of 'about one hundred gentlemen and only twenty ladies': wives were scarce among the civil and military chiefs.[14] It was said of Governor North, a bachelor in his thirties, that he liked to dine out because he would then be sure of a better dinner than he could get at home. Indeed, Viscount Valentia said of the governor that 'Mr North, though he loved good things, could never scold, and consequently his dinners were the worst in Colombo.' The good-humoured, gregarious North made a point of inviting the leading families among the Dutch residents to his dinner parties and balls. He found himself sometimes snubbed, however, by the etiquette-conscious Dutch ladies of Colombo, who were offended when the Governor invited them to a ball before he had asked them to dine with him, and refused to attend the elaborate ball he planned in honour of Viscount Valentia at San Sebastian.[15] Despite this, Valentia took away with him excellent impressions of Colombo society, which he found to be 'sufficiently large for every purpose of comfort and amusement'. He had special praise for North's officers, whom he found to be responsible and talented men, and felt that with the addition of the military, the island's society 'must be considered as equal in respectability to that of any of the Company's Presidencies'.[16]

Revd James Cordiner, who accompanied Governor North on an extensive tour of the island in 1800, would have heartily agreed with this assessment of English society in the East. Cordiner was quite overcome by the hospitality he received at the residence of the Agent of Revenue at Jaffnapatam, Lieutenant-Colonel Barbut. He seems, too, to have been much taken with the charms of the agent's wife. The governor's party was welcomed there, he wrote,

> by a most accomplished hostess: [and entertained] with a degree of luxury and elegance excelled in no corner of the world. We had heard much in praise of Mrs Barbut's charms, but after enjoying the pleasure of her society, her engaging qualities exceeded all our expectations. So much beauty and grace, combined with such

attractive sweetness, and captivating politeness, are but rarely concentrated in one person.

The Barbuts gave several public dinners and balls in honour of the governor's visit, and Cordiner noted that among the 'respectable European inhabitants of the settlement' who attended them were twenty young ladies born in Ceylon of Dutch parents. Despite their imperfect education, which was only to be expected having been 'brought up entirely in that remote corner', Cordiner found these provincial belles enchanting in their artless vivacity and innocence, and attributed such style as they did possess to 'the kind patronage of Mrs Barbut'.[17]

Respectable young women of European origin resembling the accomplished Mrs Barbut's protégées were to be found in every major town. But local women (from communities other than the Dutch or other European descendants) were officially off-limits to the young British officers. There were guidelines laid down for social contact between British people and 'natives', barriers that, even in the easy-going days of the eighteenth century, marked as eccentric or worse the individual who crossed them. This did not, of course, necessarily discourage the young and ardent. Englishmen in distant outposts (such as Delhi still was in the nineteenth century, and Kandy was in 1815, when John D'Oyly took up residence in the hill capital) were often, writes Welch, 'adventurous romantics'.

A British physician, Dr William Fullarton, was one such 'adventurous romantic'. His hookah, according to Welch,

> would have been acceptable; also his Indian bolster, carpet, sweetmeats, and native pose (as represented by Dip Chand, an Indian artist), taking his ease like a great Mughal, in a portrait entitled 'William Fullerton receives a visitor' (*circa* 1760, now in the Victoria and Albert Museum). But Fullarton lived in the Indian part of Patna, and had too many Indian friends. Fullarton was the sole survivor in 1763, when his friend Mir Kasim, treacherous son-in-law of Nawab Mir Jafar, massacred all the other British at Patna.[18]

The most spectacular instance of 'adventurous romanticism' among the British in the East in D'Oyly's time is probably that provided by D'Oyly's contemporary Sir David Ochterlony, who was made the first

British Resident in Delhi by Lord Lake in 1803. It was a position tantamount to being 'the English emperor of northwest India'. Sir David fought in the Gurkha wars in 1814 and 1815, so distinguishing himself that he was knighted. In 1818, at the age of 60, he returned to Delhi, establishing an excellent rapport with the Mughal court and occupying a pavilion in the Shalimar Gardens. By this time Sir David had come to prefer his Indian friends to the company of his fellow Englishmen. Gossip in the English community of Delhi credited him with keeping thirteen elephants in his stables, one for each of his thirteen wives.

A painting *circa* 1820 (Plate 5) shows a turbaned Sir David attired in flowing Indian robes, reclining on a carpet Indian-style, leaning against bolsters and smoking a 'hubble-bubble' (hookah). His ladies are all in the picture, as are the musicians who are entertaining the company. Four portraits of English people in English dress (one of them a woman) placed high above the windows of the room look down disapprovingly on the unseemly revelry below.

Another British Resident in India at about the same time, who would inevitably have been the subject of animated discussion in Colombo, was Captain James Achilles Kirkpatrick, who was first British Resident of Hyderabad between 1797 and 1805, and was given the title *Hushmat Jung* 'Glorious in Battle' by the Nizam. 'A colourful gentleman', writes Welch, Kirkpatrick married a Muslim lady who chose to live in strict purdah in a splendid neoclassical mansion. Since tradition forbade his wife leaving their house, the Resident commissioned a minuscule model of the house for her to admire in an inner garden. (Both house and model still exist, as part of a college for women.)[19]

Like his colleagues, D'Oyly found that promotion in the Civil Service under Frederick North was gratifyingly rapid. Arriving in Colombo in 1801 as a 'writer' (the term then used for new recruits admitted, generally through patronage, to Britain's colonial service), he found himself appointed a year later to the post of Second Member of the Provincial Court of Colombo. His observation of the Cambridge Assizes must have served him in good stead at this juncture, for a mere two years later he was appointed President of the Provincial Court at Matara, in the island's Southern Province. When, in 1805, the district of Galle was amalgamated with that of Matara, D'Oyly was placed in charge of both, with the title of 'Agent of Revenue and Commerce'. He was only 31.

CHAPTER FOUR

1801–1805: 'PROUD TOWERS' – THE ROAD TO KANDY

On every side now rose
Rocks, which in unimaginable forms
Lifted their black and barren pinnacles
In the light of evening, and its precipice
Obscuring the ravine, disclosed above,
'Mid toppling stones, black gulfs, and yawning caves,
Whose windings gave ten thousand various tongues
To the loud stream. Lo! where the pass expands
Its stony jaws, the abrupt mountain breaks,
And seems, with its accumulated crags,
To overhang the world.

Percy Bysshe Shelley, *Alastor:*
or, The Spirit of Solitude

EACH OF THE THREE EUROPEAN NATIONS that had controlled the Maritime Provinces since 1505 had in turn cast acquisitive eyes toward the forbidding line of mountains that guarded the 'Kandyan country', dreaming of the fertile valleys that were rumoured to lie beyond them. But apart from occasional arrangements made with the Kandyan court for a mutual exchange of bartered items, every European attempt to establish a trading or military post in the interior had been rejected by the King of Kandy.

Though certain intrepid travellers (including Marco Polo, the Chinese scholar Fa Hsien, and Ibn Batuta from Arabia) had managed

FIGURE 5 The fertile valleys of the Kandyan country

'The Temples of Kandy, from the hills above Mr Buller's house', pencil drawing by Andrew Nicholl. From J.E. Tennent's manuscript 'Notes and Drawings of Ceylon' (Gooneratne Collection).

in the past to visit Kandy, few Englishmen had actually ventured beyond those precipitous mountains and the wilderness that further fortified them, to reach the prosperous valleys beyond. One of these was a shipwrecked sailor named Robert Knox, whom a Kandyan king had captured in the seventeenth century and added to the palace menagerie of European wanderers whom chance had brought into the kingdom. The king regarded Knox and his companions as curiosities, and indulged their wants in every way except granting them their liberty. Free to do pretty much as he liked, Knox had lived a pleasant and active life in the Kandyan villages until, escaping after twenty years, he returned to England in 1681 and published an account of his adventures which was one of the travelogues on which Daniel Defoe drew when he wrote *Robinson Crusoe*.[1]

Another Briton who penetrated the mountains of the island's interior was Captain Arthur Johnston of the 19th Regiment of Foot, one of John D'Oyly's contemporaries and colleagues. In the belief that he was carrying out official orders, Johnston set out on 20 September 1804 to lead a military column from Batticaloa to Kandy, with 300 troops consisting of men drawn from his own regiment, from the Malay Regiment, sepoys from Bengal, and gunners of the Royal Artillery dragging along their artillery pieces with the aid of their gun lascars.

Johnston's route through the seemingly impregnable mountain barrier was by way of an 'abrupt and precipitous' secret pass hitherto untried by the British. In negotiating 'The Pass of One Thousand Steps', used by the Kings of Kandy on their pilgrimages to the shrine of Kataragama in the south, Johnston was to find that horses became a useless encumbrance. Arriving in Kandy on 6 October 1804, finding the city abandoned and the British troops he was to meet nowhere in the vicinity, he camped for three days before beating a prudent retreat to the British fort at Trincomalee. Inevitably, he was harried and ambushed by the Kandyans on his way back, but he managed to get his troops to safety on 19 October with the loss of only 38 officers and soldiers killed or missing.[2]

D'Oyly was told of European embassies that had been allowed, after months of wearisome negotiation, to visit the Kandyan court. Such parties had been met at the border of the kingdom by heavily armed guards, and conducted along such tortuous routes that they found it impossible without assistance to find their way back to the safety of Colombo. The story of an embassy that Governor North had dispatched to Kandy in January 1800 was well known to D'Oyly and his fellow civil servants, and it was not an inspiring tale.

North's choice as his Ambassador Extraordinary and Commissioner Plenipotentiary on this memorable occasion had been none other than Major-General Hay Macdowall, whom D'Oyly had met in Colombo, and whose hospitality he had, like his fellow officers, enjoyed. Macdowall had set out from Colombo on 12 March 1800 under a salute of seventeen guns, accompanying a letter intended for the king. This letter was carried under a canopy on the heads of *appuhamys* (a mode of transport insisted upon by Kandyan court protocol), and escorted by 1,164 British, Indian and Malay foot-soldiers, four six-pounder cannons, two howitzers, assorted baggage carriers, and carts laden with rice, arrack, dry provisions, Macdowall's personal belongings, and 32 cases of presents (which included a state coach to be drawn by six horses).

FIGURE 6 Delayed and irritated at every stage of his journey to Kandy

Sketch from Joinville's manuscript journal of General MacDowall's Embassy to Kandy, 16 March 1800. Figures designated: (1) Major General Macdowall, (2) Dissave of Kandy, (3) Modliar Interpreter of the Embassy. From J.E. Tennent's manuscript 'Notes and Drawings of Ceylon' (Gooneratne Collection).

Delayed and irritated at every stage of his four-week journey by heavy rain that rendered almost impassable the roads to the kingdom (which the Kandyans neglected deliberately as a matter of policy, to deter would-be invaders), the British Ambassador was further infuriated by carriers who insisted on leaving the procession when their contracted term had expired. After many delays, Macdowall was received by the king on 9 April in the audience hall adjoining the palace. Here further irritations awaited Macdowall:

> Every incident connected with the ceremony, which according to invariable custom took place at night, was regulated by a ritual almost ecclesiastical in its elaboration, devised to impress foreign

representatives with the greatness of the Ruler whom they were privileged to behold. It was half past four in the afternoon when the summons to appear was received and it was nine o'clock before the presents were all sent across the river, when Macdowall and the *Disava* who had been deputed to escort him started hand in hand from the *Tanayama*.

Within two hundred yards of the Palace Gate he rested for his dinner, moving forward at midnight to where Pilima Talavva received him in state and led him stage by stage through numerous courts to where the raising of seven successive curtains revealed the King. Little of the exhausting ceremonial usual on such occasions was omitted, Macdowall falling on his knees three times whenever he approached or retired from the Throne. The letter which he carried in both hands at the level of the eyes was received by the King himself, and a formal conversation followed, rendered wearisome by its passage through two Ministers and two Interpreters before it reached the listener.

Refreshments were served to the Ambassador in a separate room after the interview; they consisted of Sinhalese sweetmeats, fruit and water, and it was five o'clock in the morning before the exhausted man started on his way back.

Macdowall's visit to Kandy, which had kept him fuming there for nearly three weeks while proposals from both sides were negotiated and tediously renegotiated, brought the British Crown no gains. The agreement that had been proposed remained unsigned, and Macdowall returned to Colombo with a dismal report of failure, while British commentators on the embassy attempted to present the experience in such a manner that North's Ambassador Extraordinary and Commissioner Plenipotentiary did not lose face.[3]

The procedure upon which the Kandyan court insisted with regard to the conduct of foreign ambassadors brought into the royal presence had been accepted by the Dutch, but was regarded by British observers as humiliating and demeaning to the subjects of a British king. Captain Robert Percival, who published a book in 1803 about his experiences in Ceylon in which he claimed to have accompanied Macdowall on his fruitless visit, could not, apparently, bring himself to report accurately on Macdowall's embassy to Kandy: according to his version,

Macdowall stoutly refused to prostrate himself before the King of Kandy and remain kneeling in his presence as the Dutch had done. Percival declares that Macdowall won his point, and the King, apparently intimidated by the General's manner, prudently waived his royal prerogatives.[4]

Percival described the King of Kandy as 'much resembling the figures we are accustomed to see of King Henry VIII', thus unconsciously beginning a tradition among British commentators, of demonizing Sri Vikrama Rajasinha as a monster and a despot. He also gives an amusing description of the soldierly Macdowall being forced to endure an interview that 'was carried on with the most profound gravity and reserve', during which 'even the most trifling circumstances were mentioned in whispers' between five different persons (three of them interpreters) and in 'three different languages'. Percival added that, in keeping with oriental custom, 'rose-water was frequently sprinkled around from curiously wrought vessels of gold; and perfumes were handed about on salvers of gold and silver fillagree-work'.[5]

Following the failure of North's embassy, the Colonial Office was unprepared to encourage any further ideas of annexation in the government in Colombo. And so the Kingdom of Kandy remained tantalizingly on the edge of Britain's imperial ambitions in Sri Lanka, a forbidden country, ceaselessly inviting but forever destined, it seemed, to tempt, frustrate and disappoint.

In the shadow of the distant mountains that he was fated one day to conquer, innocent of any knowledge of what destiny had in store for him, John D'Oyly got on with the day-to-day work of provincial administration.

A British Agent of Revenue, or collector of rents, possessed at that time considerable personal power. The number of native assistants attached to the department of an agent, Cordiner noted, was so great that he could perform his function of collecting the revenue of a province with as much ease, and as little fatigue, as 'the richest nobleman in England experiences in receiving the rent of his estates'. But with such power and consequence came heavy responsibilities. From his observation of the lives lived by British civil servants such as Lieutenant-Colonel Barbut in Jaffnapatam, Cordiner reasoned that the happiness of the local population and the prosperity of their province depended to a considerable extent on the personal qualities of the men whom fortune had placed in situations of such high importance.[6]

His sojourn in the Southern Province introduced D'Oyly to a landscape and a way of living that were different in every way from those he had encountered in Colombo. The cities of the south are tranquil sea-coast townships with histories of trading that go back many centuries. They offer welcoming bays and inlets to fishing catamarans and (in D'Oyly's time) to trading vessels from Asia and Europe, and they contain lively markets where farmers sell their produce and fishermen their daily catch. The dry, sunny climate and invigorating sea-breezes of the province had made it attractive to the Dutch, who had established fine stonework fortresses in both Galle and Matara within which they built houses for officials and their families, and from which they had conducted the business of administration, justice and commerce.

In the Southern Province D'Oyly encountered, as so many travellers have done since his time, a striking contrast with life in a colonial city. Since 1796, when the Dutch commander of the Star Fort at Matara had handed the keys of the fortress to a young British officer, Lachlan Macquarie, life had gone on under a British administration very much as it had done under the Dutch: in an orderly, quiet and peaceful fashion that must have been for D'Oyly a welcome change from the pretentious show and noisy rattle of social life in Colombo.

On first arriving in the island, D'Oyly had played his part in the somewhat erratic social life North arranged for his young officers in Colombo, but in Matara he appears to have rapidly outgrown the comfort and amusement of such a life. 'Great loads of meat appear upon the tables of the English inhabitants of Ceylon', Cordiner noted in 1807, and reported also that madeira, English claret and English ale were freely available.[7]

Congenial companionship for officers of intellectual tastes was not quite so readily available in the capital cities of British colonies, as Leonard Woolf was to discover a century later. He complained to Lytton Strachey in 1907 that he had been walking for five days as a 'wondering ghost' through 'an interminable succession of dinners & dances' at Kandy. 'A seal of silence has fallen on my lips,' wrote poor Woolf, hemmed in by a bewildering collection of 'Governors & Colonial

Secretaries & innumerable planters . . . I am unable to talk a word to a soul . . . I wish I could talk to you for 5 minutes.'[8]

'The merit of a Government Agent in the charge of a Province,' wrote Major Thomas Skinner in 1849, 'consists (as I have known it to be estimated) in his giving no trouble, in being rarely heard of or from at headquarters.'[9] Resident at Matara, and placed at a considerable distance from the social activities of British Colombo, John D'Oyly found a unique opportunity to renew the interest in language and literature that Cambridge had nurtured in him. It was probably characteristic of D'Oyly that the first step he took in a new direction was an intellectual one.

Sinhala literary activity had suffered, as had all other forms of cultural expression, in the long period during which the Maritime Provinces had been under Portuguese and Dutch domination. In the latter half of the eighteenth century, however, there had begun a revival in southern Sri Lanka, which was less in the classical tradition of Sinhala poetry and more at the level of folk and oral literature.[10] Matara was a district in which much of the literary life of the low country was concentrated. Prominent in this revival were a number of Buddhist monks and local officials. A famous scholar-monk and former poet, the Venerable Sri Dhammarama of Karatota, was one of their number, and it was with him that D'Oyly chose to pursue his new interest. In 1805, almost as soon as he had taken up residence in Matara, possibly influenced by his association in Colombo with Gordon, Barry and Lusignan (North's three young recruits to language study), D'Oyly commenced a methodical and comprehensive study of the Sinhala language.

As a result of his Matara experience, D'Oyly altered his habits of life quite substantially. He became, writes Maureen Seneviratne,

> very much an Oriental in his habits and a recluse by choice, cutting himself away from social contacts with fellow Europeans and devoting his leisure hours to a deep study of the Buddhist religion, though there is no record that he ever became a Buddhist in actual practice. He was a strict vegetarian from the beginning of his Matara days.[11]

All things must, at this stage in his life and career, have seemed possible to D'Oyly. Life in Matara, a township located in one of the most beautiful districts of the island's lovely sea coast, was retired and peaceful, with plenty of opportunity to ride, read, shoot and study, the pastimes he had most enjoyed as an undergraduate. Pieris has noted that D'Oyly, even as an undergraduate, seems to have much preferred reading and shooting to dancing.

> He went to balls, whether at Uckfield, Lewes and Newmarket, or at private houses like Sir Elijah Impey's, though he was not attracted by dancing; on the 20th of January 1797 he writes, 'danced for the first time these 5 years'. Of the Town Ball at the Black Bear he says, 'danced & played at Whist: not so much fun as expected . . . we came away at 3 in the morning.'

On 31 January 1797 he wrote:

> Christmas Vacation spent not unpleasantly – 3 Balls enlivened the time – began to like them somewhat better – Time divided (as best suits mine & I believe everyone's disposition) between pleasure & study, tho' the former occupied the greater Portion. Shooting, my Pastime, Smith's Wealth of Nations my Study.[12]

In addition to these congenial pleasures, he was honourably employed, and had received gratifyingly rapid promotion, in the service of a country in whose imperial mission he passionately believed. He would have heartily agreed, at this period of his life, with the faith William Knighton (that other idealistic and enthusiastic young Englishman) was to express nearly fifty years later: faith in 'that invariable good fortune, which makes the British advance in the East the march of destiny, which no accident can arrest, no temporary losses retard'.[13]

Every visible sign was auspicious. The blue, tropical skies of the Southern Province shone bright and clear of clouds, over a lazy sea. The mountains of the Kandyan kingdom might loom on the horizon but, following the disappointments and humiliations of the past, storming them was most definitely not on the agenda of the British Crown. In a letter from the Governor-General in Council to North of 28 May 1800, North had been expressly forbidden to proceed to hostilities against Kandy without previous sanction.[14] 'War with the Kandyan king,' writes E.F.C. Ludowyk,

> was out of the question because it was both pointless and expensive. Nor would [consent be given to involve] the British government in

the elaboration of an embassy to the king, without which a formal
treaty of peace . . . could not have been secured.15

Archdeacon D'Oyly's son did not, perhaps, know it at the time, but
the path he chose to follow was the path of traditional Buddhist
education, according to which from the earliest times young Sinhalese
men, the scions of old Buddhist families, learned their letters in the
precincts of the temple, absorbing at the same time the moral lessons
their tutors were qualified to teach them. The instructor chosen to guide
the young Resident was an eminent Buddhist scholar, the Venerable
Karatota, who was at this time in his seventies. Despite his age, the
monk was, by all accounts, a most impressive personage whom
long experience had made a skilled and patient teacher. Under the
Thero's regular instruction, D'Oyly made rapid progress, learning first
to trace the curved and rounded Sinhala letters in a shallow tray filled
with fine sand, graduating in time to the palm leaf and stylus of the
accomplished scribe.

It was not long before the former Latin scholar was found to have
become so much a master of the local language, and so knowledgeable about the culture which had shaped it, that Sir Thomas
Maitland (who succeeded Frederick North as British Governor of the
Maritime Provinces in 1805) appointed D'Oyly Chief Translator to
the Government. This was a position D'Oyly was to hold until 1816.
As Chief Translator, and later on, in another secret and unofficial
capacity, D'Oyly was to write, send and receive many letters on palm-
leaves or *olas*, confidential messages that kept him in touch with an
extensive network of correspondents in many parts of the island and
especially within the Kandyan country, diplomatic enquiries and
carefully timed directives that led, at long last, to the capture of a
kingdom.

In later years, and especially after 1818, when his disappointment at
his failure to anticipate the outbreak of the Kandyan War of Rebellion
had come near breaking his heart, D'Oyly might well have looked back
on this eager, passionate period of his life in Matara as Marlow does in
Conrad's story, recalling his youth

and the feeling that will never come back any more – the feeling that
I could last forever, outlast the sea, the earth, and all men; the

deceitful feeling that lures us on to joys, to perils, to love, to vain effort – to death; the triumphant conviction of strength, the heat of life in the handful of dust, the glow in the heart that with every year grows dim, grows cold, grows small, and expires – and expires, too soon, too soon – before life itself.[16]

CHAPTER FIVE

1805–1810: 'THE NOBLEST CHACE IN THE WORLD'

For what's a play without a woman in it?

Thomas Kyd, *The Spanish Tragedy*

MUCH ABOUT ASIA WAS STRANGE to an English eye, but the women of the 'Orient' constituted a tantalizing mystery to most upper-class Englishmen of D'Oyly's time. Ronald Hyam and Kenneth Ballhatchet are among the numerous scholars who have marshalled a great deal of fascinating (and occasionally hilarious) evidence to establish what hardly needs to be said: that working overseas in an official capacity almost invariably enlarged a young imperialist's sexual experience.[1] This was especially true in the early part of the nineteenth century, when the hard and difficult conditions in which Britons were believed to be serving the empire discouraged many Englishwomen from accompanying their menfolk to the colonies.

First contact with Asia came, almost inevitably, as a profound shock to the system. Sexually inexperienced young men (such as D'Oyly appears to have been in 1805) found themselves visually assailed on every side by cultural artefacts which invested female sexuality with beauty and power – a phenomenon that an English gentleman, and especially one from a Church of England and public school background, would have considered profoundly unsettling at best, and at worst morally dangerous.

The iconography of Hindu mythology, notes R.G. Davies in the course of research conducted into Leonard Woolf's experience as a colonial officer, depicts female sexuality as rampant, voracious and dangerously powerful. Davies asks a crucial question:

> Was a culture that idealised women to such an extent that it denied their sexuality any less barbaric than the florid excesses of Hinduism which at least honestly acknowledged and encompassed the full range of female experience within the mythologies of the two great goddesses Kali and Amman?[2]

This is dangerous philosophical ground indeed, and the empire's loyal servants were not encouraged to venture upon it. And while their traditional beliefs were being challenged on one side, everyday life confronted them daily with new and unexpected temptations as they realized that oriental society moved to rhythms which were very different from those to which their sedate British upbringing had accustomed them.

Pictures like one that Charles Doyley included in his portfolio of engravings, of 'A Native Gentleman Smoking a Goorgoory, or Hookah, in his Private Apartments, *Attended by his Dancing Girls*', would have excited intense curiosity in Englishmen who saw it.[3] Such pictures might also have inspired ideas of emulation in the more adventurous and less repressed among European visitors and, among younger men, certainly feelings of impatience with the 'official prudery' of colonial society.

His diary shows that in his undergraduate years at Cambridge, John D'Oyly had concentrated on study and active sports. Although showing little enthusiasm for female company, he had, like most of his fellow undergraduates, acquired a limited knowledge of the town's low life. Benstead's at Cambridge, a place of doubtful reputation, is mentioned by young John in his diaries. He occasionally visited 'Codilly, alias Smith', one of the Cambridge *demi-monde*, sister of a miller's wife. At Ely he and his friend Ainslie were 'directed to Mrs Palmer, a supposed Fortune teller, to pass the Evening'. D'Oyly reported that he had found Mrs Palmer 'an old Bawd, & a cursed Whore there'. Both he and Ainslie, he added with relief, had 'got away safe'. Despite this first and censorious reaction, D'Oyly repeated the visit.

On the whole, as Pieris discreetly notes in his comments on the Cambridge diaries, D'Oyly 'passed lightly over that side of a student's life'. It is more than possible that, following such encounters, a guilty conscience troubled the Archdeacon's son: once, while attending the Newmarket races in the company of male friends, after dinner and billiards, appears the cryptic record: 'Went with them to *Hell*'.[4]

The Miscellaneous Works of Hugh Boyd with an Account of his Life and Writings by Lawrence Dundas Campbell had been published in London in 1800. It is possible that D'Oyly read it, attracted by the formidable intellectual reputation of the book's author, who had entered Trinity College, Dublin at the age of fourteen, and had taken his Master of Arts degree in 1765 at nineteen. Since Boyd had been a member of an embassy sent by the British government at Madras to the King of Kandy in 1782, his account of his experiences would have had an additional attraction for a young man contemplating a career in the Ceylon Civil Service. If D'Oyly read Boyd's writings, he would have found among them an interesting description of 'Cingalese women':

> The Cingalese woman exhibits a striking contrast to those of all other oriental nations, in some of the most prominent and distinctive features of their character. Instead of that lazy apathy, insipid modesty and sour austerity, which have characterized the sex throughout the Asiatic world, in every period of history; in this island they possess that active sensibility, winning bashfulness and amiable ease, for which the women of modern Europe are peculiarly famed. The Cingalese women are not merely the slaves and mistresses, but in many cases, the companions and friends of their husbands.[5]

Boyd appears to speak with authority, but it is not clear on how intimate an acquaintance with 'Cingalese women' he had based this appealing portrait. D'Oyly's colleague de Joinville's admiring observations of the island's rural women had focused exclusively on the charm of their outward appearance.[6] This was only to be expected: Asia was not Europe, and in neither India nor Sri Lanka did respectable women reveal themselves to strangers. Having read such an account as Boyd's, the bookish D'Oyly might well have idealized the 'Cingalese woman', yet unseen, as the romantic 'Asia' of poems and old-time maps and charts.

In pursuing his official labours as agent of the British government, D'Oyly found himself often walking, as it were, upon ground that had been already laid out and even tilled by his Dutch predecessors. The Dutch, whose main objective in ruling the Maritime Provinces had been the peaceful making of money, had had a special talent for identifying aspects of the local milieu that could be turned to profitable use, and this is exemplified in their attitude to the elephant, whose dignified presence on all important occasions had been from time immemorial an essential part of the island's cultural life. Magnificently caparisoned, elephants had an indispensable role to play in ritual processions associated with temples, palaces and wedding festivities.

Lt. William Lyttleton's coloured aquatint of 'The King's Palace at Kandy' (see Plate 6) conveys a vivid impression of the role assigned to elephants in the *Perahera* processions at Kandy. 'Processions take place from the principal temples of Buddha, through the streets of the town,' writes Lyttleton in *A Set of Views in the Island of Ceylon*. '[They are] attended by the Adikars, the Desaves, and Mohotales of different corles, and followed by thousands of people. The temple elephants on this occasion are dressed in crimson velvet and gold; the tusks of the animal bearing the sacred relic are also covered in golden sheaths, which have a very rich and extraordinary appearance. Valuable presents are offered on these occasions to Buddha, and a nightly exhibition terminates the scene.'[7]

The pragmatic Dutch put the island's elephants to new uses. In times of war these sure-footed animals transported ammunition and provisions and hauled gun-carriages up otherwise inaccessible mountain paths, and as working elephants, they lent their massive assistance to the government's agricultural and building projects.

The Dutch, whose policy it was to encourage the cultivation of cash crops in the Maritime Provinces, had constructed a system of canals to assist such cultivation, and perceiving the many and varied uses to which an elephant's giant strength could be put in assisting agriculture and hauling barges laden with cargo, instituted an entire department whose sole business it was to initiate and supervise the capture of elephants. The local official whom they placed in charge of their Elephant Department held, therefore, a post of great responsibility, and was picturesquely titled *Gajaman Arachchi* ('Lord of the Elephants'). Bellin's fine print, 'Chasse aux Elephans dans L'Isle de Ceylan'

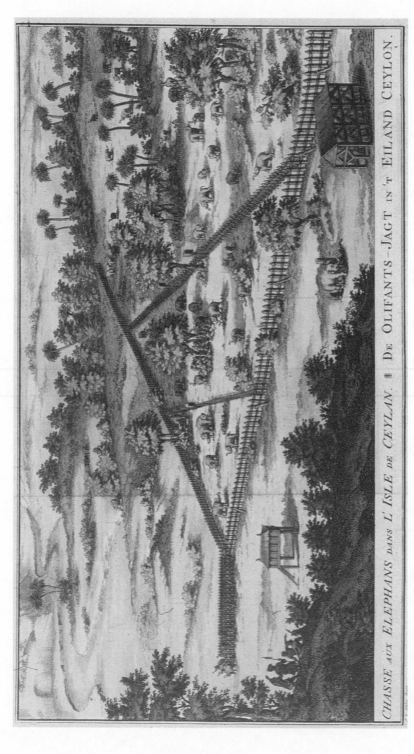

CHASSE aux ELEPHANS *dans* L' ISLE *de* CEYLAN. ‖ De OLIFANTS-JAGT in 'T EILAND CEYLON.

FIGURE 7 To hunt and capture a wild elephant alive . . .

'Chasse aux Elephans dans L'Isle de Ceylan', a print by M. Bellin, cartographer and printmaker of Paris, c.1770 (Gooneratne Collection).

(*c.* 1770), shows in detail the elaborate 'kraals' that the Dutch constructed to trap the wild elephants they intended to tame.

D'Oyly's official duties as an Agent of Revenue involved the supervision of many Dutch-inspired projects on behalf of the British Crown. The Elephant Department was within his purview, and it is evident from a letter he wrote to his brother Thomas in 1809 that his imagination had been caught by the encircling 'Net' or 'Line' in which the intrepid hunters of the region trapped their 'noble Game':

> Forced onwards [the Elephants] now approach either side in search of some Outlet, but are met by a well-guarded Line; then rush back upon their Pursuers with augmented Violence and again repulsed in the point they first attempt, run in trepidation along our Ranks, seeking if perchance they might find some Interval to pass, some weak unguarded Post to break. But here assailed from one continued Line, by many a Shot and terrifying Sound, they run forward to the Centre to obtain a short-lived Repose; and crowding together with their heads in the Centre . . . whirl round for a while in a Body, like an immense horizontal Wheel, and at length rush onward, which way one common Instinct prompts them with a Force which no human Means can resist.[8]

D'Oyly would one day describe elephant-tracking in the jungles of southern Ceylon as the 'noblest' of masculine pursuits. Captured in the forests of the Ruhuna Province and the wilder, more desolate expanse of the Vanni, and tamed by hunters renowned throughout the Maritime Provinces for their knowledge of the ways of 'the Great Ones' – men who could speak, so it was said, their secret language – elephants were more, in precolonial times, than the moving targets they were later to become for European 'sportsmen' anxious to 'bag' a prize. To hunt and capture a wild elephant alive is a dangerous task, calling for the highest degree of skill and courage in the man who undertakes it.

Such a man was Wirthamulle Don Francisco Senaratna Kumaraperumal, Vidane Arachchi of Kahawatta in Giruwapattu in the Hambantota District of the Southern Province of Ceylon, a Matara notable who had been raised to the government post of Gajaman Arachchi during the time of the Dutch administration of the Maritime Provinces.[9] Don Francisco loved literature. The interests of his wife,

Francina Grero, were of a different kind, which caused her to be known locally as '*Lansi pannakari*' (Dutch style-setter), due to her fashion sense and her skill in designing elegant dresses and accessories.

D'Oyly was 31 when he encountered Cornelia Perumal, elder daughter of the *gajaman arachchi* and his fashionable wife. Cornelia, now a young woman of formidable intelligence and remarkable personal charm, at the time of her meeting with D'Oyly in 1805 was already a poet celebrated for her skill and wit among her own people. They met in circumstances that have given rise to endless romantic speculation and formed the theme of numerous stories, poems and plays, for tradition has it in Sri Lanka that John D'Oyly's unexpected encounter with Don Francisco's witty, beautiful and poetically gifted daughter had a profound effect on her life, and dramatically altered the direction of his future career.

Cornelia Perumal had received her early education within her own family, and initially from her parents. She inherited her mother's taste and talent, together with the title of Gajaman Nona (or 'Lady Gajaman') as she was later to be called in memory of her father. She grew up to be well known in Matara as a beautiful and elegant woman with a taste for dressing herself in the fashion of a Dutch gentlewoman. Such an interest would have been regarded as entirely natural to a young woman of her culturally hybrid, partially 'Westernized' background. The degree of interest in literature Cornelia manifested, however, was most unusual in women of her community and status.

Her literary talent had shown itself at an early age when, as a child, she had composed a Sinhala verse to chide the person she believed had hidden her water pot:

> Little golden pot, filled with water
> And left on the edge of the well,
> The one who hid it is a scoundrel who can't count to
> five or eight!
> Will you give back my little pot, so that I can go home?

Delighted to discover in his elder daughter interests similar to his own, Don Francisco actively encouraged Cornelia's love of poetry. This was a branch of literature in which she was also encouraged by her uncle, Wirthamulle Don Janchi de Silva Abhayagunewardena

Samarajeeva, who, in addition to his official duties as Pattayame Lekam (Secretary and Keeper of the Grain Stores), had a local reputation as a poet. The promotion by these two elders of the young Cornelia's talent was assisted by the fact that, despite the weight of conservative opinion in some parts of the island which opposed female education, Matara had nourished from ancient times traditions of literary patronage from which women were not excluded.

English translation rarely succeeds in capturing the rhythmic felicities and plangencies of Sinhala *kavi* (verses which are, in any case, intended to be sung). Don Francisco's death, which occurred while he was on an official expedition, tracking elephants in the Ruhuna jungles, had inspired Cornelia to write one of her first poems:

> Did that fierce and maddened elephant kill my
>   beloved father?
> Ferocious was the force that tore us apart.
> Ah! The sorrow caused by your departure!
> I pass night after sleepless night thinking of you. [10]

Soon after her father's death, Gajaman was given in marriage to Merenchige Gardiyas Arachchi, headman of the village of Talpe, in the Galle district. Following the birth of a son and the death of her husband, Gajaman was married again, this time to Mohandiram Don Hendrick Siriwardena Wijayawimalasekera of Uyanwatte in Matara. She had three sons by her second marriage. Neither marriage nor motherhood, however, seem to have interrupted the steady progress of her education or affected her interest in literature.

As she matured, Gajaman set herself to learn and systematically practise the intricacies of prosody. Her chosen tutor was none other than Karatota Sri Dhammarama (1734–1822), the celebrated scholar monk of Weragampitiya Vihara who was later to become John D'Oyly's instructor. The Venerable Karatota was well known as both poet and teacher, the Dutch governor Wilhelm Falck, Don Janchi de Silva Abhayagunewardena, Mohandiram Katuwane Dissanayake, and the aristocratic poet Elapatha Disave being numbered among his pupils.

Gajaman had to break with tradition yet again in order to take instruction from this famous teacher because, from ancient times in Sri Lanka, as in many other parts of the world, the arts of reading and writing had been regarded as an exclusively male preserve. This was not, apparently, due to a cultural prejudice against female education. On the contrary, wrote James de Alwis in 1852, his countrywomen were 'taught with all possible care. Amongst the higher classes of the present generation scarcely can a single female be found, who is unable to read and write our language.' Such illiteracy and ignorance as did exist among Sinhalese women de Alwis attributed to the Buddhist rule which welcomed boys and young men into temples to further their education, while forbidding the entry of women for the same purpose.[11]

Proverbs exist in many parts of Asia which caution scholar-monks against the wiles of women, advising them to beware especially of educated women who, even though they might wear silk upon silk and move with the grace of the *houris* of Paradise, are not to be trusted if they possess the ability to press a stylus upon a palm leaf. In keeping with such traditions, conventional opinion in eighteenth-century Sri Lanka strongly discouraged the higher education of women, and women's names are absent from the list of the Venerable Karatota's distinguished students, not because they did not live and compose their poems in Matara, but because strict rules barred women from the presence of monks, unless it was for a religious purpose, such as attending a public ceremony, or donating alms.

Among eighteen sorts of monasteries the Buddhist ascetic was expected to avoid, the Methodist missionary Robert Spence Hardy listed in his book *Eastern Monachism* (1850) 'A *Wihara* near which there is an abundance of herbs, as women will come to gather them, singing all kinds of foolish songs, the hearing of which is as poison; and though they should not even be singing, the voice of a woman heard in any way is an enemy to the ascetic.'[12]

The proper sphere of a woman as yet unmarried was considered, in short, to be her parents' home; of a married woman, her husband's. There she could in safety and privacy conduct the true business of her life, the regulation of an orderly household and the bearing of children. Gajaman spurned such rules and restrictions. She is said to have entered the *vihara* alone, disguising herself as a young man in order to obtain the Venerable Karatota's literary instruction.

It was inevitable that a young woman of such an independent mind should become a target for gossip in a provincial society, and equally inevitable that not all the talk she attracted would be benign. Local know-alls hinted for years that it was not for love of literature alone that Gajaman had dressed as a man in order to enter Weragampitiya Vihara. A respectable woman to study in a temple? When it was well known that women were precluded from filling their heads with learning of any kind, and were specifically forbidden, moreover, to associate with monks? Karatota Thera had been, at the time she sought his instruction, a vigorous 49 years of age to Gajaman's 25. Clear-complexioned, six feet tall, the Thero when fully robed had appeared, so it was said, to resemble a living Buddha. Who could doubt that lust, and not literature, had motivated Gajaman's headstrong behaviour?

Popular gossip, not content with romantically linking the tutor to his beautiful student, went even further, and included one of the Venerable Karatota's most brilliant pupils in the roll-call of Gajaman's admirers. It was well known that the monk had earlier been the mentor of Elapatha Disave, a poet of aristocratic lineage who had entered the priesthood as a young man, only to later abandon his robes and his priestly title of Dhammaratana Thero. Having done so, Elapatha had entered the service of the British government. But if rumour was to be believed, an amorous passion for Gajaman Nona had contributed to his apostasy.

In the literary revival that was animating Matara at the time that John D'Oyly came into residence in the Dutch-built fort, whose massive walls and stone-flagged floors must have reminded him of the Roman shore-castles constructed along his native coast of Sussex, women poets were taking a leading part. The remarkable talents of Gajaman Nona had made her the best-known woman poet among Matara's school of singers, storytellers and poets. Inevitably, in that small society, her talents attracted envy. She became the constant target of innuendo and insult, but continued undeterred to compose poetry. Encouraged by her two male mentors, and assisted by wealthy patrons and critics who appreciated her talents, she developed a rapier-sharp wit and a quickness at riposte which earned her the admiration and the healthy respect of her literary contemporaries, both male and female.[13]

'The name of Gajaman is . . . familiar to our readers,' wrote James de Alwis in 1852, and gave the elegy on her father's death a place of honour in his survey of Sinhala literature, as one of 'several pieces of exquisite beauty' composed by the poet.[14] This was high praise from de Alwis, the nineteenth century's foremost literary critic, who regarded

Sinhala as 'a language . . . whose elegance in poetry consists chiefly in the elision and permutation of letters', and believed that 'in prose as in poetry, nothing is more to be desired than clearness and elegance of expression'.[15]

John D'Oyly and the famous Matara poet were brought together for the first time by a government proclamation which had heralded the arrival of the new Agent of Revenue in Matara. It seemed that the British government was eager to redress any injustices perpetrated by the Dutch which had caused suffering to the people of the new British colony. In order that justice should be done and reparation made, agents of government in the various districts of the Maritime Provinces were instructed to receive and enquire into claims submitted by members of the public.

Tradition has it that soon after John D'Oyly took up his appointment as Agent (*Disave*) of Matara in 1805, he received a petition from the Lady Gajaman in the form of several stanzas of richly poetic Sinhala verse.[16]

> Like Eros himself, handsome above all others, are you O
> > noble John D'Oyly, Lord of this District,
> Like the Moon itself, you light up a whole city with the
> > gentle radiance of your virtues,
> Like Lord Ganeshvara himself[17] in the range and depth of
> > your wit, you grasp the intricate meanings of poets'
> > linked verses and phrases,
> And like the Divine Tree itself your shining right hand
> > rewards with gifts their hopes and desires.

Gajaman Nona was by this time a mature 46 years of age. Widowed for a second time, she was now a notable personality in the district D'Oyly had been sent to govern. Since the Venerable Karatota had become in 1805 D'Oyly's instructor, it is most unlikely that, by the time he read her petition, D'Oyly could have been ignorant either of the literary fame of his tutor's brilliant ex-pupil, or of her reputation as a local beauty.

The stanzas submitted by the lady were accompanied by a sonorous prose preface. In it she claimed that she, her children and the other members of her family had been left without support following the death of her father, who had been killed while carrying out his duties under the Dutch regime.

> Bearing boundless riches from England,
> All-powerful *Disave*, John D'Oyly of noble birth and character:
> Possessing neither pearls nor gems, neither crops nor lands,
> I ask: by God's grace, please assist me.
> My children, who were once well fed, do not now
> Have even a little rice to still their hunger.
> With uplifted hands I implore Your Honour:
> Help me in my sad plight.[18]

Commanded to appear in person in order to formally petition the Agent of Revenue for assistance, Gajaman Nona is said to have replied that her extreme poverty made it impossible for her to come before His Excellency the *Disave* with the decorum required on such an occasion. D'Oyly then gave directions that the petitioner should receive whatever funds she needed in order to make a proper appearance before him. Having met the lady, he enquired into the case.

There is no record of what transpired at their interview, which seems to have taken place in private, but the result of it is well known. By the order of the Agent of Revenue, a grant was made to the Lady Gajaman and her heirs in the name of the British government of the Maritime Provinces, conferring upon them permanent ownership of the village of Nonagama near Hambantota, and of all its surrounding fields and grazing grounds.

Although no written records survive to support it,[19] the legend of D'Oyly's generous gift to Gajaman continues to flourish in the popular mind. The property itself is identified by popular tradition as a village on the Matara-Kataragama road, the name of which appeared for the first time as 'Nonage gama' ('Nona's village') in the village list of 1912. Similarly, the remains of a building at the top of Sri Pada is known as 'Nonage Gimanhala' (Nona's Resthouse), and is said to have been built with the revenue of the village granted to Gajaman Nona by the English Agent of Revenue. Tradition has it that Gajaman built it as a sanctuary for pilgrims in order to give thanks for her rescue when, as a small child on pilgrimage with her family, she had become temporarily lost in the wilderness surrounding the peak.[20]

Here, then, is one of those dilemmas which occasionally bedevil would-be biographers. Should they base their conclusions solely on the 'facts' available to them (which might not themselves be reliable or complete), or should they admit into their story the accumulated weight of tradition? The popular tale places its emphasis on human feeling: D'Oyly, it assures us, was genuinely and deeply moved by Gajaman Nona's helpless condition, which should not surprise since her petition was couched in terms calculated, after all, to touch the heart. The outright gift to her of the village of Nonagama, illustrative of an essentially compassionate and chivalrous nature, can be seen as the first of many spontaneous, sympathetic (and more satisfactorily recorded) actions which marked D'Oyly's later career.[21]

A second possibility is, that a shy, learned and sexually repressed young Englishman, inexperienced in dealing with women, was so completely overwhelmed by his encounter with a witty and charming woman of colour – and by her ability to appeal simultaneously to his chivalry, his compassion, and his vanity – that he perceived her as an embodiment of the 'exotic Oriental'. Judging by the accounts of her – both admiring and envious – that have survived to the present day, Gajaman – especially in the role of petitioner – might well have been hard for the 'All-powerful Disave' to resist.

Whatever the nature of his feelings on this occasion, D'Oyly's practical response to Gajaman Nona's appeal was so immediate and so extraordinarily generous that it aroused amused and cynical comment in the Sinhala society of the time. Given the imperial power wielded by one of the principals in this particular drama and the well-known personal attractions of the other, it was inevitable that such unusual benevolence on the part of an Agent of Revenue should have been interpreted by Matara society as part payment for 'services rendered'.[22] 'The expansion of Europe,' asserts Ronald Hyam, 'was not only a matter of "Christianity and commerce", it was also a matter of copulation and concubinage. Sexual opportunities were often seized with imperious confidence.'[23]

It should be kept in mind, when considering this matter, first, that the genre of the eulogistic petition has a long history in Sinhala classical literature. (It is equivalent, perhaps, to the long eulogistic prose dedications with which English poets of the eighteenth century had flattered their wealthy patrons.) In Sri Lanka as in eighteenth-century

England, the poet who went beyond the usual technical boundaries to 'snatch a grace beyond the reach of art' had often been generously rewarded by kings and noblemen.

Secondly, Gajaman's petition to D'Oyly was by no means the first of the kind that she had composed in her poetic career. She had earlier addressed a patron, Mudaliyar Karunaratne, in very similar terms:

> The constant suffering that has forcefully visited us
> You could dispel from us who are in sorrow caused by poverty
> With both hands folded in respect I fall down and worship
> Your lotuslike feet, O virtuous chieftain!

Although the grant D'Oyly made to Gajaman was not the first gift she had received from a patron, her appeal to him for help might well have been the first verse petition he ever personally received. It can hardly be doubted, however high-minded he was, that the young civil servant was flattered by being addressed in such terms.[24]

They were terms, too, the literary qualities of which he was especially well equipped to understand. D'Oyly had shown in his Cambridge ode 'Commercii Laus' that he was powerfully attracted to allusive and metaphorical language in the Western classical style. Unlike his contemporary, Dr John Davy, he would have been well able to respond as a fellow writer to the artistry of Gajaman's poetic language, the complicated elegances of which he was, as a student of Sinhala, rapidly learning to appreciate. Had he been slow to do so, it can hardly be doubted that the Venerable Karatota, pleased by this demonstration of his ex-pupil's literary accomplishment, would have pointed them out to him.

Most of these several scenarios have, naturally, been frequently canvassed by commentators on the relationship between the civil servant and the poet. If we were writing fiction we might feel justified in joining the debate.[25] But other possibilities exist, each of which leads to certain questions that relate not only to D'Oyly's state of mind at the time – a matter which must naturally concern his biographers – but to the colonial context in which his encounter with Gajaman took place.

As a young officer committed to a career in imperial politics D'Oyly might conceivably have been deliberately striving to win popularity in a newly acquired dominion by presenting himself to its people as 'a man of compassion, a man of good faith, a man of kindness and integrity'. Such was the advice offered by Niccolo Machiavelli in *The Prince* to rulers who wished to govern with wisdom and safety. It was advice which D'Oyly would almost certainly have read, either at Cambridge or in the course of his post-Cambridge study of Italian. 'The prince may either spend his own wealth and that of his subjects or the wealth of others,' Machiavelli had written,

> In the first case he must be sparing, but for the rest he must not neglect to be very liberal . . . You may be very generous indeed with what is not the property of yourself or your subjects, as were Cyrus, Caesar and Alexander; for spending the wealth of others will not diminish your reputation, but increase it.[26]

Applying Machiavellian principles to the social and political context of southern Sri Lanka in 1805, Gajaman Nona may well have appeared to D'Oyly as his gateway to the world of Sinhala literature and culture in Matara. Through his eminent tutor, the Venerable Karatota, he already enjoyed official contact with Sinhala society, but Gajaman, an attractive woman who shared his literary interests, could have seemed to him perfectly suited to act as his guide into the artistic and literary areas of his subjects' minds. The gift to her of a substantial grant of land would have certainly been a sure way of winning her friendship and support.

Another possibility is that the young Agent of Revenue, his position as sole representative in Matara and Galle of His Britannic Majesty George III going temporarily to his head, had been tempted to play the king. Had the classically trained D'Oyly been tempted by personal vanity, on finding himself resident in literary minded Matara, to emulate Maecenas? The second of these scenarios finds support in the island's established cultural traditions: as D'Oyly knew, kings and chieftains of Sri Lanka had long been accustomed to reward, with outright gifts of land titles and property, works of genius by artists, craftsmen and poets.

In the writing of biography, authorial imaginations must necessarily be kept in check by the available evidence. It is our view that no firm evidence has yet come to light that an affair of the heart between D'Oyly and Gajaman ever existed. The verses Gajaman addressed to D'Oyly function exclusively, so far as qualified critics have been able to assess them, on a level of formal courtesy and grace. There is, needless to say, no mention, however discreet, of Gajaman among D'Oyly's papers.

The possibility of a romance between two such interesting, intelligent and gifted people as D'Oyly and Gajaman cannot, however, be entirely ruled out. As the instances provided in India by D'Oyly's contemporaries and fellow civil servants Sir David Ochterlony and Captain Kirkpatrick demonstrate,[27] relationships between Englishmen and local women were by no means restricted to the lower ranks, and were treated with tolerance in the early years of the British occupation. Several British soldiers in the Maritime Provinces, and later in Kandy, took Sinhalese women as common-law wives – a fact that diarists in the officer class might not have wanted given much publicity, since the empire derived a good deal of its effectiveness from its ability to keep rulers and ruled apart:

> There may seem at first sight to be a contradiction between the care with which the military authorities provided facilities for sexual relations between British soldiers and native women and the care with which other authorities tried to discourage sexual relations between British officials and native women. In both cases . . . the fundamental concern was for the preservation of the structure of power.[28]

A craving for the exotic could, and often was, regarded as a sign of corruption,[29] a weakness that could spell danger to the British Crown in the event of an uprising against the empire.

The fact is that most nineteenth-century Englishmen of some education who had absorbed the attitudes of their race and class towards the Orient and its women seem to have found difficulty in coming to terms with sensuality openly and frankly displayed, as it is in the literature and society of many parts of Asia. An amusing example of this may be observed by comparing two of the illustrations provided in Captain James Cook's *Atlas*, which accompanied the publication of Cook's *Voyages* in three volumes. In one engraving, titled 'A Night Dance by Men, in Hapaee', lines of gesturing men disposed on either side of a central group rhythmically pounding staves are lit by moonlight and firelight. Captain Cook, immediately recognizable by his hat, is seated on the ground in the middle of a line of Hapaee males and British officers. They are facing the line of male dancers, their backs to the viewer, and Cook appears to be asking questions of his host (seated on his right), while a ship's officer seated on his left listens to the conversation. Cook's posture in this engraving is one of social ease: he leans easily on his right hand, and gestures sociably with his left. Behind the dancers, facing into the circle, are more natives of Hapaee.

In the second engraving, a companion-piece to the first titled 'A Night Dance by Women in Hapaee', Cook's attitude has undergone a complete change. He looks, in fact, almost as if he is about to take his leave, as with his left hand (now no longer used to point or to explain) he runs a finger round the inside of his collar in a distinctly embarrassed manner. And yet the two pictures are in all essential details (such as the moonlight, the firelight, and the central group pounding their staves) similar, except that two more ship's officers have joined Cook in the 'front row seats'. What makes the difference between the two pictures – and seems to have caused Cook intense embarrassment – is the fact that the lines of dancers in the second engraving consist entirely of young women whose only ornaments above the waist are the garlands of flowers in their hair.[30]

Whether a relationship closer than the official existed between D'Oyly and Gajaman or not, it is obvious that it could not have been pursued beyond the confines of the island without seriously damaging D'Oyly's career and distressing his conservative family. When, some years later, Mrs Mary D'Oyly urged her son to marry and settle down in England, it was of a suitable *English* daughter-in-law that she was thinking:

> If you must stay much longer at Kandy as you cannot have such pleasant society as you had at Colombo is there no young English young Lady who you would like to marry as I am sure you would not spend more with a wife & she could manage your own affairs for you as you say you have not time your self or if that is not the case & you chuse to stay some years longer in Ceylon would it not be better to come to England and stay one year & carry a wife back with you.[31]

The 'exotic' could be tolerated by the British, even enjoyed, in its proper place, but that place was generally agreed to be located outside England.[32]

As Gajaman's verses reveal, D'Oyly was rapidly acquiring under the tutorship of the Venerable Karatota the expertise in the Sinhala language that allowed him access to the multiple meanings of Sinhala poetry. While it is likely that D'Oyly originally approached the study of Sinhala literature as a step on the ladder of advancement in the Ceylon Civil Service, it is equally likely that he was awakened by his studies to a new reality, of life as well as of literature. His conversations with his tutor and his poetic exchanges with Gajaman Nona, both of whom were poets finely attuned to the inner life of their country's culture, must have led him, at the very least, into a better understanding of the country the British had undertaken to govern. This view is supported by evidence in D'Oyly's letters that his increasing fluency in Sinhala was bringing him into touch with Sinhalese people at every level of society.

The Sinhala poems D'Oyly read, whether by Gajaman or by her contemporaries, reveal a society characterized by passion, pride, wit, spirit and a sensuality quite unlike anything of the kind that he could have encountered in England. Indeed, the Sinhala literature D'Oyly read in Matara must have seemed at first to be the opposite of everything he had been trained to admire. But it was also the product of this unfamiliar island's finest minds, and for this reason among many others, would have demanded his close attention.

It is interesting to speculate how he would have responded, as he read the verses of the Matara poets for what he could learn from them about Sinhala literary style, and translated them into English,[33] to the well-known exchanges between Gajaman and her contemporaries. What, for instance, would he have made of their metaphorical and allusive style, and – looking beyond these – what would he have made of the society of which that style was clearly a forceful, deeply felt expression? What, even more specifically, would he have thought of the metaphors employed by them in the genre of love poetry,[34] and of the sexual relationships which were commonly said to have been the source of such passion and insult?

At least one critic has noted that Gajaman Nona's poems reveal 'a defiant woman, fighting tooth and nail, at times descending even into vulgarity, to keep her rivals, the male poets, at bay', and has described her literary career as having been largely a 'struggle for a niche in a male-dominated world'.[35] Despite these obstacles, Gajaman found generous patrons in the district. She returned thanks for their benevolence in verse, making modern use of a time-honoured classical tradition with a poetic grace that was admired by all her contemporaries and envied by many among them. In one poem of this genre, which consists in all of 50 stanzas and is addressed to a low-country notable named Mudaliyar Tillekeratne who had supported and encouraged her writing, Gajaman Nona ostensibly praises the beauty of a banyan tree for which the district of Denipitiya in Weligama was at that time famous.[36] Her composition is in reality a song which celebrates the generosity of the *mudaliyar*:

> Pleasing every eye that sees
> By the river flowing fair
> Rising over lowlier trees
> Spreading shadow everywhere
> Like dark rain-clouds massing high
> As a sheltering canopy
> Leaves that quiver in the breeze
> Loud with bees that cluster there . . .

In writing such a poem, Gajaman Nona 'was eulogizing her patron's munificence – as she was expected to do'.[37]

Gajaman Nona's poetry, deservedly honoured in Sri Lanka to this day, combines the folk idiom of the era with traditional Sinhala poetic forms. In this regard it is a true reflection of the changing times in which she lived and wrote. In verse 'dialogues' that are well known in Sri Lanka, she had conversed poetically with her first husband, warning him in one playful exchange of the dangers of lethargy –

> She: Those who sleep till the dawn of the sun,
> Were they possessors of all the earth's countless wealth,
> They will end up empty, like the *divul* fruit the elephant
> swallows.[38]
> Sages of old have prophesied their poverty!

She reminded him in another verse that constancy on her side must be earned by constancy on his:

> He: If I am delayed on this journey,
> Do not look at anyone else till I return!

Like the yam leaf, warding off waterdrops,
Remember my advice and wait for me.

She: There, in that village to which my lord is travelling,
Let not the charms of other women delay you!
Lord, I will keep in mind the advice you give me,
But let us hope Cupid remembers it too!

Gajaman Nona's poems dealt either with the harsh conflicts present in the society of her times, poised as it was between an indigenous cultural revival and the growing impact of Western modernizing attitudes; or with erotic love, continuing in this latter genre one of the favourite themes of ancient Indian and Sinhala poetry.[39]

Among examples of Gajaman's best work in the first of these genres, Sinhala critics frequently cite a verse that she is said to have written in poverty and depression:

She: There are no parents to give comfort to the body and mind
Relations do not care when one is poor.
For worry and sickness I have no cure.
There is none to protect us now.

It is said that on one occasion Gajaman's mentor, the High Priest of Karatota, had lodged with persons who were not on good terms with her. When she was informed that the monk had complained of her neglect of him, she sent him her excuses in verse:

She: Lord Buddha said association with undesirables brings sorrow.
I know well that separation from those I love also brings sorrow.
Today, since you lodge with those who are not my friends,
I sorrow that I cannot come to see you.[40]

Among Gajaman's most famous compositions in the genre of erotic verse are a series of love poems, part of an exchange that gossip credits her with having conducted with her rumoured admirer, the former monk Elapatha Disave:

He: Your face, bright as the sun and the moon!

> Your pouting breasts, glowing like blue sapphires!
> Like a lamp lit in a dark room, Lady,
> Why do you sleep alone?

She: Since the death of my dear husband,
       A lonely bed has been my refuge.
       I have forgotten the meaning of sensual pleasures –
       What right have you to ask me such a question?

In one of the poems ascribed to Elapatha, a powerful and unusual metaphor compares the devastation wreaked by a passionate woman upon a poet's spiritual life to the destruction caused by a rutting elephant set loose in a plantation. Making skilful play with the multiple meanings of words (including that of Gajaman's name), and comparing *arahat* (the last stage of spiritual evolution in which humankind overcomes all desire) to carefully tended banana orchards, the writer describes the 'elephant' as blowing through her long trunk in all the ten directions as she lays plantations waste, crazed by the madness of desire.

    Later, when their love had ended, the two poets were to attack each other mercilessly in verse:

He: Wise in the Buddha's teachings, and most beautiful,
      Lives a woman nearby known by the name of Gaja.
      Following the custom established by all women
      She continues her dalliance with paramours.

She: Branches of learning, tender leaves of love
       Grew from my lover's famous family tree,
       Heavy with ripened fruit of pleasant virtues.
       All, all, destroyed by the winds of passion!

       The current of fourfold desire, swelled by heavy rain,
       Floods and bursts the riverbanks far and wide.
       This ancient bund, built strongly out of the nine *Dhammas*,
       Was breached, and surrendered at the haven of woman.

He: Hear, all living beings, of Gajaman's virtuous deeds!
      To attain the five fruits, she gave grand alms.[41]
      Though this was brainless folly on her part,

96

May all share in the merit so acquired!

There were many others besides Elapatha Disave, so rumour said, who loved the irresistible Gajaman. These relationships too had yielded poetic exchanges:

He: In your land, Lady, is not merit earned with alms?
Don't your people ever open their doors?
Don't frogs play among the lilies in your lakes?
If I die of unquenched desire, will you not weep?

She: Is the use of this open road restricted to a chosen few?
Do travellers stir the river mud before they drink the water?
Do pleasure-loving women send out invitations?
Can't masters of adventure find their way past warning bells?

He: When I first saw you love was strong in my heart -
It vanished by and by for you were so unyielding.
Let me give you a piece of information:
Woman! till I reach Nirvana I do not want you!

She: The love that began on the day I saw you
Grew by and by into a rock of granite.
Your words, Sir, are very surprising!
For, till you reach Nirvana, who is there better than me?

When a rejected lover called Gajaman Nona 'a whore with no virtues', she lashed back in verse:

She: You, desiring not me nor love but lust,
Call all gentlewomen prostitutes!
For giving birth to such a scoundrel,
Go, insult the hill of flesh that bore you!

'The starkness of the insults', writes one critic of the stanza we have quoted above, 'eludes translation.'[42]

How would John D'Oyly have regarded this unusual woman? How would he have responded to the earthy realism of her occasionally scabrous verses, not to mention the well-established rumours of the poet's relationships with Elapatha and others? Would the unblushing directness of her poetic expression – the opposite of everything he had been trained to expect and admire in English poetry by and about women – have appalled D'Oyly, or intrigued him? She was obviously quite unlike any other woman of his acquaintance, whether in Sri Lanka or in England. As for her verses, readers at the rectory at Buxted would most certainly have regarded them as indelicate at best, and at worst morally indefensible.

Gajaman's poetry, being what it was, may have opened D'Oyly's eyes for the first time to the realities of female character. It is likely to have had a deeper and more significant impact on him by providing intimations of the complex nature of the society in which he had elected to serve. John D'Oyly's contacts among the Sinhalese had probably begun with the pandit or 'Native Professor of Languages' who, according to custom, had been hired to teach him his letters and visited the official residence several times a week so to do.[43] Later, as we have seen, those contacts extended to relationships with scholars and poets. By the time his Residency in Matara and Galle neared its end, D'Oyly had acquired the ability to converse with the utmost ease, not only with the *literati* of his district, but with its commonest folk.

'I believe my Friends in England will not give me much credit for the Talents of a Huntsman,' D'Oyly wrote to his brother Thomas on 18 June 1809,

> but Fortune which delights to sport, has made me on Ceylon, Chief Hunter of the Noblest Chace in the World.

He was describing an elephant hunt in the jungles of Sri Lanka's Western Province. The tropical vegetation that now surrounded him was very different indeed from that of Ashdown Forest, yet the experience itself had 'called to mind', he wrote, 'the early Days of my Retired Life, when I was accustomed to wander through the Sussex Woods in quest of Game'.[44]

D'Oyly's boyish experiences shooting rabbit and pheasant in England's tranquil woodlands would hardly have prepared him for the perils of the jungles of Sri Lanka which were, in those early years, richly populated with a variety of wildlife: leopard, deer, sambhur, wild pig, black bear, jungle fowl, peacocks, flocks of vari-coloured birds, and above all elephants, offered constant delight to eyes and repose to minds that were not obsessed with thoughts of slaughter.

Through translation from the Greek geographers, and the descriptions of travellers such as Marco Polo and Ralph Fitch, the elephants of Sri Lanka had entered the European imagination as wise inhabitants of an Eden of almost unearthly beauty and matchless wealth, an island fragrant with cinnamon and spices, blessed with plenty and peace. Such were the terms in which Samuel Purchas had described the island of 'Zeilan' in his *Pilgrimage*, recording the legend according to which the elephant of Sri Lanka, *elephas maximus,* occupied pre-eminent status among others of its own kind which, on encountering it, had been observed to bow their knees and lower their massive heads before it in spontaneous homage:

> The Heauens with their deawes, the Ayre with a pleasant holesome-nesse and fragrant freshnesse, the Waters in their many Riuers and Fountaines, the Earth diuersified in aspiring Hills, lowly Vales, equall and indifferent Plaines, filled in her inward Chambers with Mettalls and jewells, in her outward Court and vpper face stored with whole Woods of the best Cinnamon that the Sunne seeth, besides Fruits, Oranges, Leimons, &c., surmounting those of Spaine; Fowles and Beasts, both tame and wilde *(among which is their Elephant, honoured by a naturall acknowledgement of excellence, of all other Elephants in the world.)* These have all conspired and joyned in common League, to present unto Zeilan the chiefe of worldly treasures and pleasures, with a long and healthfull life in the inhabitants, to enioy them.

'No maruell then,' concluded Purchas, 'if sense and sensualitie haue here stumbled on a Paradise.'[45]

In neighbouring India, as in Sri Lanka (though to a lesser extent), the observation of pitched battles between well-matched fighting elephants had traditionally been a favourite pastime of rulers and their guests. The ruler of Lucknow had 'often expressed his surprise,' wrote Captain Thomas Williamson in 1813,

> that our Governor-General did not amuse himself and his court in a similar manner. He might have learnt, from experience, that the

British government was intent on contests of much greater importance![46]

So, indeed, it was. But, following the establishment of empire, the tigers and elephants of Asia came to be regarded by many British 'sportsmen' in the East as the biggest of big game, their wholesale slaughter an unsubtle symbol of imperial power. By mid-century the Sri Lankan jungles had begun to attract bloodthirsty 'sportsmen' from all parts of Europe. Count Emanuel Andrasy published a volume of hand-coloured lithographs in 1853, which he titled *Scenes of the Island of Ceylon*. In one of these, 'Stalking elephants, Bibile, 6th May 1853' (see Plate 7), two European sportsmen, immaculate in white, and attended by native gun-bearers, take on and apparently decimate an entire herd of forest elephants at point-blank range.[47]

In the early years of their rule, however, the tracking and capture of elephants was to the British still a matter of practical necessity, rather than an 'amusement' for an idle hour. When Governor North began to plan a possible incursion of British troops into the Kandyan district, hunts were organized in the south and west, not to kill but to capture the animals required to haul the heavy cannon which must necessarily accompany a military force.[48]

D'Oyly's involvement in the elephant kraal of 1809 which he described in detail to his brother Thomas in England had been occasioned by the fact that in the seven years since 1802, elephants had enjoyed a free and undisturbed range through the forests of south and west Sri Lanka. They had become so bold and numerous, D'Oyly wrote, 'as to occasion considerable injury to Agriculture and Terror to the Inhabitants in parts of the Districts of Colombo and Matara'. As a result, the government in Colombo had directed at the beginning of 1809 that elephant hunts should take place in both districts, and as Agent of Revenue for the District of Colombo, 'the charge and Conduct' of the exercise in Colombo had fallen to D'Oyly's lot.

To his description of an elephant hunt in his letter to his brother Thomas, D'Oyly added a note: 'My Acquaintance with the Habits & Language of the Singhalese affording every facility of intercourse,' he wrote, 'I joined these rude Savages in their Native Forests, & shared with them the Fatigues of the Chace.' As in most literary documents, the language is revealing. The hunters he was describing were still 'rude

Savages' to D'Oyly's English upper-class eye, not because they were Sinhalese, but because they were Sinhalese of a lower social class than the people of the district with whom he had hitherto had regular contact. But D'Oyly's studies had helped him, in some degree at least, to break through the limitations of race, class and colonial politics, and obtain new insight into the minds of the people. He realized very early – and was one of the very few Englishmen who did so – that 'The Sinhala language could become indeed the key to the heart of the native'.[49]

One of D'Oyly's most able colleagues, Captain Arthur Johnston, was among the few who were aware of the importance to British stability in the island of a knowledge of local languages. Johnston was soon to record in print his own conviction that 'a knowledge of the [Sinhala] language . . . enables us to converse with the men of education among the natives, who are generally communicative and well-informed, particularly with what relates to their own country – a species of knowledge of which we stand the most in need. It farther enables us to peruse the writings, and, by instructing us in their origin, teaches us to respect prejudices of which the Indians are extremely tenacious, and which we are too apt at first landing to despise.'[50]

Knowledge of the local language had made it possible for a British agent of government to do more than sit in his official quarters in Matara or Galle and have his orders to the hunters of the Elephant Department conveyed to them through an intermediary. He could now actually enter into the spirit of a local occasion and, as D'Oyly evidently did in the June of 1809, join his inferiors in the hunt, sharing with them their weariness and exhilaration.

This was something new in the British colonial experience. Sir Thomas Maitland, second son of James Maitland, seventh Earl of Lauderdale, who arrived in Ceylon on 17 July 1805 to replace Frederick North as Governor of the Maritime Provinces, was quick to recognize his conscientious officer's remarkable talent and abilities and to make use of them. D'Oyly was appointed Chief Translator to the Government and *Disave* of Colombo, in which post (since Maitland distrusted the high Sinhalese officials of the Maritime Provinces) it now became his responsibility to communicate on behalf of the Crown with the court of Kandy.

In D'Oyly's letter to the Venerable Móratota, Chief Priest of Kandy, he formally announced Maitland's appointment and gave the first hint that the British government in Colombo insisted on the restoration of certain officers presently held hostage by the King of Kandy:

> Invested by the Great Supreme King of Great Britain, His Master, with the highest authority both in Civil and Military Affairs, His Excellency the Governor, General Maitland, is arrived in *Lankawa*. Tho' War has been his habit from early youth, it hath entered into the considerations of His Excellency, whether it were possible to carry into effect the benevolent intentions of the Great Supreme King of Great Britain, His Master, to give peace to all nations having spread his victories in every region by the valour of his mighty fleets and armies. Therefore, ere he despatches his armed forces into the field, it hath pleased His Excellency the Governor to declare, that if all the English officers and soldiers now resident in the territory of the King of Kandy be restored, then shall negotiations commence in order to open the barriers for the commercial intercourse of the subjects of both Powers, and to conclude a Treaty of Peace, which may endure as long as heaven and earth shall endure.
>
> In many conversations with His Excellency the Governor having learnt these sentiments, I make known the same to thee, the Chief of Priests and Lover of the World's and Religion's Good, in order that you may communicate them to the Great Gate in a happy hour.[51]

The scholar monk of Weragampitiya Vihara had trained his pupil well: the formal diction of Sinhala courtly address has been captured here in masterly fashion, and a threat of imminent military intervention skilfully veiled in the polite language of diplomacy. Keen chess player at Cambridge and 'Chief Hunter' of elephants in Sri Lanka's Western Province, D'Oyly was learning rapidly how to 'dip the pen of diplomacy in the ink-well of his masters' interests, and inscribe their messages on the parchment of stratagem'.[52] He would soon find ample space to exercise his new skills in an updated version of 'the Noblest Chace in the World': the game of imperial politics which Kipling would one day call 'the great Game', and which, in the forms it took in Asia, Britain's representatives there were rapidly learning how to play.

CHAPTER SIX

1811–1815:
OBEDIENT SERVANT

The rebel Knave, who dares his prince engage,
Proves the just victim of his royal rage.

Alexander Pope, *The Rape of the Lock*

ON 11 SEPTEMBER 1811, Brigadier-General John Wilson wrote to the Earl of Liverpool to inform the home government of alarming developments rumoured to be taking place in the Kingdom of Kandy. Wilson had just arrived in Jaffna, a stage in a circuit of the island that he was making in his role as officer in charge of British affairs in Sri Lanka until a new governor arrived to succeed Maitland. Affairs in Kandy, he reported, had grown increasingly threatening since he had last written (on 15 July). He had received intelligence that active preparations for war were being made in two Kandyan provinces, and that the King of Kandy was in active communication with the French settlements on the coast.

'I trust,' Wilson added, 'that His Majesty's ministers will be strongly impressed with the danger of allowing this valuable colony, intended as it would appear to be rendered still more important by the establishment of a Naval Depot at Trincomalee, to be harrassed by a treacherous and irreconcileable Enemy, occupying the centre of the Island.'

The Bay of Trincomalee, on the eastern coast of the island, had indeed become, in British eyes, a most important part of the 'valuable colony' of Ceylon. This was due partly to its unique position in the

Indian Ocean, virtually commanding the sea routes between the West and East, partly to its capacious harbour which could easily accommodate a large number of seagoing ships. Trincomalee had come into the possession of the Dutch East India Company. Its crucial importance to European trading and military ambitions in Asia was, as T. Vimalananda points out, no secret among the contending naval powers of the West:

> The possession of Trincomalee Harbour became an object of major concern in the global British naval strategy, and when this had at length been achieved, its protection and defence against any possible attack by the French. The latter possibility was especially to be feared, as the ever-present prospect and possibility of its transfer into French hands with the support and help of the Dutch who were in possession of it would presage dire consequences to the concept of Empire which the British were building up on the Indian continent.
>
> In this context the British realised that the co-operation of the King of Kandy was essential to expel the Dutch from Ceylon and establish British naval supremacy in the Indian Ocean with Trincomalee as its base. Thus the political situation both in Europe and in India obliged the French and English alike to be uncommonly solicitous towards the wishes of the Court of Kandy.[1]

While assuring Liverpool that nothing but an actual attack on the part of the French would induce him to involve the British Government in hostilities against them, Wilson warned that the Kandyans were not to be trusted: 'Your Lordship will forgive me for expressing my opinion that their conduct towards all the European Powers established here evinces that there can be no effectual security from their machinations, but by reducing them under His Majesty's Dominion.'[2]

Wilson's view of Kandyan treachery and unreliability echoes the opinion expressed by Captain Arthur Johnston, whom experience had made anxious to guard his countrymen 'from ever reposing an unlimited confidence in the natives of Ceylon . . . It is necessary that while we make use of them in their various situations, we should, as much as possible, prevent their penetrating into our designs', wrote Johnston in 1810.[3]

The 'intelligence' to which Wilson referred in his letter to the Earl of Liverpool had been secured for him by John D'Oyly, now Chief Translator to the Government, through whose growing network of well-placed contacts and informants the British government in Colombo was being kept in touch, officially and unofficially, with developments in the Kandyan kingdom. Two amicably worded letters, composed for Wilson by D'Oyly, had already been sent through official channels to the king at Kandy. These remained unanswered. With D'Oyly's diplomatic assistance, Wilson dispatched yet another letter to the King, in which repeated assurances of his personal respect for the Kandyan ruler's 'high dignity' and the British government's 'moderate and pacific views' masked a series of threats and warnings.[4]

He had been informed, Wilson told the king, that Britain's old enemies, the French, had been holding out to the Kandyan kingdom 'fabulous promises of assistance'. He warned him to be on his guard against such dangerous friends 'whose practice it is to ruin every Country with which they form any Connexion'. Citing the fall of Mysore and the death of Tippu Sultan as instances of the results attending French 'perfidy in India', he described the French as universally considered in Europe to be 'disturbers of the World and the Enemies of all nations, sacrificing the treasures, the people and the Government of every Country where they are admitted to their own insatiable ambition and rapacity'.

If provoked, Wilson warned, Britain would surely wreak a terrible vengeance: 'For what nation so remote and uninformed as not to have heard of that Navy which Commands the Ocean and of those Armies which pervade every quarter of the globe?'

As a further and telling disincentive he reminded the king that the government in Colombo was perfectly able to call up at short notice troops of 'Caffres' from the West India colonies to reinforce the two battalions already stationed in Ceylon: D'Oyly knew well that rumours which had been circulating since the period of Portuguese occupation, of Africans' taste for human flesh, had made 'Caffre' soldiers greatly feared by the Kandyans.[5]

A new governor, Lieutenant-General Robert Brownrigg, succeeded Maitland in Colombo in 1812. In his very first despatch to the home government, Brownrigg referred to information he had received from 'Mr D'Oyly the Chief Interpreter of Government' that public feeling

FIGURE 8 The soldierly Brownrigg

Portrait of Sir Robert Brownrigg, Bart., Governor of Ceylon. Frontispiece to John Davy, *An Account of the Interior of Ceylon* (1821).

towards the British among the Kandyans was favourable, and that perfect quiet prevailed on the frontier.[6] This good news had been inferred by D'Oyly from the tenor of a regular private correspondence he had been conducting for some time with two Kandyan chieftains, Ehelepola Maha Nilame, the First Adigar of the Kandyan court and *Disava* of Sabaragamuwa, and Pusvella Disave, Chief of the Seven Korales.

It is evident, viewing past events from the standpoint of the present day, that from the time of Brownrigg's appointment as Governor of the British Maritime Provinces in Ceylon, John D'Oyly's position as Chief Translator to the Government had undergone a major change. He was still nominally in charge of the *disavani* of Colombo, but the main task assigned to him by Brownrigg was the organization of a reliable intelligence network that would keep the government informed on every aspect of Kandyan affairs. In this capacity D'Oyly was entrusted with all the negotiations the British government conducted with the court and chiefs of Kandy.

It is likely that John D'Oyly would, by 1811, have read Robert Percival's book *An Account of the Island of Ceylon*, which had been published in 1803 and reprinted in 1805. Percival had accompanied General Macdowall on his embassy to Kandy in 1800[7] and was one of the few Englishmen who had visited the court. 'The Civil and Military Establishments of the Kingdom of Kandy' gives an account of the king, his titles and manner of government, concluding with advice regarding relationships with the Kandyan people that D'Oyly might well have taken to heart:

> It will require many years of perseverance in a mild and steady policy to obliterate those prejudices with which imprudent cruelty (on the part of Portuguese and Dutch invaders) has inspired them against Europeans. But the advantages which may be derived from their friendship and co-operation, certainly render a new system at least worth the experiment.

Where, previously, only the uneasiest and most hostile of relationships had existed between Colombo and the interior, D'Oyly set himself painstakingly to create friendships. Unfailingly courteous in all his dealings with members of the Kandyan nobility, paying due regard to their status in their own society, he made himself at once agreeable to them and indispensable to his master, Brownrigg.

D'Oyly's correspondence with the chieftains was one of the means by which he had been patiently trying for some time to obtain peaceful access to the Kandyan country. Improved knowledge on the British side of the Kandyan terrain was advisable, indeed imperative, in case British soldiers should have at some future time to fight there. But a more specific and urgent incentive existed at the time: the hope of securing the return to Colombo of Major Davie, an English officer whom the Kandyans had captured in 1803, and who had since then been held prisoner in the Kandyan Kingdom. The desperate tone of a letter sent by Major Davie to D'Oyly had made him extremely uneasy regarding the state of the officer's health, since it appeared to contradict the impression (earlier conveyed to him by Pusvelle Disave, Chief of the Seven Korales) that the major had recovered his health after having been placed in the care of the court physicians.[8]

'My health weak and my body weaker,' Davie had written in a secret appeal to D'Oyly, who had contrived to send him some wine, tea, medicines and articles of European clothing through the good offices of Pannala Unnanse, a Buddhist monk who was one of his regular couriers. 'My supplies of food are small and in arrears. For heaven sake send quickly Laudanum and opium my torture is (un)indurable.'[9]

Between 1812 and 1815, D'Oyly patiently built up personal links with court and temple that were based on common interests and – seemingly – mutual respect. Robert Percival had recommended civil attentions paid to Kandyan leaders, together with 'some well-timed presents and concessions' as likely to be more effective than war.[10] Accordingly, D'Oyly opened the correspondence with Kandy by informing the *maha adikaram* of his wish to obtain specimens of certain medicinal herbs that were to be found only in the forests surrounding Sri Pada (the sacred mountain reputed to bear on its summit the Buddha's footprint being located in the first adigar's province). This desire, whether genuine or not, Ehelepola had courteously satisfied, requesting on his own behalf that he be sent a pair of geese and a pair of fan-tailed field-grouse.[11] D'Oyly responded with alacrity: he promptly sent the chieftain not one but two pairs of geese, with a promise of several pairs of fan-tailed field-grouse to be sent on as soon as they should become available.

D'Oyly's polite exchange of gifts with Ehelepola may have been inspired by a timely reading of Percival, but it is worth noting that on his own initiative D'Oyly styled himself in his letters not simply as 'Chief Translator' or 'Chief Interpreter' to the British government, but as '*Disave* of Colombo', expanding this later to the even grander title of 'Great *Disave*'. In this he may have been taking his cue from Ehelepola's own magniloquence (much as his countrymen were, at about the same time, building viceregal abodes in India on a scale intended to equal the splendour of the maharajas' palaces). However, the grandeur D'Oyly assumed satisfied more than a mere personal vanity: it effectively maintained the tone of his correspondence with the chiefs at an appropriately dignified and cordial level, as taking place spontaneously between persons with common interests and of equal rank and status.

Having established friendly relations with the powerful chieftain, D'Oyly now enquired of him whether a Mr Hooker, an Englishman resident in Colombo, could possibly be permitted to tour the Sabaragamuwa Province while Ehelepola was resident there. The gentleman in question being a botanist interested in the herbs that had been sent to Colombo, he was 'anxious', D'Oyly said, 'to see the nature of their growth in the forests themselves'.[12]

The botanical 'Mr Hooker' and his scientific interests were probably as much an artistic invention on D'Oyly's part as his strategically assumed titles. According to Sir Paul Pieris, Hooker did not in fact visit Sri Lanka.[13] On the other hand, as we know, D'Oyly was himself interested in both botany and ornithology: the letters of his brother Thomas, especially after 1815 when D'Oyly was resident in Kandy and had access to the jungles of the Seven Korales, are filled with references to plants that D'Oyly was collecting and bird skins that he was attempting to cure prior to shipping them to England for examination by British scientists.

D'Oyly was aware that Governor Brownrigg, who was very much in favour of extending British control over the Kandyan kingdom, by force if necessary, was disappointed by the lack of enthusiasm such ideas elicited from London. Rather than go to battle with the court of Kandy, Brownrigg was urged to make 'every attempt consistent with the honor of the British name to preserve Tranquility by measures of conciliation'.[14] A policy of conciliation did not appeal to the soldierly Brownrigg. In his subsequent correspondence with the King of Kandy, conducted through D'Oyly (who had, Brownrigg wrote to Lord Liverpool, 'so long and so ably conducted the Candian Correspondence and . . . whose knowledge of the motives of action and policy of that Court is superior to that of any person here'), he made the release of Major Davie a test of Kandy's good intentions.

I cannot refrain from expressing my sentiments of regret [Brownrigg wrote] that . . . whilst other powerful sovereigns of the earth deem essential to their glory, and the dignity of their crowns the immediate Restoration of Prisoners unfortunately captured in War, there should arise in the breast of Your Majesty just causes for withholding this purest token of pacific disposition.[15]

The Kandyan court dealt with the whole question of Major Davie and his return by blandly ignoring it. Instead, there now followed a long-drawn-out correspondence on a topic which the Kandyan officials evidently regarded as being of much greater importance: the proper method by which correspondence from Colombo with the King of Kandy was to be addressed and conveyed. D'Oyly did not regard the matter in the same light but, being sensitive to the punctiliousness of the Kandyan court with regard to matters of protocol, he did not of course say so. Brownrigg, on the other hand, clearly regarded the fuss over correspondence as a trivial matter, transparently a devious method the Kandyan officials had chosen to avoid being forced to a direct discussion of Major Davie's state of health. He was convinced that Davie was, in fact, dead, and that the Kandyans were refusing to admit it.[16]

Brownrigg's letter of 1812, written to the King of Kandy, announcing his appointment as Governor of the Maritime Provinces, remained unacknowledged on 15 March 1813. His irritation at this breach of courtesy surfaced in an unusual diatribe addressed to Lord Bathurst and directed at 'this strange people' and their 'strange way':

> Their treachery and cunning is such that appearances are never to be relied upon, but they are so contemptible as a military power, that no serious consequences are to be apprehended from any change in their present dormant position. – The King, whose disposition is tyrannical, and was considered to possess activity of body and mind, is now said to have become sensual and indolent, indulging in the use of spirituous liquor, and his having added two to his former number of wives has recently been celebrated at Kandy.[17]

The weaknesses of British royalty were well known to the British public of the time, so that Brownrigg's malicious description of the King of Kandy as sensual, indolent, alcoholic and licentious must have rung somewhat hollow in the ears of the Earl of Bathurst as he read it. George III had had fifteen children, eight sons and seven daughters. The daughters were virtually unknown to the public, but all the surviving sons were generally disapproved of, though in varying degrees. The Duke of Cumberland was a scoundrel, widely suspected of having murdered his valet. The Duke of York had been involved in a disgraceful business, through his mistress, of selling army commissions when he was commander-in-chief. The Duke of Clarence had lived off the earnings of *his* mistress, the successful comedy actress Mrs Dorothea Jordan, by whom he had ten children, before casting her off to marry a German princess. The Duke of Kent's life followed a similar pattern, and when he finally brought his bride back to England, he had to borrow £5,000 from Earl Fitzwilliam and Lord Dundas. Parliament was constantly being asked to vote money to rescue George III's sons from bankruptcy and to keep them in idle profligacy. As Liverpool frequently complained, no other kind of business was so difficult to get through the House of Commons. Nor was this surprising. Wellington calculated that the brothers between them 'at one time or another' had 'personally insulted every gentleman in the kingdom'.[18]

As for Brownrigg's comments regarding rumours of the King of Kandy's weakness for liquor, a weakness that was to increase in future years as his courtiers intrigued against him and obtained from British sources the means to further befuddle their master,[19] Bathurst could not but have been aware that from the 1790s onward it had been the habit of the Prince Regent, later King George IV, to spend from 6 pm to midnight at the dinner table, beginning with 'ten Bumber toasts': there were six bumper glasses to a bottle.[20]

While drinking was a national weakness – a compassionate Moghul emperor is reported to have decreed that the households of British ambassadors to his court should be allowed liquor by special dispensation since the British lived in alcohol as fish lived in water, so that to deprive them of liquor was to deprive them of life[21] – polygamy was regarded by the British in the nineteenth century with a mixture of fascinated curiosity, horror and envy. Sensuality, openly displayed and joyously celebrated (as it still is, in many oriental societies), was a phenomenon with which many Britons in Asia found it difficult to come to terms.

The harems maintained by 'Orientals' of wealth and power had, of course, been a topic of perennial interest for Europeans ever since contact had first been made with Asian courts. The possibility that one or more women might be kept secluded, under strict guard, for the private sexual pleasure of a single, all-powerful male was a titillating idea in itself. Add to it the legendary luxury of an oriental court, the thought of dozens, nay hundreds of beautiful women whose sole desire was to please a 'vastly rich [and] imaginatively sensual' nawab or raja, and it is not hard to perceive the source of Brownrigg's irritation and envy. Shuja-ud-daula, who reigned in Oudh from 1731 to 1775, a physically powerful ruler who proved his capacity by resisting the pressures upon his kingdom of the Marathas, the Rohilla Afghans and the British, was rumoured to maintain a harem of seven hundred wives.[22]

Of course, the British were not without their own 'Orientals': we have seen that Brownrigg's contemporary Sir David Ochterlony (1758–1825), the first British Resident in Delhi, maintained a household of thirteen wives.[23] The licentiousness of the Kandyan king appeared to have been practised on a smaller scale than Sir David's, yet the four queens known to dwell in the royal palace at Kandy were regarded by Brownrigg, and by most of his countrymen in Colombo, as being evidence in themselves of their husband's wicked 'sensuality'.

Did D'Oyly work deliberately, under Brownrigg's instructions, to alienate the chiefs and the priesthood from their king, and ultimately win Kandy for the British Crown? It is impossible to provide an answer to this question, since the detailed records he kept of his transactions tell us only what occurred from day to day: they reveal nothing of his intentions or plans, or of the conclusions he drew. Historians are forced, therefore, to judge D'Oyly only in relation to his ultimate achievements. Despite this, at least one historian is convinced that D'Oyly aimed to bring about the ruin of the Kandyan kingdom. Gaining by degrees a firm insight into the principal forces that were threatening the stability of the ancient monarchy, D'Oyly, according to the view put forward by T. Vimalananda, applied his knowledge to the task in hand with 'a Machiavellian coolness and calculation', and did everything in his power to undermine the king's influence and authority.

The espionage work D'Oyly conducted had several branches: to ascertain the identity of the important Kandyan noblemen and aristocrats who were not well-disposed towards the king, and to fan their feelings of ill-will to the sovereign; to ascertain the names of the members of the Kandyan court who remained loyal to their monarch, and wherever possible to neutralize them; to secure the trust and support of the *sangha*, or Buddhist clergy; to gain a comprehensive knowledge of strategic points of the realm and of the various secret routes leading from the Maritime provinces by which they could be reached, and Kandy itself approached; to obtain information regarding personal antipathies and clan rivalries among the leading families in the Kandyan Provinces; to originate and bring into existence in the remotest part of the king's dominions such situations and tensions among the people as might justify British intervention; to find out the exact military strength, supplies, arms and ammunition available for the defence and protection of Kandy; to obtain information regarding the whereabouts of hiding-places in which the royal treasure was usually hidden during political upheavals; and last but not the least important, to convey through various agencies, British liquors of all sorts to the king.[24]

In many ways the Kingdom of Kandy must have seemed to D'Oyly (and no doubt to others in Colombo who were acquainted with the wider political world of Europe) like a toy kingdom, a Lilliputian state. Tennekoon Vimalananda has described how the ancient monarchy of Ceylon, 'unique in the history of nations', became in these years a political and military factor on the 'chess-board of international rivalry'[25]. The metaphor of chess can be justly applied, not only to the sphere of international relations, but to the administrations of Colombo and Kandy between which it became D'Oyly's responsibility to maintain good relations for as long a period as possible. Here was an exotic game of chess in which the rules were reversed, and saffron-robed Bishops and knights with cushioned hats and ornamental swords could be made into pawns of the British government. D'Oyly, who had enjoyed chess as a student, brought to his negotiations with Kandy the skills he had polished in playing that game. An ambitious minister could be encouraged with subtle words to dream of a coronation, while D'Oyly's strategy where that minister's royal master was concerned seems to have been to isolate, and finally check, the king.

Among the chief pieces on that board with whom D'Oyly had to deal was Kandy's sonorously titled *maha adikaram* (first *adigar*, or chief minister). Ehelepola Wijesundera Wickramasingha Chandrasekera Seneviratne Amarakoon Wasala Panditha Mudiyanse Ralahamy was a year older than D'Oyly himself, and the most powerful official of the Kandyan court. His father was the *disave* of the Uva Province, and his mother a daughter of the ancient Pilimatalawe family. Like all Kandyan youths, Ehelepola had been brought up under the influence of the *maha sangha*, in this case of the Yatawatte and Kobbekaduwa Nayake Theras. He had married the daughter of the previous first *adigar*, Maha Adikaram Pilimatalawe. Due largely to this impressive background, Ehelepola held a number of important appointments under both King Rajadhi Sri Rajasinha and the present ruler of Kandy, Sri Vikrama Rajasinha. During the early years of Sri Vikrama Rajasinha's reign he had served as the *disave* of the Seven Korales, and later as *adigar* of Udugampola and as *maha adikaram*.

Other key pieces on D'Oyly's chessboard were Molligoda Maha Nilame (the second *adigar*), Kobbekaduwa Maha Nayake Thera of Poya Malu Maha Viharaya, Yatawatte Maha Nayake Thera of Asgiri Viharaya, Dunuwille Disave of Wellassa, Kapuliyadde (second *adigar*). On the side of the British Crown, the principals included James Sutherland and Edward Giffard, who occupied the posts respectively of Chief Secretary and Chief Justice in Colombo, the low-country chiefs Illangakoon Maha Mudaliyar and De Saram Maha Mudaliyar, Tamby Mudaliyar (chief of the British intelligence service), and Talgama Unnanse (the chief intelligence agent for the British among the Buddhist priests).

Maintaining a personal system for meticulously checking and double-checking the veracity of their statements, D'Oyly manipulated this large cast of characters with remarkable deftness, winning the trust and confidence of the men he knew personally, and extracting as much information as he could about the one individual he did not, the principal actor in the tragic drama of Kandy's last days, His Majesty King Sri Vikrama Rajasinha.[26]

The King of Kandy (formerly Prince Kannasamy) was a member of the Aravidu royal dynasty of South India, to which region the Kingdom of Kandy had for many generations been accustomed to look for its royal rulers. After the death in 1785 of Prince Kannasamy's father, Venkata Perumal, chief officiating priest of the Rameswaram *devale* in South India, the prince and his mother Subbamma Perumal had come to Sri Lanka on the invitation of her sister the queen Upendramma, consort of the reigning king, Rajadhi Sri Rajasinha.

Although a South Indian and a Hindu, Prince Kannasamy received his primary education from the erudite Sinhalese scholar-monk Venerable Moratota Rajaguru Siri Dhammakhanda Mahanayake Thera of the Buddhist Pushparamaya (Malwatte) Vihara and later from another Sinhalese prelate, the Venerable Kobbekaduwe Rajaguru Sirinivasa Mahanayake Thera of the Malwatte Chapter, before he was elevated to the throne at the age of eighteen.

On the death of King Rajadhi Sri Rajasinha in 1798 it had become necessary to choose a successor to the throne. According to royal court etiquette, responsibility for the choice lay in the hands of the *maha adikaram*, who at the time was Pilimatalawe Wijayasundera Rajakaruna Seneviratna Abayakoon Panditha Mudiyanse (1780–1811), a most ambitious courtier.[27] According to custom, the High Priest of the Malwatte Chapter had to be consulted before the making of a final decision. Dr John Davy records a conversation which took place between the high priest and the *maha adikaram* during the king's last sickness, in the presence of a *disave* who became, presumably, Davy's informant:

> **Nayake Thera:** The king's case is desperate; he can live only a few days. What are your plans respecting his successor?
>
> **Adigar:** I have a good plan in view. We will have a king who will listen to us and not ruin the country.
>
> **Nayake Thera:** Yes: such a one as you contemplate will attend to advice and be tractable at first; but if his education be not good, your plan will fail: he will finally follow his own bent, and the country will suffer.
>
> **Adigar:** There is a remedy for the evil you anticipate: if the king turn out ill, we can apply to the English; they will check him.
>
> **Nayake Thera:** What you propose might have answered in the time of the Dutch, but now it is out of the question. Be assured, if the keeper does not take care of the elephant, not only the lives of others, but his own will be endangered. In choosing a king, do not proceed a step forward without deliberation: you must choose one who will take care of religion, the country, and yourself.

Despite the warnings of the *nayake thera*, the *maha adikaram* succeeded in raising Prince Kannasamy to the throne. The individual selected by the minister, according to Davy,

> was a young man, only eighteen . . . a sister's son of one of the queens-dowager; uneducated, and having nothing to recommend him but a good figure. He was, as usual, regularly proposed to the chiefs and the people; and, as usual, accepted, and publicly acknowledged.[28]

The coronation was performed according to tradition within the precincts of the Natha *Devale*, a building that was a part of the palace complex and dedicated to the divine spirit Natha, Guardian of the City. Here the rulers of Kandy received the golden sword that was the emblem of their kingship. Lt. William Lyttleton's coloured aquatint, giving a 'View of part of the Palace' (Plate 8), was painted in 1821 (i.e. after the fall of Kandy), and includes an imposing octagonal building (the *Patirippuwa*) which was constructed by the new king in the last years of his reign as an addition to the two-storeyed temple that had been built by King Narendra Singh in the eighteenth century to house the sacred relic of the Buddha's Tooth.[29]

Whether the result of careful planning or of D'Oyly's response on a day-to-day basis to events as they occurred, there can be no doubt that D'Oyly's efforts and his ultimate achievement were made significantly easier by the personality and actions of the king. Sri Vikrama Rajasinha, though educated by Venerable Moratota of the Malwatte Chapter, was young. He married into South Indian royal dynasties, and brought numerous members of his Indian relations into the country, where they exerted formidable influence in the Kandyan court, and enjoyed residence in a street exclusive to their use which neighboured the palace. Encouraged by his relations, Sri Vikrama saw an opportunity of establishing Hindu customs and forms of worship in Kandy. This became obvious and offensive when Hindu customs were introduced into the daily life of Kandy that included the slaughter of goats near the sacred Temple of the Tooth, *Sri Dalada Maligawa*. Buddhism forbids the act of killing, and the king's decision stunned the *maha sangha*, but they could do very little to protest due to the South Indian influence at court.

The resentment and anger of the Sinhalese at the king's obstinacy, his increasingly voluptuous habits, and above all the Tamil domination of the court of Kandy, gradually reached the point of open revolt. All that was necessary, it seemed, was a leader who would take the initiative to remove from the ancient throne of Ceylon an individual who had proved himself unworthy to occupy it.

D'Oyly was well aware that Sinhalese Buddhist monks had twice visited the court of the King of Burma, to request a Burmese Buddhist prince to be sent to replace the tyrannical Tamil king. Not only did he know of these secret missions, but he is believed to have encouraged them, and even to have provided, courtesy of the government in Colombo, the facilities necessary for such distant journeys.

When the expeditions to Burma proved fruitless, D'Oyly, demonstrating the tenaciousness of character which popular tradition compares to the Wealden clay of his native Sussex,[30] patiently continued his friendly correspondence with Ehelepola Maha Nilame at Sabaragamuwa. He sustained by this means a cordial relationship between Colombo and the Kandyan chiefs, while obtaining from the *maha adikaram* and noting with meticulous care all the information the powerful official had to give regarding the convoluted intrigue and mounting discontent which complicated court life in Kandy. He learned that the king became quickly hostile to anyone who opposed him or offered advice contrary to that given him by his relatives, and had proof of it when, as the high priest had warned, the sword of the royal executioner fell on the neck of Maha Adikaram Pilimatalawe. On 26 August 1811, under the sal tree at the Kumarahapuwa execution grounds in Kandy, Pilimatalawe met his end, to be succeeded in the office of *maha adikaram* by his son-in-law Ehelepola.

The royal youth Kannasamy had grown into an impressive figure of a man. According to Dr Henry Marshall, Inspector-General of the Army Hospital at this time, the king was 5 feet 9 inches in height, and possessed broad shoulders, a fine beard and a manly figure.

> Having been placed on the throne by a professed friend, but in reality an inveterate intriguing enemy, for the intriguer's own aggrandizement, his situation as king was attended with insuperable difficulties. Like a man blindfolded and in fetters, he could neither see nor move but as the adikar directed him . . . Not having a minister in whom he could place any confidence, he lived under the constant fear of conspiracies . . . He trusted none of his courtiers; and it is doubtful if any one of the chiefs deserved his confidence.[31]

Here was a notable weakness in the situation of the Kandyan king, and D'Oyly would soon exploit it to his master's advantage.

King Sri Vikrama Rajasinha's compassion for the poorer classes of Kandyan society and his inclination to protect them from oppression by high officials displeased Ehelepola, and no doubt coloured his view of certain other actions and initiatives of the king that he interpreted as

FIGURE 9 Sri Vikrama Rajasinha, the last King of Kandy

From John D'Oyly, *A Sketch of the Constitution of the Kandyan Kingdom* (1975 edn).

personal slights to him and to his family. Convinced that the Nayakkar king must go and be replaced by anyone other than a member of the Nayakkar dynasty, Ehelepola poured his grievances into the sympathetic ear of his friend John D'Oyly, who was now becoming, increasingly, his confidant. It was in this way that D'Oyly learned the names of the nobility who had suffered at the hands of the monarch, the names of persons whose lands the king had confiscated, and the causes for public discontent of which the chieftains complained.

According to T. Vimalananda,[32] the climax to the chiefs' dissatisfaction with their ruler occurred when Sri Vikrama Rajasinha, surrounded and advised by the host of Tamil relatives he had invited to Kandy from his south Indian homeland, planned a complete reconstruction of his capital. Kandy, the ancient city which had been the centre alike of Buddhist learning and traditional arts and crafts, and was, above all, venerated as the home of the sacred Temple of the Tooth, was to be fashioned into a faithful copy of the Indian city of Madura. Ornamented with royal pleasure gardens, royal baths, and lakes of large dimensions, it would become a city from which every vestige of Buddhist religious worship was to be removed.

One of the main features of the project was the king's plan to shift the Malwatta and Asgiriya Chapters, monasteries which were the sources of continuing Buddhist scholarship and devotion, together with the four *devales*, to Peradeniya. The removal had been ordered of Poya Malu Maha Viharaya from Kandy. Aware of a saying that disquietude and death would stalk any who touched the Temple Square or the precincts of the Maha Maluwa with a motive that was not in keeping with the traditional aspect of the area, the royal plan preyed on the mind of the *adigar*, who saw in it yet another instance of the injustices and licentiousness of an increasingly uncontrollable and irrational ruler.

Having established friendly and cordial terms with Maha Adikaram Ehelepola, and also with the *disaves* Ekneligoda and Pusvella, D'Oyly was well aware of what was going on in Kandy. Between September 1810 and April 1815 he kept a diary in which he recorded the negotiations he conducted with the chiefs, and made detailed notes about information brought to him by informers from the interior. Thousands of Sinhalese were being forced, he was told, in the name of *rajakariya* (royal service), to construct an ornamental lake in the heart of the old city. Two Buddhist monks, Paranatala Unnanse and Suriyagoda Unnanse, who were known for their piety and scholarship, had been summarily executed.[33]

In March 1814 D'Oyly met by arrangement with Ekneligoda, and informed him that the British were not interested in subjugating the interior of the country to the British Crown. They were interested only, he said, in trade and the social well-being of the people. Two months later (in May), Ehelepola communicated again with D'Oyly. He required help from the British, he said, to wage war against an unjust and unprincipled king. D'Oyly did not reply, but conveyed the request to Brownrigg, who by now was more eager than ever to invade the Kandyan kingdom. Deteriorating relations between Ehelepola and the king clearly made this a possibility, and further unpopular actions by the king, including the execution for treason of Moratota Kuda Unnanse, a learned and pious monk, had further alienated the *sangha*.

D'Oyly had explained to Ehelepola that military action against the ruler of Kandy was out of the question unless there was unequivocal proof of a general wish of the people, for the British wanted not conquest but peaceful friendship and commercial intercourse. 'The British Nation', he wrote,

> will ever be ready to contribute Relief to a distressed People, as far as may be consistent with Propriety and Justice. But under the present circumstances, having no such grounds for action, and especially at a season when the rains are fast approaching, it cannot voluntarily and without provocation enter upon hostile operations.[34]

Ehelepola, kept thus on tenterhooks by D'Oyly, was desperate for a straight answer, and he seems to have read into D'Oyly's discreet ambiguities what he wanted to find there. He believed that by inviting the British to intervene in the affairs of the kingdom, he would be initiating merely a change of kingly identity: Sri Vikrama Rajasinha would be deposed, and he would himself take his place as King of Kandy. Ehelepola did not envisage any change, either of government or of the political system. When it was ultimately conveyed to him by D'Oyly that the British were prepared to assist him, provided it was understood by all concerned that they were only responding to a request for help against injustice, and that nothing of this transaction was to be made public, Ehelepola took this as a firm assurance of British military support for his cause and declared war on his king.

The punishment for treason under Sinhalese law was well known:

> When a King demanded the assistance of his Chieftains who held their positions by Feudal Tenure, and they appeared remiss in their

exertions or traitorous in their intentions, that not only the unfortunate man was doomed to expire by the most horrid and lingering of deaths (impaling alive) but also the whole of his family, his wives, his children, his nearest and tenderest connections, were doomed to suffer with him, even in his presence.[35]

Ehelepola knew the danger to which, by his treasonable actions, he was exposing the family he left behind when he fled from Kandy to what he knew would be a safe refuge in Colombo. He had discussed the question with D'Oyly beforehand, but neither of the two men had envisaged the swift and terrible justice that would be wreaked by the king on the *adigar*'s family. Mistakenly, Ehelepola had concluded that the king, however angry, would stay his hand since the punishment of a blameless family was almost without precedent.

Ehelepola Kumarihamy, wife of the first *adigar* and mother of his four children, entered the history books on 17 May 1815. Dr John Davy, who was the physician in attendance on Governor Brownrigg and Lady Brownrigg in Colombo at this period, gave in his *Account of the Interior of Ceylon* (1821) what might be termed the 'Government House' version of the events which had led to the fall of Kandy. Governor Brownrigg was understandably anxious to justify British intervention in Kandy, and Davy gives the Ehelepola family tragedy – terrible enough in its own right – the dramatic tension of successive scenes in a contemporary production of Shakespeare's *Macbeth* or *Richard III*:

(Ehelepola) was ordered to return to Kandy, and bring with him the people of his district, who had neglected the payment of various dues to the king, particularly on the occasion of his marriage. The Adikar's answers were not those of a submissive subject, and widened the breach. A favourite in his district, which is almost entirely cut off from the other Kandyan provinces by mountains inaccessible, excepting by two or three difficult passes, he began to think of opposition: he opened a correspondence with Colombo, and made preparations for defence, with the concurrence of the people, who promised to risk their lives in his support. Intelligence soon reached the king, who instantly deprived him of all his offices, imprisoned his wife and children, appointed Molligoda First Adigar and *Disave* of Sabaragamuwa, and ordered the invasion of the province by the new minister. Molligoda obeyed with alacrity, he entered Sabaragamuwa over the loftiest point of the island, and the most difficult pass – the summit of Adam's Peak. The hearts of the natives failed them on his approach; and he met with but little opposition. Ehelepola, with some of his adherents, fled to Colombo, and Molligoda returned to Kandy with a crowd of prisoners, forty-seven of whom were impaled.

This happened in 1814. Now, one scene of horror and bloodshed rapidly follows another, till the tragedy is wound up, and retributive justice again appears on the stage. Pusvella, *disave* of Nuwarakalaviya, had excited the king's displeasure, by a present that, through the ignorance of his brother, was offered in a disrespectful manner. The brother was imprisoned: the *disave* was soon suspected of corresponding with Ehelepola, and a letter from this chief, abusive of the king, having been found in the possession of one of his attendants, Pusvella was considered guilty, his eyes were plucked out, his joints cut, and after this torture he was beheaded.

The old offence of the Seven Korales was again ript [*sic*] open; all the headmen supposed to have been concerned in the rebellion which Pilima Talawa suppressed, were summoned to appear at Kandy. They were tried by a commission of three chiefs, of whom Molligoda, whose authority they had opposed, was one, and were condemned to death: after a severe flogging, about seventy were executed, all of them men of some consequence in their district. These transactions are horrible; but what remains to be related is worse.

Hurried along by the flood of revenge, the tyrant, lost to every tender feeling, resolved to punish Ehelepola who had escaped, through his family, which remained in his power: he sentenced the chief's wife and children, and his brother and his wife, to death, – the brother and children to be beheaded, and the females to be drowned. In front of the queen's palace, and between the Natha and Maha Vishnu *devales*, as if to shock and insult the gods as well as the sex, the wife of Ehelepola and his children were brought from prison, where they had been in charge of female jailors, and delivered over to the executioners. The lady with great resolution maintained her's and her children's innocence, and her lord's; at the same time submitting to the king's pleasure, and offering up her own and her offspring's lives, with the fervent hope that her husband would be benefited by the sacrifice.

Having uttered these sentiments aloud, she desired her eldest boy to submit to his fate; the poor boy, who was eleven years old, clung to his mother, terrified and crying; her second son, nine years old, heroically stepped forward; he bid his brother not to be afraid, – he would show him the way to die! By one blow of a sword, the head of this noble child was severed from his body; streaming with blood and hardly inanimate, it was thrown into a rice mortar; the pestle was put into the mother's hands, and she was ordered to pound it, or be disgracefully tortured. To avoid the disgrace, the wretched woman did lift up the pestle and let it fall. One by one, the heads of all her children were cut off; and one by one, the poor mother – but the circumstance is too dreadful to be dwelt on. One of the children was a girl; and to wound a female is considered by the Sinhalese a most monstrous crime: another was an infant at the breast, and it was plucked from its mother's breast to be beheaded; when the head was severed from the body, the milk it had just drawn in ran out mingled with its blood.

During this tragical scene, the crowd who had assembled to witness it wept and sobbed aloud, unable to suppress their feelings of grief and horror. Palihapane Disave was so affected that he fainted, and was expelled his office for showing such tender sensibility. During two days the whole of Kandy, with the exception of the tyrant's court, was as one house of mourning and lamentation; and so deep was the grief, that not a fire (it is said) was kindled, no food was dressed, and a general fast was held. After the execution of her children, the sufferings of the mother were speedily relieved. She, and her sister-in-law, and the wife and sister of Pusvella Disave, were led to the little tank in the immediate neighbourhood of Kandy, called Bogambaraweva, and drowned.

Such are the prominent features of this period of terror, which, even now, no Kandyan thinks of without dread, and few describe without weeping.[36]

Sri Vikrama Rajasinha's behaviour in this matter, though notably lacking in the quality of mercy, was in strict accordance with Kandyan law and the Kandyan code of honour as they existed at the time and had been administered by the Kandyan kings. The king had vowed solemnly at his investiture to uphold Kandyan law and custom, and he invoked them when he was called upon later to defend his actions: 'The Kandyan laws are well known . . . Did I make those laws?'[37]

Brownrigg made sure that every blood-stained detail of the punishment meted out to the members of Ehelepola's family obtained maximum publicity in Colombo, where the executions were received, not as justice but as murder, and were seen as the latest spectacular example of the Kandyan despot's devilish cruelty to his subjects.

The demonizing of Sri Vikrama Rajasinha as a 'tyrant king' and the routine comparison of his character to those of Shakespeare's most famous monsters in the Crown's official bulletins need not surprise: such parallels were part of the constitution of literate Englishmen of the period, who instinctively 'used (Shakespeare's) similes, and described with his descriptions'.[38]

Pity for the Ehelepola family and horror at their plight was so great as a result of Brownrigg's well-timed and imaginative propaganda that no objections were raised to his mounting an expedition to Kandy. It had become the clear duty of the British Crown to rescue the Kandyans from the oppression of such a tyrant. The terrible suffering bravely endured by a Kandyan noblewoman who was not only innocent of any crime against the state but a daughter of the ancient clan of Pilimatalawa raised, meanwhile, deep resentment among Kandyans of every district, among whom the memory of the steadfast behaviour of her heroic younger son quickly became a legend that inspires history, song and story to the present day:

> Ehelepola Kumarihamy and her children and Pusvella Kumarihamy and her daughter were brought for execution by order of the King to the Mahamaluwa. The sentence of death was read out. On hearing it, Ehelepola Kumarihamy cried aloud: 'Am I and my children to answer for the wrong of my Lord and husband?' To this the King replied: 'Thy husband is an ungrateful and despicable dog.' Loku Banda, the Kumarihamy's eldest son, frightened at the sight of the executioners, and falling at his mother's feet, began to sob. The nine year old Madduma Banda exclaimed, 'Elder brother, there is nothing to be gained by tears. They disgrace the Sinhalese race. Therefore it is right to give up our lives for our father.' With these words . . . he

advanced to the executioners and said, 'Fellows, you may strike off
my head' and lowered his neck. The executioners rushed to Loku
Banda and struck off his head. Next they snatched Dingiri Menike
who was at the hip of her mother and struck off her head and put it
into a mortar. They snatched the infant child which was in her arms
and struck off the head.[39]

As for the renegade minister: despite widespread sympathy in
Colombo for his family, by mid-March the attitude of the British had
changed towards Ehelepola, who was now useless to them. On two
occasions between 2 and 18 March Ehelepola sought interviews with
Brownrigg, asking that some sort of official recognition be given him
now that he had lost everything that belonged to him. As a last resort
he craved that Brownrigg would give him, since he was marrying the
widow of Meegastenne (the eldest daughter of Pilimatalawe Maha
Adigar), a gift of two or three thousand pagodas.

Brownrigg, hoping by this means perhaps to rid himself of Ehelepola
for ever, promised him 5,000 pagodas. The former *maha adikaram*,
trying vainly to rehabilitate himself, now humiliated himself still further.
He requested a title not inferior to that of the Great Disave of Colombo,
Mr John D'Oyly, so that he could live with a sense of honour. Brownrigg
then administered the cruellest of snubs: he suggested that Ehelepola
present his case in writing. A letter from him, said Brownrigg, could
certainly be considered: it might even be dispatched to London, for the
attention of His Majesty the King of England.

All that was needed now was some kind of provocation which would
justify the movement of British troops into the interior. The Kingdom
of Kandy, ripe as a sun-warmed mango, was ready to fall. Keeping
patient vigil as he moved between safe houses at Sitawaka and Hanwella,
receiving and sending messages inscribed on *ola* leaves and carried by
his army of well-paid spies, D'Oyly wondered if the moment had come
to shake the tree.

In Colombo Brownrigg waited, his hands outstretched.

CHAPTER SEVEN

1815: 'THE PORTALS THROWN OPEN'

Beneath him with new wonder now he views,
To all delight of human sense exposed,
In narrow room Nature's whole wealth, yea more –
A Heaven on Earth: for blissful Paradise
Of God the garden was, by him in the east
Of Eden planted . . .

John Milton, *Paradise Lost*

ON 25 OCTOBER 1814, it seemed that Governor Robert Brownrigg and John D'Oyly had at last secured what they wanted: an excuse that would justify a British invasion of the Kandyan border. Ironically, it was the king himself who provided that excuse when, by royal command, officials of his court detained and mutilated members of a party of traders from Puttalam who had entered the Kandyan kingdom to barter goods. D'Oyly held an inquiry into the matter, and learned that the king, suspecting the traders to be spies of the British, had had them treated in this manner, after which they had been told, 'Now go to Colombo and tell Ehelepola, the *Disave*, and the British what happened to you for your secret mission. This is the order of the King.'

To make assurance doubly sure, however, Brownrigg waited for further provocation.

When the king's troops chased a band of insurgents across the Sabaragamuva border into British territory, Brownrigg chose to treat

126

this as an invasion. No opportunity was given to the king to apologize for the incident, and this 'violation of British territory' was treated as a sufficient cause of war.[1]

On 10 January 1815, an invading force of British troops under the personal command of Governor Robert Brownrigg set out for the hill capital. The army consisted of eight divisions, totalling 2,762 troops, and marching along five different routes. They were accompanied by carriers, pioneers, gun-lascars, cooks, servants, wagon-drivers, pack-bullocks and horses, together with baggage-elephants and their keepers. What this invasion actually meant for the troops involved, who had to move themselves, their provisions and their heavy equipment through such difficult terrain, can be surmised from the observations made some years later by young Thomas Skinner when, travelling in the opposite direction, he surveyed the country through which, in 1815, his father had taken heavy artillery intended for the destruction of Kandy:

The next day we proceeded on our march towards Colombo. The country was truly beautiful, and I was not too young to appreciate it. The second day's march was down the old Ballany Pass, over which, four years before, my father had brought up his battery of heavy guns, one of them a 42-pounder, for the taking of Kandy. It was a marvel to me how he could have accomplished it; I subsequently learnt that he had parbuckled the guns from tree to tree. I can scarcely imagine anything better calculated to expunge from a son's vocabulary the word 'impossible' than this feat: the mountain path was so narrow, broken, steep, and rocky, that it was quite impassable for any horse and rider. My father was an officer full of resources and expedients, and it would have been a strange country through which he would fail to take a battery.[2]

In his *Expedition to Candy* (1810), Captain Arthur Johnston had laid particular stress on the 'steep and lofty mountains, in many places covered with impenetrable forests' which had for centuries barred attempts at invasion, and which the Kandyans used to their advantage. It can hardly be doubted that this earlier experience of invasion and warfare in the Kandyan country, recorded by the resourceful Johnston following his remarkable expedition to Kandy from Batticaloa in 1804, proved very useful to the British in 1815. The light-weight dress and equipment of Kandyan fighting men, their knowledge of the terrain and their familiarity with the climate, their practice of delaying assault until the enemy was trapped in a defile admitting no more than one or two men abreast, and then attacking from a point of vantage, had all been carefully studied by Johnston. The strategies he advanced to counter these methods, based on first-hand and painful experience, merited careful attention from any person directing or commanding a future foray into the island's mountain country.[3]

That person, as far as the invasion of Kandy in 1815 was concerned, was a scholarly civil servant who had never had any military training or experience. John D'Oyly was attached to the troops as Commissioner to the Governor in the field, and accompanied the army on its journey into the mountain country. Johnston's first principle, 'the expediency of European officers learning the native languages', had probably influenced D'Oyly's appointment.

Once in charge, D'Oyly's diary reveals that he did far more than control his network of spies and messengers and negotiate with the Kandyan leaders. Such activity would have been expected of any civil servant placed in similar circumstances. But, as Geoffrey Powell has noted, the duties of 'the ubiquitous Mr D'Oyly' grew, during the course of the campaign to capture the king, unusually wide in range and scope. Much of the military planning for the 1815 expedition was done by D'Oyly, and he directed many of the movements of the forward columns, seemingly on his own initiative, issuing instructions not only to the various column commanders but also to Major Willerman, the senior military staff officer in the field.

'Anomalous though his position may have been,' comments Powell, 'none of the participants seem to have criticized either the propriety or the effectiveness of D'Oyly's role, unconventional though it was. Probably this was because the arrangements worked; their failure would have produced complaints enough.'[4]

The British troops met with no resistance. Chieftain after chieftain crossed over to the British, until the progress of the army began to resemble a triumphal procession. What, one might wonder, were D'Oyly's thoughts as he crossed the mountain barrier which had for so long resisted the attempts of Europeans to penetrate it? Satan's vision of paradise could well have been in his well-stocked mind as he moved at last beyond that 'steep wilderness' with its 'wild and hairie thickets' to receive his first view of the breathtakingly beautiful valleys which lie at the heart of an island Europe had long regarded as the original Eden.

On 2 February, D'Oyly and Colonel O'Connell rode on horseback through Molligoda, the paternal village and family residence of the *adigar* and *disave* of the Three Korales, and posted a detachment near it in what D'Oyly described admiringly as 'a beautiful Romantic Valley abounding in well cultivated Paddy fields & Gardens'.[5] But when, on 12 February, the British entered Kandy, they found that the king and his court had fled, leaving the capital empty and desolate. 'We . . . found this City entirely deserted,' wrote D'Oyly, '& the Houses destitute of all property, except Mats, Baskets, Chatties &c.'[6]

This had been Captain Arthur Johnston's experience in 1804, too, though with a grim difference. Setting up temporary camp in the empty palace, waiting anxiously in the deserted capital for reinforcements that would never arrive, Johnston had had to keep up the spirits of the men of his regiment, in whose minds the loss of many of their comrades in the massacre of 1803 was still fresh: 'They saw displayed in savage triumph in several of the apartments of the palace, the hats, shoes, canteens, and accoutrements of their murdered comrades, most of them still marked with the names of their ill-fated owners,' Johnston wrote.[7] Matters were very different now, thanks to D'Oyly's meticulous planning. With Kandy in their hands, all that now remained for the British to do was to capture its king.

While describing an elephant *kraal* in the Western Province six years earlier, John D'Oyly had been fascinated by the skill of the hunters, and the methods they employed to capture their 'noble Game'.[8] What 'game' could have been nobler than the royal Majesty of Kandy? D'Oyly seems to have found the hunt irresistible.

According to D.B. Kappagoda's exciting account of the king's last moments of freedom, nearly 500 men from Sabaragamuwa followed Ekneligoda Mohottala to the spot (indicated to them by a terrified boy they had captured in Medamahanuwara) where the king was rumoured to have taken refuge. The *appuhamy* of the bedchamber, who was pacing up and down in the compound of the house with a lance in his hand, saw Ekneligoda approach.

'Ha! Ekneligoda Rala, where are you going?' he exclaimed.

'Yes, we too have come here,' replied the noble.

When Ekneligoda walked up to the door of the house and ordered the king to open it, the king did not open the door.

'Is it our relative Ekneligoda who is there?' he asked.

'Yes, it is I,' replied Ekneligoda. 'Open the door.'

The door remained closed, and Ekneligoda's men broke it down. Inside was the king, with his four queens. Then followed a revolting scene, as the intruders tore clothes and jewellery from the members of the royal family. Two of the queens clung to Mohandiram Dias, a low-country notable who had come up with the British forces to act as an interpreter. Dias, managing to free his hands, wrote a note to D'Oyly, requesting immediate assistance. His message ran:

> The Sinhalese king has fallen into our hands and Ekneligoda Mohottala
> is fetching him on and has bound him and is subjecting him to much
> ill treatment and ignominy. Therefore it is of paramount importance
> that you should come to meet us with three palanquins. Some wearing
> apparel is also necessary as the queens are almost naked.

Within half an hour D'Oyly had sent Colonel Hardy and Colonel Hook to the spot, together with a number of officers, 50 foot-soldiers, 100 English cavalry and eight palanquins. They found the captive King lying in a meadow in which the Sabaragamuwa men had thrown him down when, having been pushed along by them and dragged along the ground for some distance, the king had said at last that he could walk no further. Seeing the humiliation and torture to which the king was being subjected, the two colonels and the officers used their horse-whips to drive away the Sabaragamuwa men in all directions. They then dismounted from their horses and, uncovering their heads, they knelt before the king.

The fallen ruler showed no fear.

'Is this the way to treat a King?' he asked with dignity as the officers untied his hands and tried to comfort him.

When the officers asked him if he were hungry or thirsty, Sri Vikrama Rajasinha replied that he was thirsty and tired. He said he would like to have a drink. He was offered Madeira, drank nearly a pint of it with water, and refused to take anything else. The queens drank claret and water.

The king and queens were then dressed in the white garments D'Oyly had procured for them, and were placed in palanquins. On the journey back to the English camp, the two colonels mounted their horses and took up positions on either side of the king's palanquin, their swords drawn and ready. They were followed by other officers, who took up different positions round the palanquins, also with drawn swords in their hands. Fifty soldiers and 100 cavalrymen with their muskets loaded and bayonets ready took up positions at the front of the procession and at its rear. Neither up-country Sinhalese nor Malays took part in the march. Only three men belonging to the English regiments and a few of the low-country Sinhalese, including Dias, the interpreter, accompanied the king's party.

The sun was setting when the party neared the camp. The king and two queens in palanquins and two women of the *arachchi* chamber who had proceeded on foot presented themselves to D'Oyly, who came forward to meet them, received them courteously and gave orders for their rest, refreshment and appropriate accommodation. Military tents were quickly furnished with beds suitable for royalty. Sentries were placed around the tents, who changed guard every few hours.

The elaborate precautions taken for the protection of the royal family suggest that D'Oyly feared an attack might be made on the king by Kandyans eager to avenge what they saw as the fallen monarch's many savage injustices. He knew that such an attack, if successful, would result not only in further humiliation of the king, but possibly in either his capture or murder. No such incident occurred, however, and two days later the king and the other members of the royal family were transferred under armed military escort to Kandy.[9]

On 14 February the British forces, under the personal command of Governor Robert Brownrigg, had entered Kandy,[10] and five days later D'Oyly had the satisfaction of writing to Brownrigg from the King's Granary at Teldeniya:

> I have the sincerest Joy in reporting to Yr. Excellcy., that the Object of your anxious Wishes is accomplished & the King of Kandy a Captive in our Hands.

On 19 February 1815 tidings of victory reached Colombo. Brownrigg's eyes filled with tears as he rose from the dinner table to proclaim the news and thank those around him. Feeling against the tyrannical and 'licentious' king ran high in Colombo, fanned by British propaganda. Victory over the decadent Kandyan despot must have seemed to the governor to be truly a triumph of light over moral darkness, of good over evil. On 1 August 1815, British officers and staff gave a ball in Colombo to celebrate the invasion of Kandy, and landscapes in colour of the royal city and its environs, based on sketches made on the spot by a Captain Stace, were the main theme of the elaborate decorations. They included a picture of the lake constructed by the deposed king and of the pavilion in its centre where his refractory wives were said to have been kept in retreat.[11]

Colour-Sergeant George Calladine of the 19th Foot, a young British soldier who served in Sri Lanka during Brownrigg's Kandyan campaign, has left an interesting record of the fall of the Kandyan kingdom as a ranker saw it.[12] 'On the 22nd of February,' Calladine wrote,

the news arrived in Colombo that the King had been taken on the 18th of the month. The whole of the guns in the garrison were fired, and every soldier was served out with a double allowance of liquor. There was great rejoicing throughout the country, not only among the soldiers and the inhabitants in our districts, but also with the subjects of the King, he having been a great tyrant, and they were glad to have a chance to try another government.

At the capture of the King of Kandy the whole island became subject to His Britannic Majesty. Not only was there a large territory of land, but, it was supposed, there were three millions of money, besides immense quantities of valuable things. The King had a chair of solid gold, which was sent to England with a number of very valuable ornaments.

The kingdom of Kandy had never been conquered before, although the Portuguese and Dutch, when they had possession of the island, had several very hard trials, but at this time the British army certainly had the greatest success that it was possible to expect, as they ascended the tremendous mountains, and penetrated the dreadful jungles, and marched into the capital of the kingdom without the loss of one drop of British blood. The victory gained over the Kandian King brought the whole of the island under our government, and added to the crown of England one of the richest islands in the universe.

Shortly after the capture of Kandy . . . On the 6th of March the King arrived himself [in Colombo] with a number of his attendants and three or four of his wives. It was surprising to see the fellow's presumption to say he would not enter the garrison till the soldiers and people were ordered from the rampart that he had to pass under, as he could not allow anybody's feet to be over his head. A house was in readiness to receive him and his guests, and he was guarded by European soldiers till further orders were received to determine his future destination.

He remained at Colombo till orders arrived for his removal to Madras, where, I afterwards heard, he died in prison. His chief officer, when he was King, afterwards turned Christian, the Governor and the Governor's lady standing sponsors for him.[13]

One task had been accomplished. Another, of the utmost importance and urgency, had now to be fulfilled by D'Oyly: the drafting of an agreement in Sinhala and English to be signed by the British governor and the chieftains of the Kandyan provinces, in which would be set out the terms upon which the district would be administered in the future. It was an agreement that must find clear and unreserved acceptance on both sides if it was to hold, and its preparation was a task that no one but D'Oyly ('the only Cingalese Scholar in the Ceylon Civil Service') could perform.

Two other responsibilities, however, took immediate priority over the drafting of the agreement. One of these was to ensure that the former King of Kandy and his family suffered no indignity while they remained in the care of the British government. This was a task that required endless tact and patience since the king, in his position of humiliating dependence upon the protection of a foreign power, was more insistent even than usual that all due respect should be paid to him. For eight days following the capture of the king, D'Oyly was in constant and courteous attendance on the royal family. He made it his personal responsibility to have a military detachment conduct the King's mother and two more of his queens (then at Hanwella) to Teldeniya, and 'secure from Plunder any Treasure & Valuables which may be found'. He informed Brownrigg that he had 'written Olas to be sent to the King's Relations & Nayakkaras, informing them of these Events & inviting them to come without Fear'.[14]

The location of suitable clothing, food and transport for the royal family presented a difficult problem. D'Oyly was keenly aware that every aspect of such matters was hedged about with court protocol, the least deviation from which would result – now, more than ever before – in injured feelings. Innocent mistakes would almost certainly be misinterpreted as malicious insults. For example, the king was accustomed to being served a certain number of dishes at his meal: this was not merely a matter of personal taste, but of protocol. Clean white linen, for a second example, was required to be spread over any seat or palanquin on which people of consequence were invited to sit. A host who accidentally omitted such courtesies revealed himself and his countrymen to be ignorant, uncultivated barbarians at best, at worst as intentionally rude.

The situation was made more difficult for D'Oyly by the fact that Ehelepola and other chieftains who felt themselves to have suffered at Sri Vikrama Rajasinha's hands showed little sympathy or enthusiasm for the Englishman's desire to treat the king and his family with proper decorum. At times, indeed, they seemed positively anxious to obstruct him, and to humiliate his charges. The extreme delicacy of D'Oyly's predicament and the patient tact with which he resolved it are revealed in his *Diary*.

'As the King is entirely without suitable or even decent Apparel (which has been sent for, but is not yet arrived) & the Afternoon has been rainy he has not set off on his Journey,' wrote D'Oyly in his *Diary*.

On 20 February he requested that '2 Doolies [palanquins] fitted up with White Cloth in a decent Manner may be sent with Bearers from Kandy . . .' for the two queens.

'Tho' the King in his present fallen Condition should carry with him no Insignia of Royalty,' he wrote to Brownrigg on 23 February,

himself & the Royal Family should be treated with all the Respect due to Persons of High Rank – It is essential to our Credit, that White Cloths should be hung in the Rest Houses, & Provisions furnished without Deficiency & Apparel suitable to their Dignity. The Adikar, I perceive, is disposed to allow as little Respect & Attention, as possible, & I think, an Intimation from Yr. Excelly. would be advisable to ensure proper Treatment during the Remainder of their Journey to Colombo – I was ashamed to go near them last Night . . . I wrote to the Adikar to furnish as many Bearers as possible – I hope the King's Apparel will not be forgotten.

On 24 February, D'Oyly let Brownrigg know that his fears had been justified:

I recd. late last Night from the Adikar, a Cap, Jacket & Shirt designed for the King, which are in very bad Condition & entirely without Buttons. I sent them to the King's Resthouse, & they are returned with Answer, that it is impossible for him to wear them –

A second problem which was very much on D'Oyly's mind during these crucial eight days was the fact that the fleeing king was known to have taken with him many valuable jewels, including the royal regalia, when he left Kandy to go into hiding. Marco Polo and other early travellers had spun colourful tales of wondrous sapphires and of rubies as large as saucers taken from the island's mines. As Calladine's account indicates, the King of Kandy was popularly believed to possess untold wealth, and it was D'Oyly's duty to discover the whereabouts of this royal treasure, retrieve it if he possibly could (without putting into the king's mind any fears that the British entertained ideas of plundering his property), and transport it to Brownrigg in Colombo.

Following the entry of the British force into Kandy, all the senior officers, including D'Oyly and the general commanding the troops, had taken up residence in the palace of the fallen King of Kandy: a very grand 'barrack' indeed.[15] The royal family were also assigned some space in the palace until they could be transported 'with decency' and decorum to Colombo, and D'Oyly's *Diary* entries show how much tact and circumspection were required of him in this situation.

'Much valuable property belonging to the King is said to have been plundered by the Kandyans who seized him,' wrote D'Oyly in his *Diary*. 'He complains of the insulting language and ill-treatment experienced from them, but otherwise shows no symptoms of hurt feelings or depression at his fate.'

His surreptitious search for the king's hidden treasure had, D'Oyly wrote, been 'interrupted by the Residence of the King & his Queens in the adjoining Room . . .'[16]

Matters then took an unexpected turn. In a letter to the governor dated 22 February, D'Oyly reported that 'The King having desired to speak to me the night before last, took me by the hand and requested my assistance':

[He] said [wrote D'Oyly] that he would discover to me places where royal treasures are concealed, unknown to any but himself, intending, as I understand, to offer them as *douceur*. I told him that any account of concealed property which he gave me would be laid before Your Excellency, and that all royal treasures would of course belong to the Government.

Sri Vikrama Rajasinha had evidently concluded from his private conversation with D'Oyly that this Englishman was one who could be trusted, for on 25 February D'Oyly was able to report that he had 'called on the King in the morning – long conference, in which he gives accounts of the valuables belonging to the Maha Wasala.'

The chieftains, too, showed trust in D'Oyly's unshakeable integrity, for on 2 November 1816, D'Oyly wrote to Governor Brownrigg to inform him that 'the unrecovered Regalia' had been safely delivered into his possession by Ehelepola and the Disave of Uva. Trust on one side was to be rewarded by trust on the other, and D'Oyly set down in plain terms in his letter the solemn promise with which he had received the royal treasure on behalf of the Crown:

The Dissave renewed his expressions of fidelity to the British Government on the part of Ehelepola and himself and stated their request that the Regalia which they hold in great respect, should not be exposed to sale or exhibited to common persons, or to those Chiefs who under the King's Government were never admitted to see them. I promised that they would not be exposed to sale and in general terms that they should be treated with every respect by the British Government.

I propose with Your Excellency's permission to notify to the Kandyan Chiefs the recovery of these valuables and assure them that the Government is well aware of the high honour and estimation in which they are held by the Nation, and that having become the property of the king of Great Britain, they will be preserved with the same respect as the Regalia of the British Crown.

I have, etc.,

J. D'Oyly.

Several years were to pass before D'Oyly recovered, by dint of patient enquiry of courtiers and chiefs, the regalia of the King of Kandy and the other items of royal treasure that had been secreted in various places during the months and weeks preceding the British invasion of Kandy. Accompanied by his detailed and meticulous inventories, these were sent under armed guard into the keeping of the British governor in Colombo. And so the question must be asked: Was D'Oyly insincere and cynical, then, in his dealings with the Kandyan chiefs in this matter? Was he aware, even while he invited the chiefs to trust him, that the assurances he offered regarding the safety of these most precious and sacred objects were absolutely worthless?

For in the event, despite the promise D'Oyly had made to the chiefs on behalf of the British Crown that the royal regalia would never be sold, nor even exposed to unworthy eyes, the King of Kandy's treasure was publicly auctioned in London in 1820 by authority of the British government.[17]

It should be pointed out in this connection that appropriation of Kandy's royal regalia was only one among the many spectacular thefts and frauds that mar the story of the British in Asia from the time of Clive to that of Queen Victoria.[18]

The question of whether or not John D'Oyly was complicit in the plunder of Sri Lanka's royal regalia will never, probably, be satisfactorily resolved. But it should be recognized, before adverse judgement is passed upon his character, that the matter was out of D'Oyly's hands from the time he sent the various parts of the royal regalia to Brownrigg. As an experienced and 'obedient servant' of government, he must have known that it would be. Such being the case, it is worth examining closely the care with which he set down, in his letter to Brownrigg, the precise terms of his undertaking to the chiefs. For, unlike Brownrigg, who would certainly not have been prepared to assign any special sanctity to objects associated with heathen ceremonial practice, judging them entirely on their carat value as gold and precious stones, D'Oyly understood well the veneration and awe with which the regalia were

FIGURE 10 The melancholy queen

'The Queen of Candy', a portrait attributed to William Daniell, RA, engraved by R. Woodman. From Hobart Caunter, *The Oriental Annual* (1834).

regarded by the chiefs. The detail in which he spelled out his promise to the chiefs in the final paragraph of his letter suggests that he was indicating, as clearly and uncompromisingly as a civil servant *could* presume to indicate such a thing to a colonial governor, where the Crown's responsibility lay.

There is some irony in the possibility that it was in connection with his supreme triumph, the annexation of the Kandyan kingdom in the name of his country, that D'Oyly had his first experience of promises broken in the imperial cause, of illusions dissolved regarding the benefits of empire itself.

For our final glimpses of Sri Lanka's last royal family, we must go to sources other than official records. In 1834 there was published in London a volume titled *The Oriental Annual, or, Scenes in India.* Dedicated by gracious permission to 'Their Royal Highnesses the Duchess of Kent and Princess Victoria, it contained 25 engravings stated to have been made from original drawings by William Daniell, RA, together with a descriptive account by the Revd Hobart Caunter, DD. The thirteenth engraving in the volume is a portrait of a woman, and is titled 'The Queen of Candy'. If that title is to be believed, the subject of the portrait is Venkatta Rengammal, the youngest of the four queens of Sri Vikrama Rajasinha, deposed by the British in 1815.

Despite the attribution of the portrait to William Daniell, a member of the family of distinguished artists who travelled in India and adjacent countries recording aspects of what they saw there,[19] controversy surrounds the identity of the artist.[20] The photograph of the queen's portrait (Figure 10) merits close study for several reasons, not all of which are connected to that debate.

It is of some interest, for one thing, that the subject of the portrait faces the artist, but her gaze does not meet or challenge that of the viewer in the style of many European portraits of this period, being directed obliquely instead at a point to the viewer's right. Her face, the perfect oval of which is accentuated by shining black hair drawn smoothly back from a centre parting, and the tiny hand that emerges from her draperies to lie sedately on her knee, are the face and hand of a child or of a very young girl. Her small and well-shaped features are highlighted by the small dot of a *tilak* on her forehead that marks her as Hindu by religion.

The impression created by the portrait of an extreme, almost doll-like innocence is belied by the unexpected fullness of the young woman's figure and the mature dignity of her coiffure and her dress. A shawl, the edge of which is broad and heavily embroidered, is formally arranged over a garment which seems to be a European-style dress. Her jewellery is spectacular. On her breast is a five-strand necklace of pearls and precious stones, while two jewelled earrings frame her face and appear to completely cover the lower part of her ears. A heavy bracelet weighs down her wrist, and an elaborately jewelled throatlet decorates her slender neck.

There is not a hint of a smile on that lovely face. Instead, the expression of the sitter's dark eyes is quietly serious, even melancholy. This might, of course, have been a passing mood that the artist has successfully captured, a mood to which the engraver has responded with remarkable sensitivity. But a viewer who is aware of the sitter's sad history would ascribe other reasons to it, reading more than a decorative significance into a thin chain she is wearing from which are suspended two large circular pendants that might, since they have the dull sheen of metal, be protective amulets.[21]

The story of Venkatta Rengammal is a sad one. Taken from her family home in south India at the age of fifteen or sixteen in order to be married to the young King of Kandy, she lived the secluded life of oriental female royalty until, without warning, she found herself involved in the terror and humiliation attending that dramatic moment in the island's history related earlier in this chapter, when her husband was taken prisoner by his own nobles, she and her sister were stripped half-naked, their jewels were torn from their bodies by acquisitive hands,[22] and they themselves were placed, together with their husband, under the 'protection' of a British army of invasion.

For eight days after their capture by General Brownrigg's army, the royal family resided in the palace at Kandy under the watchful care of John D'Oyly, *Disave* of Colombo, until he was able to send them to Colombo in palanquins under military guard. It has been reported that they were then accommodated in a manor house in Maligakande, the residence of Maha Mudaliyar Adrian de Abrew Wijegunaratne Rajapaksa. There they awaited their exile to Vellore in south India.

As previously mentioned, the portrait of 'The Queen of Candy' has been the subject of considerable controversy. Caunter accompanies it

with an account of a visit he claims to have made to the mountain capital
of the Kingdom of 'Candy', during which visit, he states, the portrait of
the queen was undertaken and completed.

> Whilst we remained in the neighbourhood of his Candian majesty's
> residence [writes Caunter], Mr William Daniell was permitted to
> make a portrait of the queen, from which the accompanying
> engraving is taken; it may be relied upon as a most admirable
> likeness. She was very young, extremely pretty, of engaging manners,
> familiar without being free, and appeared much delighted at seeing
> her features transferred to paper. Her dress was becoming, her figure
> graceful, and her gait elegant.[23]

Is Caunter's account reliable? Relations between the British government
in Colombo and the Kandyan court had become – as we have seen –
extremely strained by 1811 (when Caunter claims the drawing was
made). At a time when even British ambassadors were forced to observe
the court's strict rules of etiquette, and approached the kingdom's
borders under military protection and with considerable pomp,[24] a
casual visit to the royal palace in Kandy by British tourists hardly seems
probable. An interview with a member of the royal family would have
been most unlikely.

The fact that the royal personage in question was female renders
Caunter's claim to have been either in her presence, or near it,[25] even
more dubious. English travellers who made a Grand Tour of Europe at
this time generally began their adventures with a visit to Paris, from
which city it was *de rigueur* to drive out to Versailles in order to view the
two principal sights on offer there, the palace and the royal family.
Allowed entree to the court of Brunswick, the young James Boswell
recorded with pride that he had had the honour of dancing with a
hereditary princess.[26] Asia, however, was not Europe. In neither India
nor Sri Lanka did women of high rank reveal themselves in the
nineteenth century to casual strangers.

During a recent debate in Sri Lanka over the identity of the queen's
painter, an 'eye-witness account' was contributed to the discussion,
according to which Governor Brownrigg had asked Maha Mudaliyar
Rajapaksa to attend to the needs and welfare of the royal family. The wife
of one of the *maha mudaliyar*'s nephews who came with her husband

to stay at the Rajapakse walauwa soon after the royal family arrived there made frequent visits to that part of the property in which the queens resided. According to her report, the queens required new clothes before they left for India, and the *maha mudaliyar* engaged the services of some 'white ladies'[27] to prepare the necessary garments.

The sewing was carried out at the walauwa, and the *maha mudaliyar*'s niece had assisted the ladies in their work, which took several months to complete. On several occasions the ladies and the *maha mudaliyar*'s niece visited the queens for the necessary fittings. There was heavy rain at the time, the roads were under water, and the party had sometimes to make the journey by boat. During one of these visits the *maha mudaliyar*'s niece observed a painter at work on a portrait of one of the queens. He was accompanied by his wife, and it was she who had persuaded the melancholy queen to pose for the portrait, wearing the new clothes that had been made for her.[28]

The next, and final view that we have of Sri Vikrama Rajasinha is obtained from the captain's cabin of *HMS Cornwallis*, the battleship on which the royal family set sail for Madras on 25 January 1816. Accompanying His Majesty were his mother, his four queens Venkatta Rengammal and Venkatta Jammal (daughters of Gampolasamy), Muttukannamma and Venkattammal (daughters of Degalsamy), and several servants. After some days at sea, Captain O'Brien received a message from Sri Vikrama Rajasinha, expressing a desire to observe the ship's officers at dinner. According to a report made by one of them, the king

viewed us through one of the windows (in the panelling which divided the stern gallery from the cuddy), which was lowered for the purpose. We could only see his head and shoulders, while he was able to discern the whole of our cabin. We arose on his making his appearance, when he desired us to be seated, begged we would begin dinner, and requested we would eat our meal as though he were not present. Our appetites being excellent, the ceremony was soon dispatched. After the cloth was removed, Captain O'Brien proposed His Majesty's health in a bumper. On our compliment being interpreted to him he appeared much pleased with it, and returned thanks in a loud voice, laughing heartily. He at the same time inclined his head slightly to each of us, and wished Mrs Sewell health and happiness.

The officers noticed that the king carefully observed the management of knife and fork, 'sometimes (thrusting) his head and shoulders through the aperture to regard more distinctly the materials of which the dishes were composed'.

The same officer (who kept a journal of this journey) reported that the king was greatly incensed one afternoon on finding that only five sorts of vegetables were served to him.

> He never forgot his birth and former dignity of station, nor asked a question which could betray ignorance, except in regard to things which he had never seen before. Even in these cases he quickly repaired any error he made by the rapid introduction of fresh observations, full of prompt sagacity and discretion.[29]

From Madras the royal family were taken to Vellore Fort. The splendid mansion of Tippu Sahib Sultan of Mysore was taken over by the Governor of Madras, and given to the king, who lived there with his family and retinue for sixteen years.[30]

It was only after the deposed king and his family had arrived safely in Colombo that D'Oyly could give his mind to the formulation of the Act of Settlement between the Crown and the Kandyan chiefs which brought to an end 2,357 years of Sinhalese independence. Lengthy discussions between D'Oyly and the principal chiefs preceded the making of the final draft, but by 1 March all was complete. On 2 March D'Oyly noted in his diary: 'At 4 pm the Governor gives audience to the Adikar, Disaves and other Kandyan chiefs – the Proclamation or Act of Settlement of the Government of the Kandyan provinces is read in the Magul Maduwa – afterwards read to the Mohottales and other inferior chiefs without – and the Royal Standard hoisted – and a Royal Salute fired.'[31]

An unexpected incident had occurred during the ceremony that D'Oyly, being inside the audience hall at the time, did not witness and therefore failed to record. It concerned a Buddhist monk, Wariyapola Sri Sumangala Anunayake Thera of the Asgiriya Maha Viharaya, who pulled down the Union Jack which a British ensign had prematurely hoisted when Governor Brownrigg entered the audience hall. Placing his foot on the flag the monk had shouted, 'The Treaty is not signed'. A sword was drawn, but it went back into its sheath. The Union Jack remained lowered until the ceremony was over.[32]

On the same day, 2 March, Brownrigg appointed D'Oyly 'the accredited Agent of the British Government in the Kandyan Provinces with the more convenient and summary appellation of Resident'.

'In this choice,' Brownrigg wrote,

I can have no difficulty. Your general attainments and those in particular of which you have possessed yourself in the Cingalese Language your extensive Knowledge thro' that medium of the Kandyan people & their customs and manners and the whole economy of their Civil Institutions eminently qualify you for the exercise of public Functions amongst them – while the zeal and judgment with which you have for some time back applied your Talents in the furtherance of those measures which have so happily terminated in the extension and consolidation of His Majesty's Ceylonese possessions by the accession of the Interior Country give me the most perfect confidence in committing this great charge into your Hands.

Brownrigg also nominated D'Oyly for the time as a Member of His Majesty's Council in the island. On 5 March, on a 'Fine hot clear Day', D'Oyly's commission was read in the Hall of Audience in English by Mr Sutherland, and its substance explained in English to the chiefs by Mudaliyar A. de Saram.

On 6 March D'Oyly sent Brownrigg his reply.

If my Endeavours [he wrote] have in any Degree contributedto the brilliant Success which has attended Yr. Excy.'s Measures, this alone is a Subject of heartfelt Satisfaction: but to have earned so honourable & public a Notice of them from the Govt. of this Island, is the highest Praise to which I could aspire . . . In Return for this flattering Distinction, I can at present only tender my Assurances, that if my Health will permit, my best Exertions shall never be wanting, in the Attempt to realize the Benefits expected to flow from the Acquisition of the Interior Provinces, & to establish His Majesty's Govt. upon its surest Basis, in the Affections of the Kandyan Nation.

D'Oyly's mention of his health introduces an ominous note into the celebrations attending this moment of his great personal triumph – the fruit of years of patient negotiation. For D'Oyly, now 42 years old, was a sick man. On 6 March he recorded in his diary that he was 'seized with ague at night which continues all night with violent discharge of urine'. On the next day matters had not improved. On 7 March he wrote: 'Sick all day with fever and dysentry. Molligoda first Adikar visits me this afternoon and gives some account of the royal revenues. Took tincture of rhubarb and salts this afternoon and bark (quinine) at night.'

Several factors, besides hard work, anxiety and the possible onset of malaria, might have contributed to D'Oyly's state of health. The early weeks of 1815 brought news of the sickness and ultimate death (on 14 December 1814) of the poet Gajaman Nona, whom he had known in Matara. His respected mentor, Venerable Karatota, had also begun to fail in health.[33] Four months after the signing of the Act of Settlement, on 2 July 1815, Thomas D'Oyly wrote to inform John that their younger brother Francis D'Oyly had been killed at Brussels, two weeks after the English victory at Waterloo. Henry D'Oyly, who had also borne arms at Brussels, had been wounded but had survived.[34]

A month later, on 5 August 1815, Thomas wrote again, this time to congratulate his brother John on the part he had played in the peaceful annexation of 'the interior country':

> I have read the detailed account in the Gazette of your success at Candy – your name is mentioned several times – and the thing seems to have been well done, I hope it may lead to something advantageous to you.

Thomas's pleasure was genuine and sincere, if restrained. He prudently warned his brother that he should not let his hopes ride too high:

> Just at this moment when such momentous scenes are acting on the continent, I apprehend that your victories at Ceylon however important will not attract all the notice they merit.[35]

Thomas was quite right. As Britain rejoiced that its own involvement in the greatest carnage Europe had ever seen had at last been brought to an end, Waterloo was the word on every English tongue. The bloodless English 'success at Candy' which marked four years of patient effort on D'Oyly's part went almost unremarked. The Waterloo Medal was struck within six months of the victory, but Thomas's letter of congratulation took over a year to reach his brother in Kandy.

D'Oyly's mother, Mrs Mary D'Oyly, was not quite so restrained in *her* rejoicing as her eldest son had been in his. It is not known whether she had been altogether enthusiastic about John's choice of a career in the Ceylon Civil Service, but now, following his 'success at Candy' she seems to have used every argument in a limited armoury to get him back to England. On 18 August 1815, having been visited by Frederick North with news of the British success in Kandy, Mrs D'Oyly wrote:

> We hope to see your name in the Gazette every day I am only afraid that this appointment will prolong your stay in Ceylon but if it is for your advantage & you are happy & in health I shall be content I do hope in the unhealthy season you will go to Colombo & stay there till it is over & not stay at Kandy to injure your health I hope & think you will be a blessing to the natives after having such a tyrant as a King as they have always had I know that you are very generous but I hope & I think you ought to take care of your own affairs & that you will save as much as you can that you may come home & enjoy yourself in England.[36]

On 29 August 1815, Mrs D'Oyly wrote again, urging her son to marry:

> I should have said nothing about your marriage now but I hope you do mean to do it & at your age I think the sooner you do the better.[37]

By the time D'Oyly received these letters in 1816, he was very far indeed from contemplating either marriage or a return to England. A board of three commissioners had been set up by Governor Robert Brownrigg to administer the newly acquired Kandyan kingdom, and he had been appointed First Commissioner of the Board, in addition to his position as first British Resident of Kandy.

CHAPTER EIGHT

1815:
'A COMMON BOND
OF PEACE'

The people never give up their liberties but under some
delusion.

Edmund Burke, 1784

TO ASSESS D'OYLY'S PART in bringing about the fall of the Kandyan
kingdom is not an easy matter, partly because the success of Governor
Robert Brownrigg's strategy depended on his principal agent's
maintaining continuous and effective cover. The results of that strategy,
when viewed from the vantage point provided by hindsight, suggest
that between 1811 and 1815 D'Oyly was not merely maintaining
communications with the Kandyan court, but doing his best to
effectively isolate the king and undermine the respect and affection his
people felt for him.

Aware of Brownrigg's desire to capture the Kingdom, it is possible
that D'Oyly advised Brownrigg on the uses of timely and effective
propaganda. The King's fondness for liquor seems to have been
deliberately encouraged by the British in Colombo, and his maintenance
of several queens was made into a subject of disapproving and fascinated
gossip. Whether D'Oyly had a part in bringing this about or not, by
1815 Sri Vikrama Rajasinha was well established in the minds of
Colombo's British community as a black-hearted oriental despot,
licentious in his private life and, like Macbeth, a tyrant to his people.

When First Adigar Ehelepola defected to the British, the punishment meted out to the traitor's family provided Brownrigg with the 'one single instance' he needed that would encompass all the flaws of the royal character. The Official Declaration of the Settlement of the Kandyan Provinces declared that the 'deplorable', 'savage' and 'cruel' execution of Ehelepola's family by the king's order included 'every thing which is barbarous and unprincipled in public rule', and portrayed 'the last stage of individual depravity and wickedness, the obliteration of every trace of conscience, and the complete extinction of human feeling'. This official account of events in Kandy, depicting Sri Vikrama Rajasinha as crazed and murderous, while omitting to mention that the punishments meted out in the Kandyan kingdom to traitors were those prescribed by Kandyan customary law, prepared the ground for Brownrigg's next step.

To carry out an invasion in defiance of commands from Downing Street that war with Kandy must at all costs be avoided, Brownrigg had needed an excuse, some act of provocation that could be legitimately interpreted as hostile to British subjects or territory, and justifying a British reprisal. We have seen how the king, increasingly under the influence of alcohol and incapable of controlling his temper, himself provided the excuse Brownrigg needed. Brownrigg could now piously 'accede to the wishes of the chiefs and people of the Kandyan provinces',[1] lead British troops unopposed through the once impregnable mountain passes, and hoist the British flag in the mountain capital of Ceylon.

According to T. Vimalananda's assessment,

North's successor Sir Robert Brownrigg was singularly fortunate in having the services of John D'Oyly. The swashbuckling Brownrigg ... could not easily reconcile himself to the ignominy suffered by the might of British arms, and came resolved to succeed, if possible by craft and guile, where the show of valour had so signally failed. In this design he found available on the spot, ready to hand, a most able, faithful and conscientious assistant in John D'Oyly, prototype of the later and more widely publicised Lawrence of Arabia and 'Glubb Pasha'.

A versatile linguist and administrator who had organised a most efficient system of espionage covering the Kandyan Court with the assistance of Mudliyars [sic] of the Colombo and Matara districts, D'Oyly contrived to hearten the dissident elements in the Kandyan provinces already exasperated by the brutality and barbarism bordering on lunacy, of Sri Vikrama Rajasinha, to rise in revolt against the demented tyrant. The precise character of the role that John D'Oyly played in the annexation of Ceylon to the British Crown still remains to be assessed and evaluated. In the whole history of British colonial expansion in the East, it is difficult to find such a variety of documents, of the highest social and political importance covering all aspects of the life and habit of the population in the territory to be administered as are contained in the voluminous letters, diaries and memoranda of D'Oyly.

It would be no exaggeration to say that the thoroughness of D'Oyly's work more than any other single fact made it possible for the British Governor Robert Brownrigg to cause the Sinhalese nation which had remained free for two thousand, three hundred and fifty years, to lose its independence and become a subject territory of the British. Where the Portuguese and Dutch had failed in their efforts to subjugate the Kingdom of Kandy, D'Oyly's astuteness, cunning and efficiency succeeded in securing for the British the possession of this ancient Kingdom without a single shot being fired and without loss of any soldiers.[2]

Not every Briton resident in Ceylon in 1815 was taken in by the propaganda generated by Government House. Among those who seemed to have treated it with a healthy scepticism was Dr Henry Marshall who arrived in Ceylon in 1809 to serve with the 2nd Ceylon Regiment, participated in the invasion of Kandy, and was later to have first-hand experience of the Kandyan War of 1818. His comment on the reasons Governor Brownrigg gave to justify the invasion of Kandy is typical of the common sense Marshall habitually brought to the assessment of what was passing before his eyes:

As to the reason assigned for seizing the country, namely, to relieve the inhabitants from oppression, it may be observed, that civilized nations assume a sort of inherent right to regulate the policy of the more barbarous communities, humanity being frequently assigned as the pretext for subjugating a country, while conquest is the real and ultimate object of commencing hostilities. There seems to be room to suspect some lurking fallacy in an argument which gives a specious colour of humanity and beneficence to the gratification of a passion so strong and so general as the love of conquest.[3]

This passage from Marshall's account of his experiences, published in 1846, illustrates his uncompromising honesty and lack of bias. Marshall wrote with equal bluntness of relations between the Kandyans and their new rulers, as he observed them after 1815, accurately indicating the immense gap which separated Kandyan and British points of view on that all-important document which was intended to forge their unity, the Act of Settlement of 1815.

The *adigars*, the *disaves*, and the *sangha* wished to protect the country and the religion from the wicked and arbitrary rule of a foreign tyrant. They wanted to ensure that it was governed according to the ancient laws and custom of the people, with no outside interference, even in the hour of crisis. Brownrigg and D'Oyly, on the other hand, wanted to establish British sovereignty over the ancient Kingdom of Kandy. Since their main purpose in annexing Kandy was to strengthen their control over the Maritime Provinces, and to protect the British outposts in India against attack by the sea from a foreign power basing itself in Trincomalee, they were willing to leave internal administration of the newly won territory to the representatives of the people.

The meaning of the Act of Settlement as understood by the Kandyans was that Sri Vikrama Rajasinha was being replaced by the King of England. No innovations needed to be introduced since the British governor, acting on behalf of the English king, was expected to govern the country according to its time-honoured institutions and customs. For the protection thus afforded to the people, he would be entitled to claim dues from the royal villages in the same way that Sri Vikrama and his predecessors had done. If the British governor acted contrary to the Convention, he would be required to withdraw, leaving the Kandyans to manage their own affairs.[4]

No wonder, then, that Marshall could report of the Kandyans he encountered after 1815, that

For many reasons, [they] disliked the English. Differing in race, language, religion, customs, habits and modes of thinking the British

PLATE 1 How matters stood between Britain and the 'King of Candia' in 1802

Map of Ceylon by Major A. Allan (1802). Published by William Faden, Geographer to King George III and to the Prince of Wales (1803) (Gooneratne collection).

PLATE 2

'A vision of perfection'

'View of Colombo,
taken from the end of
Sea Street, leading to
Mutwal', drawn on the
spot by Hippolyte
Sylvaf. From J.E.
Tennent's manuscript
'Notes and Drawings of
Ceylon' (Gooneratne
Collection).

PLATE 3 Local dignitaries required attendants

'Kandyan chief, with servant', watercolour by Arthur Fairfield. From J.E. Tennent's manuscript 'Notes and Drawings of Ceylon' (Gooneratne Collection).

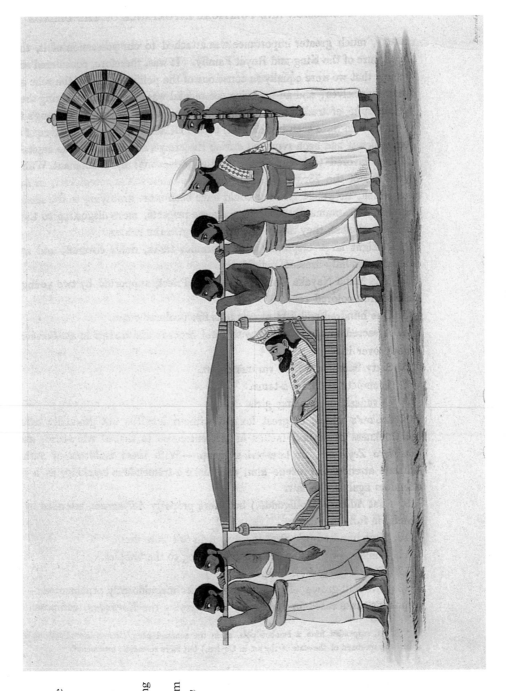

PLATE 4

It was considered demeaning not to be carried about in a palanquin

'A Kandyan dissave in his muncheel (palanquin)', drawing by an unknown Sinhalese artist. From J.W. Bennett, *Ceylon and its Capabilities* (London 1843).

PLATE 5
An English Oriental

'Sir David Ochterlony
watching a nautch'.
North India, c. 1820.
From S.C. Welch,
Room for Wonder:
Indian Painting during
the British Period
1760–1880 (1978).

PLATE 6
Temple elephants . . .
dressed in crimson
velvet and gold

'The king's palace
at Kandy', by Lt.
William Lyttleton.
Coloured aquatint
from W. Lyttleton,
*A Set of Views in the
Island of Ceylon*
(1819).

PLATE 7

'The noblest chace in the world'

'Stalking Elephants, Bibile, 6th May 1853', hand-coloured sepia lithograph by Count Emanuel Andrasy. From *Reise des Grafen Emanuel Andrasy in Ostindien. Ceylon, Java, China und Bengalen* (Herman Geibel, Pest 1859).

PLATE 8

Here the rulers of Kandy received the Golden Sword, symbol of their kingship

'View of part of the Palace, including the Paterippooa and of part of the Nata Dewale, from the great Square', by Lt. William Lyttleton. From John Davy, *An Account of the Interior of Ceylon* (1821).

rule could not but be for a long time highly unpalatable to them . . .
The Kandyans used to inquire when the English intended to return
to the maritime provinces. 'You have now,' said one, 'deposed the
king, and nothing more is required – you may leave us.'[5]

Naturally, the British had no intention whatever of 'leaving', i.e.
withdrawing from, Kandy. In formulating the Act of Settlement, D'Oyly
was in effect devising a constitution for the government of the Kandyan
provinces. Among the several clauses of the Act, the most important
by far to the Kandyan chiefs was one which formally guaranteed
protection under the British Crown to Buddhist places and modes of
worship. This clause, to a greater degree than any other, reassured the
Sinhalese leaders that they had done right to remove their tyrant king
and install a just (if foreign) government in his place.

What the Kandyans did not and could not know, of course, was that
Buddhism and Hinduism seemed to many British people of the time
(and to missionaries in particular) to be Satanic manifestations of all that
was gross, grotesque and evil. A document dated 'Kandy, 3rd March
1815' which was probably written by Brownrigg and was published
together with the Official Bulletin that contained the Act of Settlement,
makes elaborate excuses to English readers for the inclusion in the Act
of clauses guaranteeing religious protection to the island's indigenous
religion:

> The treaty . . . comprises, though in a very summary way, the heads
> of a constitution carefully adapted to the wishes of the chiefs and
> people, and with a more particular degree of attention to some
> prejudices, the indulgence of which was plainly understood to be a
> *sine qua non* of their voluntary submission to an European power.
>
> The preservation of the religion of Boodho was the first; the other
> (hardly inferior in their estimation) was the recognition and
> continuation of their local institutions.[6]

Neither the governor nor his military advisors, writes Hulugalle,
shared D'Oyly's genuine interest in the life of the people.[7] For that
reason among others, the Act of Settlement D'Oyly drew up was unique.
Wearing down opposition from his master, Governor Brownrigg (and
presumably from his Civil Service colleagues Sutherland and Giffard,

too), D'Oyly had written into the formal clauses of the Act the unique insights into Sinhalese life and thinking that he was acquiring through his ability to communicate directly and cordially with the Sinhalese people in their own language.

In doing so he was, however, working against the grain of British colonial life. Many of his compatriots interpreted respect for the indigenous religions of the island as a wicked and quite unwarranted pandering to the grossest superstition. To at least one of them it already seemed that, between misguided and over-educated Englishmen who took a fashionable interest in deviant religion, and demonic natives who worshipped false images, the cause of sound 'British' Christianity was in danger of being irretrievably lost in the colonies. In September 1814, the Revd Benjamin Clough had warned Methodist Mission Headquarters in London that the missionary who chose to serve a Christian God in Ceylon would find himself forced

> to mix with two Classes of people; the first is English Gentlemen all of whom have had a Classical education. And sometimes he will have to contend with a little fashionable D-ism, delivered in rather a pretty manner. The other Class is the Natives who though they are Strangers to the corruptions of Europe . . . have . . . received educations which he will find it his duty to counteract.[8]

The Kandyan Convention (as the Act of Settlement is popularly known) was formulated by John D'Oyly, literally, 'on the run'. It was devised in the ten days between 19 February 1815, when D'Oyly announced to Governor Brownrigg with 'the sincerest Joy' that the King of Kandy was at last a captive in British hands, and 2 March, when the Act he had drawn up was publicly read and signed. During eight of those ten days, D'Oyly had been, as we have seen, in constant attendance on the Kandyan royal family.

The Act has been described as 'a masterpiece of statecraft in which the vastly conflicting interests of the different signatories were at least temporarily reconciled in a treaty which on the face of it seemed both just and reasonable'.[9] Such a description implies that the Act was a deliberate confidence trick, devised by a master diplomat to mask Britain's real intentions and beguile the Kandyan leaders into unquestioning acceptance of its terms and conditions.

Was this in fact the case?

'We begin our public affections in our families. No cold relation is a zealous citizen,' wrote Edmund Burke,[10] whose classic and influential views on the nature and function of the English Constitution D'Oyly had read at Cambridge. On 6 March 1815, as the newly fledged constitution-maker, flushed with delight and satisfaction at his success, sat down in the king's palace in Kandy to respond to the governor's letter appointing him First British Resident of Kandy, it would seem that Burke's celebrated words were not far from his mind. His best exertions would never be wanting, D'Oyly assured Brownrigg,

> to establish His Majesty's Govt. upon its surest Basis, in the Affections of the Kandyan Nation.

In pledging himself to base his future rule of Kandy on warm personal relationships between the British government and its Kandyan subjects, D'Oyly was expressing a confidence in the Kandyans, and a sympathy for them, that few of his countrymen shared. (Even the exceptionally fair-minded Henry Marshall would have told D'Oyly that he was setting himself a difficult, indeed, an almost impossible task.) That D'Oyly wrote so confidently of 'affection' between the Kandyans and their rulers was due, perhaps, to his intention to strengthen such good feeling where it existed, and his determination to create it where it did not. But his confidence owes something too, probably, to certain changes that had been taking place over a period of time in his own ways of living and thinking.

The very qualities that made D'Oyly unique in his sympathy for the Kandyan people had begun to set him apart from the generality of his countrymen. His experience of life in Matara appears to have wrought profound changes in his style of living. During his term of service in the Southern Province, D'Oyly seems to have moved away from a British diet so rapidly and so far that in a few years his gentlemanly, 'sporting' image had altered considerably – so much so that Sir James Mackintosh (who met him in 1810) could not recognize in him the young man who, with two other undergraduates, had rowed him from Cambridge to Ely in 1799.

'He is the only Cingalese scholar in the Ceylon Civil Service,' wrote Sir James in his journal on 2 March 1810, 'and like many Orientalists, has almost become a native in his habits of life. He lives on a plantain, invites nobody to his house, and does not dine abroad above once a year; but he is generally esteemed, and seems amiable and honourable, though uncouth; a recluse. When I saw him come in to dinner at Mr Wood's[11] I was struck with the change of a Cambridge boy into a Cingalese hermit, looking as old as I do.'[12]

It was well known, of course, that the East did tend, occasionally, to go to a man's head. Barbara Strachey, in her book about her family *The Strachey Line* (1986), gives us an account of an amiable eccentric, George Strachey (possibly a relative of the George Strachey who had been one of John D'Oyly's particular group of friends at Cambridge), who went out to India at about the same time that D'Oyly went out to Ceylon. George Strachey spent only five years in the subcontinent, between the ages of 19 and 24, yet he insisted for the rest of his life (which was spent 'at home' in England) on regulating it by Calcutta time, which he considered the only trustworthy time in the world, breakfasting at tea-time and lunching at midnight:

> Breakfast, moreover, he preferred to eat standing, and off the mantelpiece, where it was laid for him, and he liked his eggs cold. He finally took almost entirely to the nocturnal life and was rarely seen.[13]

The changes in D'Oyly's appearance and manner were by no means symptomatic of disloyalty to his country and its interests, but they could not escape the notice of his colleagues and associates. It was an understood thing among the English community in the island that, 'even in the humid tropics' (or perhaps, *especially* in the humid tropics within which so many British colonies were located), an English way of life should be kept up. Conformity was encouraged, nonconformity was not. What was quintessentially 'English' could apparently apply to behaviour across an astonishingly wide range, including regular church-going, participation in social activities (especially sport), a vigorous appetite for food and drink, taste in colours, gardening and furnishing, and of course a uniform style of dress. A stoic British refusal to 'go native', despite the temptations of the 'Orient' and the trying conditions imposed by its climate, was regarded as proof in itself of superior stamina and high moral character. It explained British invincibility and justified British rule.

The lyrics of Noël Coward's 'Mad Dogs and Englishmen', that English ballad which enjoyed immense popularity in the heyday of the Raj, wittily make this very point, and deserve to be looked at attentively in the colonial context:

> It's such a surprise for the Eastern eyes to see
> That though the English are effete,
> They're quite impervious to heat.
> When the white man rides every native hides in glee,
> Because the simple creatures hope he
> Will impale his solar topee
> on a tree . . .
>
> In a jungle town
> Where the sun beats down
> To the rage of man and beast,
> The English garb
> Of the English sahib
> Merely gets a bit more creased.
> In Bangkok
> At twelve o'clock
> They foam at the mouth and run,
> But mad dogs and Englishmen
> Go out in the midday sun.[14]

Coward based his lyric on the fact that an expected conformity to an 'English' pattern provided a useful way of drawing a line between the ruling class and the native subject. At a more serious level, an Englishman who held a high position in the Civil Service but did not eat, dress or behave as his colleagues did, preferring a 'native' way of life – and worse, showed a quite unnecessary respect for 'native' customs and public reverence for 'native' gods, as D'Oyly had begun to do when conducting temple affairs in Kandy, a duty that was part of his responsibility as Resident – was obviously not drawing such a line. He was, therefore, necessarily suspect.

Modern British commentators often find eccentricity excusable and even endearing, especially when it occurs 'at home' in England, even more especially when it is manifested by scions of old (and presumably inbred) families.[15] But a personal preference which might have been regarded as a harmless foible in an Englishman 'at home' could acquire very sinister connotations in a colonial context. The sum of British cooking, as practised in households throughout the British Isles, and wherever the British travelled abroad, were 'the roasts of beef, mutton and lamb, the various meats cooked in salt water in the manner of fish and vegetables, fruit preserves, puddings of all kinds, chicken, turkey with cauliflower, salt beef, country ham and several similar ragouts'.[16] As Maureen Seneviratne rightly observes, 'In those rumbustious days of Roast Beef and Yorkshire Pudding consumed in gargantuan quantities by Englishmen abroad, even in the humid tropics, it was difficult for his own people to imagine a man could prefer a diet of fruit and vegetables.'[17] In such circumstances, it is most likely that his British superiors and fellow officers in Colombo or Kandy would have regarded D'Oyly's 'abstinence' as extremely odd, and even un-English.

This would have been especially true of Governor Robert Brownrigg's successor, Sir Edward Barnes, who had a taste for good living and who had, at the age of 48, married a young and frivolous wife. During their time in Ceylon, government house became the scene of elaborate and noisy festivities very different from the lavish, but rather sedate, entertainments that Lady Brownrigg had arranged.

A Mrs Smith of Baltiboys, who dined at the governor's house on every evening except two during her three-week visit to the island, was shocked by the doings there, which she considered 'certainly extraordinary':

> One night there was a ball and making speeches, then more dancing, or rather romping, from which we were glad to get away. Next night it was a play in the pretty private theatre, 'The Honeymoon'. Supper, of course, in the same style as before. We then had a fancy ball, very well done, a few groups very good. Colonel Churchill was a perfect Henry IV, his wife such a pretty, impudent Rosalind, with a stupid Celia, but such a Touchstone! some clever young officer. The rooms were large, numerous and well-lighted; a grand supper and great noise towards the end. These were all grand affairs; the ladies and gentlemen romped about, playing *petit jeux* with strange forfeits, hunt the whistle etc.

It was 'a whirl of riotous folly,' said Mrs Smith disapprovingly, adding that in her opinion it was all 'very unlike the propriety of a Government House'.[18]

It seems that Mrs Smith was not the only person glad to get away from the extravagant doings at Government House. D'Oyly seems to have constantly absented himself from Colombo's social life, pleading pressure of work. Governor Barnes noted that the civil servant's 'society [was] much more desired by all who were acquainted with him, than his laborious zeal in the execution of his public duties would allow of their enjoying it'.[19]

Circumstances, however, had now winkled D'Oyly out of his self-chosen isolation as orientalist recluse. The board whose activities and deliberations he was to direct had a great deal to do, since it exercised both administrative and judicial powers, and heard all appeals from the provincial courts.[20] His colleagues on the board administering the Kandyan provinces were Simon Sawers, the Judicial Commissioner, and Colonel Kelly, the officer commanding the troops. James Sutherland was Secretary.

The administration of justice was entrusted to a Great Court consisting of the Board, the *adigars* and the principal chiefs. All civil authority in the Kandyan provinces was exercised as before by the first *adigars*, Molligoda, who was *Disave* of the Seven Korales, Kapuvatte, the second *adigar* and *Disave* of Sabaragamuva, and the *disaves* of the Four Korales (Pilimatalawe), of Uva (Keppetipola), of Matale (Ratwatte), of the Three Korales (Molligoda), of Nuwarakalaviya (Galgoda), of Walapane (Dulleve) and of Tamankaduva (Galagama); and the *ratemahatmayas* of Udunuwara (Mampitiya), of Yatinuwara (Pilimatalawe), of Ulapane (Kobbekaduwa) and of Vellasa and Bintenne (Milleva).[21]

These appointments had been decided at a meeting on 19 March 1816 that D'Oyly had held in Kandy with the chieftains. We owe the only portrait we have of D'Oyly (see frontispiece) to Captain William King of the Royal Staff Corps, ADC to Governor Brownrigg, who attended the meeting and sketched D'Oyly in conference with Ehelepola and the *adigars* Molligoda and Kapuwatte. The chairs on which the chiefs are seated are covered with white linen in accordance with Sinhalese etiquette. D'Oyly, a long, lanky figure, leans forward towards the three chiefs, his top hat on the floor beside him. Behind D'Oyly stands a bespectacled Sinhalese *mohottala*, who is recording the conversation with a stylus on a strip of palm leaf.[22]

D'Oyly entered upon his new role as 'Chief of Chiefs' with great enthusiasm. It was noticeable, states Hulugalle, that in carrying out his duties, D'Oyly 'conducted himself more like a Sinhalese chief than as a bureaucrat representing a foreign ruling power. For example, he joined in ritual processions and carried the sacred insignia; he also distributed "Panduru" (offerings) customarily sent by the King to the four temples.'[23]

Hulugalle's view is borne out by a report that appeared in the *Asiatic Journal* of a ceremony which had been conducted in April of 1815, to mark the restoration of the Sacred Relic of the Buddha's Tooth to its place in the Dalada Maligava at Kandy. As official representative of the governor, Archdeacon Matthias D'Oyly's son had walked in the mile-long procession in the company of the chiefs, to demonstrate the Crown's respect for the Buddha's sacred relic. Arriving at the temple,

> Mr D'Oyly, &c. being also invited to enter (we did so), first taking off our shoes; after a few complimentary words, Mr D'Oyly intimated, that he wished to make an offering to the temple, in the name of His Excellency the Governor, and would retire to bring it. After a short interval, he returned, and presented as an offering to the temple, a most beautiful musical clock, which was sent out during the government of Governor Maitland. The burst of applause which continued for some minutes, upon this beautiful work being produced (which so fully showed the superiority of our countrymen as mechanics), proved the high estimation they put upon the present; but when, as if by magic, this little machine was put in motion, the expressions of delight, by both priests and chiefs, exceeded all belief.[24]

It is an interesting story, with an even more interesting subtext. The reporter stresses the 'delight' and 'high esteem' with which the gift of the clock was received by the priests and chieftains present, yet to the modern reader the gift appears to have been a diplomatic afterthought on D'Oyly's part since he would surely have carried it with him to the temple if he had intended to present it. Were the chiefs and temple priests being polite in pretending not to notice the improvisatory nature of the gift? Or were they merely naive provincials, overawed by the tinkling music that came out of the little magic machine?

On the other hand, D'Oyly could easily have feigned ignorance, as a foreigner, of the custom of formal presentation. It is worth noting that he did not take that easy way out of the situation but personally covered the distance between the temple and the palace twice, probably in the heat of the day, so that his government would not be disgraced by its failure to present a worthy gift at the temple on this most important and significant occasion.

D'Oyly had found himself in 1815 on what is called today 'a steep learning curve'. The temple ceremony described in the *Asiatic Journal* is one example among many of the lessons in personal relations that had to be mastered. Every day that D'Oyly spent in Kandy, administering the affairs of what was still a medieval society, acquainting himself with its complicated system of customary law and, inevitably, formulating plans for its future stability and prosperity, must have brought forth its share of new ideas and new experiences, and offered fresh opportunities 'to establish His Majesty's Govt. upon its surest Basis, in the Affections of the Kandyan Nation'.

'At a distance of over a hundred and fifty years it would seem to us,' writes Hulugalle,

> that [the Board appointed to administer the Kandyan Provinces] was a precarious and temporary arrangement. But whether D'Oyly thought so too, we shall never know. The rebellion of 1817 and what followed must have been a shattering blow to his hopes and ideals. He probably believed that the ancient system could be continued. He had certainly studied it carefully and spared no trouble to get to know the chiefs and the people.[25]

Making the decisions that would shape the future of a people he had come to know better than did any other officer serving the British government at this time, full of hope that he would be able to guarantee to them the independence they valued and had temporarily lost to a tyrannical king, D'Oyly had in 1816 reached the pinnacle of his career.

Surrounded by the wild and beautiful scenery of the Central Province, all of which was now within his jurisdiction, D'Oyly would have agreed with Dr Johnson that the thoughts 'excited by the view of an unknown and untravelled wilderness are not such as arise in the artificial solitude of parks and gardens'. But he would discover, too, that even in such a setting, the highest hopes might fail, as man is made 'unwillingly acquainted with his own weakness, and meditation shows him how little he can sustain, and how little he can perform'.[26] A baronetcy would come to him six years later, in tardy recognition of his services to the Crown, but by the time the honour came to D'Oyly, it had ceased to matter very much.

The agent of empire was soon to become the victim of imperialist insularity and chauvinism. In D'Oyly's case, of course, his loyalty to crown and country were not in doubt. He had, besides, proved himself a hard and conscientious worker. But the community gossiped, and D'Oyly's reputation among his fellow countrymen suffered. It would not be long before a British missionary, writing to Methodist Missionary Headquarters in England about an uprising in the Kandyan provinces that destroyed some 1,000 British soldiers in 1817/1818, seriously attributed British reverses in battle to the ungodly (and therefore un-British) activities of the British Resident in Kandy.

We have every reason to expect this is a judgement to a Christian nation for their iniquity. The Chief Civilian Servant in Kandy has for a long time been a worshipper of Budhu, & Gen. Jackson told me & Mr Erskine that Mr D. was a Budhite. He takes off his Shoes & offers flowers &c. &c. to Budhu. Will not a Holy God visit for these things.[27]

CHAPTER NINE

1816–1817:
TRANSLATING THE NATION

> I, too, am a translated man. I have been *borne across*.
> It is generally believed that something is always lost
> in translation; I cling to the notion – and use, in
> evidence, the success of Fitzgerald-Khayyam –
> that something can also be gained.
>
> Salman Rushdie, *Shame*

IN A THOUGHTFUL ARTICLE published in 1995, the translator Chris Berry draws a distinction between what he calls 'hunter-gatherer translators' and 'cultivator translators'. The former, Berry writes, 'believe the aim of translation is to capture the most highly prized specimens in the original culture, bring them back, and then display them in a case with a label on it carefully explaining why they are so highly regarded in their culture of origin'. The latter, on the other hand, see their task as 'transplanting live literature and helping it thrive in a new environment'. Interestingly – and employing a simile that is strikingly relevant to our study of John D'Oyly and some of his 'orientalist' contemporaries in the Civil Service – Berry compares the activity of 'hunter-gatherer translators' to the approach adopted in the nineteenth century by

the imperial adventurers of high colonial Europe, setting out for the heart of darkness and bringing home exotic prizes for the great Victorian museums of the metropolis.[1]

In 1815, soon after the acquisition of the Kandyan kingdom by the British, a translator who had been trained in 'hunter-gathering' in the manner of 'high colonial Europe' was set a task that involved him in the very different activity of 'cultivation'. This situation came about because, by the terms of the 1815 Act of Settlement, the Kandyan provinces were to be administered under King George III exactly as they had been administered under the Kings of Kandy whose line had now ended with the British accession.

'I say nothing of their laws,' Governor Brownrigg had stated of the Kandyan people in the document he had had published together with the official Government Bulletin in 1815, 'because I should find it hard to point out what they are.'

It was imperative, however, that the new British rulers of the Kandyan kingdom should hasten to inform themselves as fully as possible on the esoteric subject of Kandyan customary law. Although, according to Brownrigg, the customs of the Kandyans, their 'estab-lished gradations of authority' and the 'forms of justice' known to exist among them had fallen out of regular use for some time, he had given his word that the treaty drawn up for mutual agreement between the Kandyan chieftains and the British government would be based upon a 'general re-establishment' of Kandyan custom, social organization, and law.

As Dr Henry Marshall perceptively observed at the time, this was not at all the way in which the Kandyans themselves viewed their relationship with the British. The people, Marshall wrote, seemed to entertain a superstitious notion that Englishmen could not live in Kandyan territory.

> They made no complaint of oppression or misrule, contenting themselves with expressing a wish that we should leave the country. Conversing on this subject, a subordinate chief observed to an officer, that the British rule in the Kandyan country was as incompatible as yoking a buffalo and a cow in the same plough.[2]

The urgent desire of the British government to establish a workable legal code for the newly annexed Kandyan kingdom could be seen as the result of a distinctively English preoccupation with legislature. 'If there is one thing by which the English are peculiarly distinguished from all other people in the world,' wrote Robert Southey in 1807, 'it is by their passion for exercising authority and enacting laws.'[3]

The English 'passion' for law-making needs to be seen in its colonial context too, however, especially in relation to procedures that had been adopted in India. One of the first problems that the English East India Company had faced, after taking over Bengal, had been related to the kind of legal system that was to be put in use. Nathaniel Halhed had been asked by Warren Hastings to prepare an English commentary on Hindu law, and his rendering had been published in 1776 under the title *A Code of Gentoo Law*. Less than four months after consolidating his position in Calcutta, Hastings himself prepared the 'Judicial Plan of 1772', according to which 'in all suits regarding inheritance, marriage, caste, and other religious usages or institutions, the laws of the Koran with respect to Mahometans and those of the Shaster with respect to Gentoos shall be invariably adhered to'.[4]

We have seen that in order to make Brownrigg's promise a reality, a board of three commissioners was formed in 1816 to administer the Kandyan kingdom. The board had both administrative and judicial powers, and heard all appeals from the Provincial Courts (which were supervised by the *disaves* till 1818, and after that by the government agents). Since John D'Oyly has been appointed First Commissioner of the Board, in addition to his position as Resident, he and his assistant Simon Sawers,[5] the Judicial Commissioner, were well placed between 1815 and 1817 to undertake the task with which Governor Brownrigg had entrusted D'Oyly: the study and, if possible, the codification of Kandyan law and institutions.

Throughout D'Oyly's career in the Ceylon Civil Service, he had been an assiduous 'hunter-gatherer' in the colonial sense in which Berry uses the phrase in his article. He had been a keen student of natural history in his Cambridge days, and he maintained his interest in scientific investigation in Ceylon, where, as Sir Paul Pieris notes, 'agriculture and botany, geology and mineralogy, zoology and epigraphy, ethnology and hydrography, all attracted his versatile mind'.[6]

Life in the Central Province gave D'Oyly plenty of opportunity to pursue his scientific interests. It was part of his duty as British Resident to ride about the countryside, and ascertain for himself the condition of the people who had been placed in his charge and, like many other colonial officers with interests in botany, history and archaeology, he seems to have combined administrative 'business' with intellectual pleasure. His elder brother Thomas D'Oyly kept him supplied with the reference books and instruments that he requested from time to time, and he frequently sent back to England for examination by experts geological specimens and plants he had come upon in his circuits of various districts, as well as the stuffed carcasses of rare birds that he had shot in the jungles surrounding Kandy.

In a letter that is typical of their correspondence, Thomas D'Oyly wrote on 18 February 1814 to his brother John:

> I am sorry that most of your attempts [at stuffing birds] have hitherto failed, but as three of the skins of birds came over in a good state I hope you will not be discouraged. I mentioned the matter to Dr Kidd who advises to do all you can to dry them thoroughly and to expell all the moistuyre [sic] before you apply the camphor and other ingredients for preserving them.

In a subsequent letter of 7 February 1816, Thomas assured D'Oyly that he intended

> to forward to the Professor of Botany the specimens of Woods & Plants, & the creepers from the Forests around Adam's Peak; these last, I hope, have arrived in a sufficient sound state to be . . . an accession to a Hortus siccus, they have been kept dry & do not appear to have sustained injury.

From the same letter, we learn that D'Oyly was developing an interest in mineralogy, particularly that area of mineralogical study which focuses on the incidence of precious and semi-precious gems. Wrote Thomas D'Oyly:

> The large stone which you sent over as a Cat's-Eye is not of that quality, but a Chryso-beryl, which is of the nature, I believe, of the Chrysolithe . . . your specimen is, clearly, prized as a valuable addition to the collection of a Mineralogist, its money-price as a precious stone cannot be known till it is cut, but it is my intention that it should remain in its natural state till your return.[7]

The codification of Kandyan customary law was, however, an activity rather different from that of collecting minerals, drying botanical specimens or stuffing dead birds. D'Oyly and Sawers, in consulting with various Kandyan officials on the precedents that had grown thickly around well-established customs and practices, found themselves engaging with 'live' material that was an integral part of a dynamic, living culture. The task that had been assigned to them might well be seen by some as a British initiative akin to the preservation of the Elgin Marbles, whereby ancient and unique artefacts had been rescued from destruction by time and human error for the instruction and enjoyment of all mankind. But there was an important difference: the results of *these* investigations, when translated, would not be enshrined in a library or a museum, but used in the day-to-day business of governing real people.

D'Oyly's researches into Kandyan custom and law were published after his death as *A Sketch of the Constitution of the Kandyan Kingdom.*[8] It is an interesting document, different from most legal texts in drawing on anecdotal and proverbial lore as well as on precedent, and reflecting in the process a vivid image of Kandyan life and culture. It is possible that before he began work on this project D'Oyly had regarded Kandy as something of a miniature curiosity. In the course of his research, however, his attitude seems to have undergone a subtle change. Delineating the outlines of the Kandyan social system, and enquiring into the process of its development, D'Oyly seems to have developed an unusually intimate relationship with the people and their district.

It is not improbable that, in the course of his researches, D'Oyly developed an idea that he, who had 'won' and 'captured' this extraordinary medieval kingdom, and had now been given the privilege of ruling it, might be able through his labours to preserve it unchanged in a rapidly changing world. The idea of making himself into an instrument of continuity might well have seemed attractive to a man who was conservative by nature, training and background, resident in the palace of an exiled king,[9], vested by his own government with the powers of virtual kingship, and inspired by his own sense of moral duty in guiding Sri Vikrama Rajasinha's leaderless nation.

Whatever D'Oyly's private hopes might have been, they meshed very well with the practical task at hand: to uncover the structure of the Kandyan political and social system so that the society upon which it was based would be efficiently, knowledgeably and sensitively governed by British administrators. In this sense, Brownrigg's directive accorded well with his own approach to his appointment as Resident. The chief administrators of the kingdom were now to be British, so it was surely advisable that he and his colleagues on the board should inform themselves rapidly and thoroughly of the rules of custom and tradition persisting from ancient times, in order that these could be maintained in the future without a break. Here was the best, most immediate way for the British government to establish itself rapidly and as firmly as possible in 'the Affections of the Kandyan Nation'.

D'Oyly's choice of that particular phrase in his letter to Brownrigg[10] has a special interest for the contemporary reader, since it contrasts sharply with the manner in which the majority of his colleagues habitually referred to the newly acquired kingdom. Brownrigg had a coat of arms designed for himself that was embellished (in recognition of his achievement as 'Conqueror of Kandy') with representations of the crown, sceptre and banner of the Kandyan kingdom, but he nourished a contempt for Kandyan law and honour that was only thinly disguised. He usually referred to the region in his communications as 'the Kandyan provinces', a term which emphasizes the subordination of those provinces to the government established in the capital, Colombo. Most members of the English community (especially after 1818) stereotyped Kandyans as 'treacherous'. By contrast, in both D'Oyly's *Sketch* and his letter to Brownrigg, the Kandyan people retain their separate identity as members of a 'Nation'.

By the time D'Oyly began his researches, he had developed many friendships among the Kandyan chiefs. The ecclesiastical background of his family and the solidly Christian principles according to which he had himself been brought up and educated at school and at university do not appear to have hindered in the least his voluntary and enthusiastic participation in the customary rites and rituals that went with chiefdom, including those associated with Buddhist and Hindu religious ceremonies. The readiness and enthusiasm with which the Resident had taken up his chiefly role did not, as we have observed, escape the notice of observers.[11]

Among many notes D'Oyly made in the course of his discussions with knowledgeable chieftains, there is a detailed description of the character and behaviour of an ideal judge. 'He that takes the Seat of Judgment,' he wrote,

> should not be proud and haughty, and should not be disdainful and disrespectful to the Priesthood and the King – he should not appear either pleased with the good, nor displeased with the bad, but must maintain Equanimity – he should not be talkative or pronounce words of insignificance, but must utter only what is appropriate and necessary – he should imagine no evil, but be intent on doing good – where a Priest is a Suitor, he should not inquire who was his Preceptor, who was the Upaadya, who ordained him to the order of Upasampada – who his Pupils are – he should not make inquiries touching [these things]. –
>
> Severity and Lenity should be evinced on befitting occasions – In the course of Investigation, he should be gracious and disposed to do good and not be influenced with a desire of inflicting evil – he should conduct the trial in serenity and mildness, but not in Anger and intemperate impatience – whispering should not be tolerated in the Council nor sidelong looks – nor must the Judge wink or nod significantly at the Suitors – nor should he by the shaking of his head or knitting of his brows allow his thoughts to be guessed – he should circumscribe his view to about the extent of a fathom, and not extend his gaze to object(s) beyond that distance in any direction – He should be pertinaciously careful in examining the statements of interested persons and of those who are noted for cunning and falsehood, but it is proper that he should be affable and mild in interrogating those who are veracious and void of guile, and those [who] are agitated and timid because of their simplicity and ignorance must be encouraged by kind words.

Here was a model that any European jurist would have been happy to adopt for himself, even though D'Oyly probably smiled to himself at the 'quaint' and 'whimsical' elements with which oriental 'superstition' had adorned it. From the Kandyan point of view, impeachment (such as had been the punishment of Warren Hastings) was unnecessary: an unrighteous judge, D'Oyly learned, would inevitably bring about his own downfall. Ill fortune would inexorably eat away his substance, as surely as the full moon wanes to a sliver in the sky:

The prosperity of him that perverteth Justice through Love, Hatred, Fear or Ignorance, shall diminish gradually as the moon in its wane – but he that shall not deviate from Justice through Affection or Malice, through fear or from ignorance, will advance in prosperity as the moon in its Increase. Should Justice be disregarded and its Rules deviated from, and Judgment given in favour of the false claiment [*sic*], to the prejudice of the rightful owner or Heir, through affection or love induced by Relationship, Friendship, or Gratitude for benefits conferred – or through motives of personal animosity or from Fear induced by the daring and wicked character of one of the parties – or from his being a powerful personage in the State – or if Justice be perverted through ignorance, that is not being properly acquainted with the Science of Jurispudence as taught in the comments upon the Sermons [of Buddha] – the wealth, Ritenue, [*sic*] and Celibrity [*sic*] of such unjust Judge will gradually pass away as waneth the Moon – thus is declared the destruction of the Prosperity, wealth and Power of him that Judgeth unrighteously, be he a Layman or a Priest – and the gradual advancement to Dignities consequent on the celibrity [*sic*] and renown of the just Judge who escapes from these Agati or Perversion, is compared to the progressive expansion of the refulgence of the moon in its increase – it therefore behoveth the wise Judge to act constantly according to the following rules of Adjudication. –

Above all, the chieftains declared, a good judge

must strictly adhere to the Dictates conveyed in the Sacred Sermons, their context, and the commentaries thereon – for thus it is enjoined:

'The diligent Judge shall administer Justice in strict conformity to the Rules of the Soottree [*Sutra*], and the Wineye [*Vinaya*], and their exposition and commentaries.'

'That which is recorded is of greater importance than oral tradition, therefore the written Rules must be duly enforced.'

Owing to the ignorance and misconduct of Individuals the observances of their Preceptors in former generations may happen from time to time to be infringed, but the Pali Sermons recorded in books are not liable to perversion, but will remain pure, therefore it is here enjoined that the Pali Text must be made the invariable Rule of Judicial Investigation. –[12]

D'Oyly titled this section of his *Sketch* 'Rules for Administering Justice'. He would have been encouraged by the emphasis seemingly placed there on the reliability of the written word over the oral tradition, since such an emphasis could be said to justify his own researches and demonstrate his good intentions.

Some of the information D'Oyly and his colleagues gathered from their extended discussions with 'the chiefs and the people' must have astounded them. E.J. Harris notes that in England, the land from which men travelled in the nineteenth century to spread the light of civilized law among the benighted tribes of Asia and Africa, suffrage was denied to women. Englishwomen were, in addition, stripped of their property and inheritance rights when they married. For much of the nineteenth century in Britain, whatever a woman earned, inherited or owned became her husband's and, since she could neither sue nor divorce him, there was little redress in the case of marital exploitation.[13]

The Kandyan system was very different. Simon Sawers later presided over a committee of Kandyan chiefs that compiled an account of Kandyan Law, the *Niti Nighanduwa*, which was published in 1880. When the *Niti Nighanduwa* is compared with the marriage laws that were in force in England during much of the nineteenth century, the degree of freedom and mutuality given to Kandyan women is immediately striking. H.A.J. Hulugalle suggests that this freedom, to which the British were unaccustomed, is one of the roots of the culture clash between ruler and ruled in Sri Lanka. Whereas within Sri Lankan Buddhist culture, marriage has nothing to do with religion, but is a secular agreement undertaken between families for the reproduction of the race, Victorian Britain regarded marriage as a divinely sanctioned, lifelong union of one man and one woman. For the British, any other pattern would have appeared immoral.[14]

At a time when married women in England were not permitted to hold property in their own names, and polyandry was, of course, regarded with pious horror by every right-thinking Englishman, it is notable that D'Oyly recorded without betraying the least sense of surprise or outrage (and possibly with a good deal of tolerant amusement) certain customs of the Kandyans relating to inheritance and marriage which gave Kandyan women a degree of independence unheard-of in Europe:

The Proverb is, that the . . . husband should take care to have constantly ready at the door of his wife's room, a walking stick, a talipot,[15] and a torch, that he may be prepared at any hour of the day or night, and whatever may be the state of the weather or of his own health, to quit her house on being ordered.[16]

E.M. Forster has said that his experience of India was a revelation, in that it extended a mind which had been hitherto confined to the limits imposed by an exclusively Western classical education. If the years in which D'Oyly made contact with the island's literary life as Government Agent of Matara had done something similar for him, we might conjecture what it meant to a mind such as his to venture beyond Forster's experience and steep itself in the study of a living oriental society.

That he found such study congenial, we can hardly doubt. His education had introduced him to the masters of Western philosophical and political thought. He had the means, therefore, lacked by most of his colleagues and contemporaries in Sri Lanka at the time, to draw parallels and make intelligent comparisons between the political and social systems of East and West and their respective capabilities for the nurture of the human spirit.

High-minded and worthy as D'Oyly's intentions might have been, they were open to misinterpretation. According to Tennekoon Vimalananda, the governor's instructions to D'Oyly to collect and codify the Kandyans' accepted but as yet unrecorded laws, customs, precedents and traditions aroused suspicion in the minds of the people. Was it possible that the Government in Colombo was contemplating the imposition of English laws on the Kandyan kingdom?

The people of the Kandyan Province knew and understood their laws, rights and duties. What need was there to have these set down in writing? The Sword of the State belonged to the King, and this they never contested. The rest was theirs, not his. Any infringement of their own rights and perquisites was resented and opposed.[17]

Under the Kings of Kandy, the chiefs had been the repositories of customary law: when the need arose to make a decision or appeal to precedent, the Kings of Kandy had consulted them. By writing down laws that had been traditionally handed down by word of mouth, the jealously guarded power and influence of the chiefs were thought to be in danger of erosion.

There was no outward sign by which the discontent mounting among the chiefs could possibly have been detected. The orderly business of government proceeded in Colombo and peaceful prosperity seemed to be everywhere the order of the day as D'Oyly and his Kandyan colleagues worked in seeming harmony towards the establishment of a written legal code for 'the Kandyan provinces'.

So tranquil seemed the general temper of the country, and so confident had the British become in their role as the liberators of the Kandyan people, that Governor Brownrigg and his wife, attended by their personal physician, Dr John Davy, left Colombo in August 1817 on what was intended to be a few weeks' holiday, 'a party of pleasure'. Many anxious months were to pass and many lives were lost before they returned to the capital. Davy, who attended the Brownriggs throughout the entire period of the Kandyan War, provides a detailed description of that fateful journey.

Brownrigg seems to have travelled in some state, although (according to his physician and friend) he was an individual 'particularly averse to show and display'. The governor's cavalcade was led by three tusked elephants 'gaily caparisoned, each with a bell hanging from his side which made a clear and mournful sound'. Next came a party of the Ceylon Light Dragoons. The governor and his lady followed in two separate 'tomjohns', and the rear of the procession was brought up by another party of dragoons.

A procession followed the governor's entourage, led by the *disave* of the district, mounted on a horse with bells on its bridle and what Davy calls 'very gay furniture', conducted by two grooms. Behind the *disave* came his own party, bearing the insignia of his office, including flags. These in turn were followed by 'irregulars', some in palanquins, some on horseback, but the majority on foot, being chiefly servants or bearers. 'Persons of refined taste', writes Davy,

> may justly find fault with this oriental mode of travelling, and exclaim, – what barbarous pomp! The exclamation is just; but it is

the pomp which the natives are accustomed to respect and associate with power, and in consequence it would not be very politic to neglect the observance of it.[18]

Their picturesque tour took the governor and his party at first along a road 'most agreeably shaded by the fine foliage of fruit-trees'. This gave way to 'wild scenery' which Davy found very beautiful and 'most remarkable for the richness and variety of forest and jungle', and led to Avisawella, a village 'romantickly [sic] situated almost at the base of bluff hills of black naked rock, which rise precipitously from a surface of rich foliage to a height of perhaps 1000 feet'.

The travellers encountered nothing untoward on their way that might have made them in the least uneasy, or have given them warning of the violence that was about to erupt. On the contrary, the Governor's party traversed Sitawaka, 'once a royal residence, and a place of considerable consequence . . . now merely a name', and were greeted at the riverside town of Ruwanwella by a populace in a mood, seemingly, of general rejoicing.

> In honour of the Governor, the day was a holiday; the natives were clothed in their best; the street which leads from the river to the fort, was ornamented in the Singalese simple and beautiful style, with arches of young cocoa-nut leaf, scented with the sweet and elegant white blossom of the areka-palm, and supported by plantain trees, which, transplanted entire, full of leaves and fruit, looked as fresh as if growing in their native soil. In the evening, when the Governor and Lady Brownrigg visited the bazar, it was quite splendid, and like a fairy scene, ornamented as described, and brilliantly illuminated with lamps made of cocoa-nut shells, and fed with cocoa-nut oil, and placed amongst the vegetable arches and before the humble shops of the natives.[19]

Machiavelli had had certain memorable words of advice for princes acquiring new states which are very relevant to the situation of the British in 1817, as rulers of a newly acquired kingdom:

> It must be considered that there is nothing more difficult to carry out, nor more doubtful of success, nor more dangerous to handle, than

to initiate a new order of things. For the reformer has enemies in all those who profit by the old order, and only lukewarm defenders in all those who would profit by the new order, this lukewarmness arising partly from fear of their adversaries, who have the laws in their favour; and partly from the incredulity of mankind, who do not truly believe in anything new until they have had actual experience of it.[20]

Viewed from a Machiavellian perspective, it will be seen that Vimalananda has reason on his side in suggesting that fear of an erosion of their powers could have been an important reason for the disaffection of the Kandyan chieftains.

Suspecting that the writing down and codification of their traditional customary law were first steps in the direction of replacing it with a British legal system, Monerawila Keppetipola Maha Disave, a scion of one of the most distinguished and influential of Kandyan families and a colleague of John D'Oyly on the board appointed to administer the Kandyan provinces,[21] rose in revolt, with others among the Kandyan chieftains, against the British administration.

CHAPTER TEN

1817–1821: 'MADNESS OF WAR'

'When I am discharged,' said a private of the 19th Regiment in the hearing of an officer, 'I intend to become a highwayman; for one thing,' said he, 'after what I have seen in Kandy, taking the life of a man will give me no concern.'

Henry Marshall, *Ceylon (1846)*

THE REBELLION OF 1818 (now generally referred to as 'the Kandyan War') started with the shooting of a British official in the Uva Province. It delayed Governor Brownrigg's return to Colombo for over a year.

On 3 October 1817, Brownrigg and his 'party of pleasure' arrived in good spirits in Trincomalee on the island's eastern coast. After two weeks of sun and sea air, they left Trincomalee for the cooler clime of Kandy. Davy records that at the time they resumed their tour, the wet season was about to begin: rain poured down in torrents at Nalanda, and the Mahaweli Ganga was so swollen that they had difficulty crossing it. Near Lake Minneriya the governor had the first news of the rebellion. Hastily retracing their steps, Governor Brownrigg and his party re-entered Kandy on 26 October 1817. Martial law was declared over the Kandyan provinces. The governor's party remained in Kandy until 25 November 1818, when they left the hill country for Colombo.

The rebellion lasted nearly two years and cost about a thousand British lives. Ten times that number of Sinhalese fighting men died before the rebellion was put down and British power consolidated in Kandy. At the centre of the battles which raged throughout 1817 and 1818 in the hill country was the Province of Uva, the home of Monerawala Keppetipola Maha Disave.

Keppetipola had been appointed *disave* of the Uva Province by the British after the annexation of the Kandyan kingdom in 1815. When the alarm was given the chief was ordered by his British overlords to quell the uprising which was known to be burgeoning in the areas of Uva and Wellassa. Keppetipola advanced, at the head of a force which included a few British militiamen armed with guns that had been delivered to them from the military stores at Kandy.

The *disave*'s march, undertaken ostensibly to quell the disturbances, seems to have been in reality part of a preconceived plan fostered by him and his compatriots to give support to the rebels. Joining the rebel force that was awaiting him in Uva, Keppetipola dismissed the British soldiers who had accompanied him with the following words:

> It is not proper for us as Sinhalese to shoot you down with your own guns – go, therefore, return your guns to your Governor and tell him that the whole of Uva, Wellassa and Bintenne has risen in rebellion.

Keppetipola's defection was unexpected, even by John D'Oyly, his colleague on the board appointed to administer the Kandyan provinces. It was a stunning blow to the British, who had begun to settle confidently into their role as rulers of the whole island. On 6 November 1817, an official proclamation placed a price of 2,000 Rix-dollars on the rebel leader's head, and offered 500 Rix-dollars for the capture of any others directly involved in the hostilities.

The early successes of the rebels were negated by fresh arrivals of British contingents from India in September and October 1818. Strong auxiliary forces, augmented by conscript native militiamen, staged a three-pronged drive on the interior from Trincomalee, Batticaloa and Colombo. The rebellious provinces were successfully subdued, and Madugalle Disave was one of the notables captured by the British.

On 13 November 1818, Keppetipola, Madugalle, Pilimatalawe and several other leaders of the uprising (including Ihagama Thera, a Buddhist monk who is said to have been a particular friend of John D'Oyly's) were taken captive and arraigned before a British court martial. All the accused were condemned to death, the punishments of

Pilimatalawe and Ihagama being commuted to sentences of banishment. Keppetipola conducted himself with such composure, it is said, that even his English captors acclaimed him as a hero, a born leader of men.

Dr Henry Marshall, Inspector-General of the Army Hospital, whose friendship with Keppetipola was of several years' standing, visited him in prison several times. During one such visit the condemned rebel leader had shown his drab prison clothing to his European friend and remarked, with good humour and some wistfulness: 'As you know, this is not the way I have been accustomed to dress.' Marshall, visibly moved, had lowered his head and dabbed his moist eyes with his hand. A Highland Scot, and a great admirer of the Kandyan aristocracy, Marshall compared the fate of Keppetipola with that of his native hero, Sir William Wallace, beloved patriot of Scotland, whose struggle and sufferings five centuries earlier for the deliverance of his people from the yoke of Edward I, King of England, had made him the guiding star of the oppressed Scots.

Keppetipola, a devout Buddhist, took some comfort from the conviction that his present impasse was the outcome of his own delinquencies in a previous incarnation. On the morning of 25 November 1818, the two prisoners Keppetipola and Madugalle were conducted to the front of the Dalada Maligava, which, it will be recalled, houses the palladium of the Sinhalese Buddhists – the Sacred Tooth relic of the Buddha. Here Keppetipola recounted before the high priest the various meritorious actions he had performed during his lifetime.

He prayed silently for the supreme bliss to which every ardent Buddhist aspires – the attainment of nirvana, the bliss that arises from the cessation of craving. The *mahanayake*, conferring on him the blessings of the noble Triple Gem, consoled the fallen nobleman with the benediction:

> You will receive your due reward for all the meritorious acts you have performed in this birth, as surely as the stone that is tossed up into the air inevitably falls back to the earth.

The *disave* then turned to Simon Sawers, the government agent of Badulla, who was present, and offered a part of his last religious offering to him as a token of remembrance. It was the upper covering of his prison garment. He removed a part of the rest of his vestments and offering these to the priest, remarked with great composure:

> This is all I have to offer now, let not the merit of the offering be lessened by it being so meagre and befouled.

Sawers, who had served as government agent in Uva when Keppetipola was *disave* in that province, had worked with the condemned chief and had apparently found much in common with him, was deeply affected. He dropped his gaze, and stared at the ground, later declining Keppetipola's request that he should accompany him to the place of execution.

Madugalle, whose heroic deeds in the field of battle had been one of the sustaining legends of the rebellion, lost his composure and broke down when the priest ended his sermon. He implored the mercy of the sacred Tooth Relic to save him from death, and collapsed. Unnerved and limp, he had to be bodily removed from the temple precincts by Lieutenant Mackenzie, the superintendent of the gaol, and his assistants. Keppetipola, taken aback, is said to have commented dryly, 'What has possessed the once valiant Madugalle, that he makes such a fool of himself? He should set a better example.'

The prisoners were conducted to the bank of the Bogambara Lake, which would be the place of their execution. Their last wishes having been attended to and the religious rites completed, Keppetipola tied up his long hair neatly on the top of his head and sat down on the ground with his legs crossed in the posture of meditation. He produced a holy book of the sacred verses – a *Bana potha* – from the upper folds of his remaining garment and recited a few Pali verses from the text. He then handed the book to a friend standing near, requesting him to give it to Sawers as a token of gratitude for his kindness and friendship when they were official colleagues at Badulla.

The priest in attendance continued the religious litany that the occasion demanded, and the executioner raised his sword. His blow struck the neck of the chieftain from behind. Keppetipola uttered his last word, '*arahan*'. The first blow failed to sever the head from the body, and a second stroke was necessary. Keppetipola's body slumped to the ground. According to Sinhalese custom, the head was then placed on the breast.[1]

S.M. Nanayakkara, author of the above account, adds that Dr Henry Marshall, 'a man intent on scientific pursuits' – yet another 'hunter-gatherer', perhaps – took the skull of Keppetipola along with him when he returned to Britain, and presented it to the museum of the Phrenological Society of Edinburgh. Marshall's purpose in subjecting Keppetipola's skull to scientific examination is not clear. Perhaps he believed that Keppetipola displayed qualities of character so unique among the natives of Sri Lanka that they seemed almost British, and imagined that examination of the hero's cranium might reveal some 'scientific' reasons for this.[2]

The British, too, were not without their heroes. The 19th Regiment lost in the year 1818, from various causes, 114 men.

An opportunity to view the Kandyan War of 1818 from the British side has been provided by a British soldier, Colour-Sergeant George Calladine of the 19th Foot, who served in Sri Lanka during the rebellion, and whose regiment was camped near Kandy during its final months. Calladine kept a record of his experiences and impressions [3], recording in 1818 that

> At this time there was seldom a day passed but we had parties out scouring the country for a distance round, burning all they came across and shooting those they could not take prisoners . . . Their instructions were to burn down every village they came across where the inhabitants had not protection to show . . .[4]

From these 'search-and-destroy' parties Calladine, who held the position of hospital orderly, was fortunately exempt, except on those occasions when the camp doctor accompanied the soldiers on their mission of punitive destruction.

It is not known whether the activities described by George Calladine inspired any outbursts of poetic fervour in the senior officers who gave him his 'instructions' (or, indeed, in the civil servants who, reluctantly or otherwise, authorized those instructions). But Calladine himself on at least two occasions was visited memorably by his Muse. The dark Kandyan nights, when any moving shadow might turn out to be a guerrilla armed to the teeth, were, it seems, especially productive of poetic inspiration in the soul of the young sergeant. 'About this time,' he writes, when on sentry, I composed a few verses, which I presented to Mr Robinson, and for which he made me a present of his German flute. The lines are as under:-

List, ye lads of British courage,
    To these lines which I'll unfold
Of our campaign in the interior,
    Where there's many a soldier bold.
In the month of last October,
    From our stations we did go,
For to range the dreadful jungle
    In pursuit of the rebel foe.

In the beginning of November,
    When our troops were in the field,
We travelled o'er those lofty mountains
    Thinking to make our foes to yield.
But the cruel arrows flying,
    As through the jungle we did go,
Many a young and gallant soldier
    Was killed in pursuit of the rebel foe.

But British courage still prevailing,
    Soon we made our foes to fly,
And, their villages assailing,
    Caused some hundreds for to die.
See their villages a-burning,
    And their temples soon laid low,
This, the wretches got for joining
    With the jungle rebel foe.

There is brave McDonald[5] on the mountain
    In pursuit of the rebel King,
And the day that he is taken
    We with heart and voice will sing.
Success unto our British forces,
    As on our journey then we'll go;
And when we're stationed in Colombo,
    We'll drink bad luck to the rebel foe.[6]

The second occasion on which the young sergeant was moved to poetic expression occurred a few days later. Once again on sentry-duty, Calladine 'amused himself' by composing a song which the following night, 'being in the canteen, and some one calling on me for a song, I gave it them to the tune of Waterloo, and they, not knowing that I had a song of that description, I was nearly drowned with porter and arrack for my composition'.

SONG

Come all ye lads of courage bold and listen to my song,
I'll sing to you a ditty which will not keep you long,
Concerning of our late campaign shall here related be,
Where Britons fought like heroes in the Kandian country.

Our forces then proceeded to where this fray begun,
And many a day we've marched from rise to set of sun,
O'er Dombra's lofty mountains and Wellasses' watery plain;
But Briton's [sic] sons, like heroes bold, all dangers still
        disdain.

Our enemy we did pursue for many a weary day,
Along with those black rebels we'd many a bloody fray,
O'er hills and lofty mountains where troops ne'er marched
        before,
And many a rebel Kandian lay in his bloody gore.

The rebel chiefs whene'er we met before us soon did fly,
And Keppetipola taken was sentenced to die.
According to his sentence beheaded soon was he,
Which closed this rebellion in the Kandian country.

Come all ye lads of courage bold and let a toast go round,
Here's a health to Governor Brownrigg who put rebellion
        down,
And unto every officer who fought in freedom's cause
For the honour of old England, her liberty and laws.

Come all ye lads that's faced with green, here's a bumper
    unto you
Who have done your duty manfully and to your cause
    stood true.
Now this rebellion's over we'll sing so merrily,
Our Nineteenth lads have bid adieu to the Kandian
    country.[7]

Displaying a pleasing modesty, Calladine judged his 'song' to have been of 'only a very indifferent' quality. During their period of service in the 'Kandian country', he and his fellows were not so preoccupied with fighting in what he rather curiously terms 'freedom's cause' that they did not seek other ways of amusing themselves. 'To keep myself from doing worse,' writes Calladine,

I made up my mind to take a black girl, and I was not long before I got one. All a man had to do was to get the officer of his company's leave in writing, and he was then allowed to be out of the company's mess and to sleep out of barracks.[8]

The end of June presented George Calladine with some personal problems:

I was some time before I made up my mind whether I would volunteer or go home with the regiment, but having at last resolved to return with it, I turned away my black girl as soon as possible to prevent anything occurring which some of them would be guilty of doing, though I don't think my poor little Dingy[9] would have been guilty of injuring me, as I always behaved very kind to her, and I was very sorry when the cook of our company (who was our interpreter on this occasion, as I had never given myself to learning much of their language, and the girl did not speak any English) told her my intention of going home. She cried bitterly, but I believe her sorrow was of short duration, for the next day one of our men who had volunteered into the 73rd Regiment took up with her, and she went off with him shortly afterwards to Trincomalee, where in a few months she died.[10]

. Since John D'Oyly was discovered, after his death in 1824, to have used his salary to support and educate the children of British soldiers who had returned to England when their period of service in the island was ended, Calladine's remarks on the sexual activities of his regiment ('which left more children than any regiment leaving the country before'), and on his own departure from Ceylon[11] are of some interest:

> Having embarked on the 7th I was wishing to be away, for there is nothing scarcely so uncomfortable as to be laying in harbour. You never can get settled properly, but all is confusion and bustle, and indeed in this case it seemed very miserable, and it was a happy thing we remained only till the next day, as we had such a number of black women coming alongside, who were left behind, some with three and four children, and although they were only blacks, still I conceive they felt as keen a sorrow as if they had been white. I suppose the 19th Regiment left more children than any regiment leaving the country before, as it was so long in the island, between twenty-four and twenty-five years. Some of them were grown up, and girls were married, while boys who had been brought up at the Government School at Colombo were filling respectable places as clerks, or otherwise had entered the army. We had a number sent to the school when the regiment came away.[12]

The story of Calladine's little 'black girl', Dingiri Menike, of her 'kind' protector's desertion of her, and of her subsequent early death, deserves (it seems to the authors of this book) to be disinterred from its burial-place in the 'his/story' of Calladine's memoir and resurrected as 'her/story' in its own right. There were many such young women who gave themselves to British soldiers and suffered a similar fate; the only record of their ever having lived or loved being, as in the case of Calladine and his 'Dingy', a fleeting impression in the minds of their departing men that, although 'black' as regards complexion, 'they felt as keen a sorrow as if they had been white'.

The defeat of the rebels was finally sealed by the recapture by the British of the Relic of the Tooth (rightly termed by Geoffrey Powell 'the mystical affirmation of a [Kandyan] king's regality'), which was said to have been abstracted from the Dalada Mandapa by a *bhikkhu*, and exhibited in July by Keppetipola at Hanguranketa. Brownrigg, however, had had doubts about Keppetipola's claim that he held the true Tooth. How, reasoned Brownrigg, could the Relic have been stolen from the Temple, closely guarded as it was by British troops? The situation was further complicated, first, by the realization that no one could have recognized the Tooth if he had seen it, and second, by the sincere doubts expressed by the loyal Adigar Molligoda as to whether the British had ever, in fact, taken possession of it.

Had a fictitious article been deposited in Kandy in 1815? The real relic, the *adigar* suggested, might well have been hidden by Ehelepola for use when he might need it to support his ambitions. It was D'Oyly who produced the solution to the dilemma. A state of uncertainty, he suggested, might well be preferable to confirming that Keppetipola did indeed possess the true relic. The advice was shrewd, and Brownrigg accepted it, albeit a little grudgingly.

Some months later, British soldiers caught a *bhikkhu* lurking among some trees. Inside a bundle of clothing he was carrying they found the Relic of the Tooth in its jewelled container. This was the final blow to the Kandyan resistance. The people, already crushed into submission, saw in the loss of the Tooth Relic a divine demonstration that the British were destined to rule them. In two thousand years, it was the first time their Relic had passed from their possession. In Molligoda's opinion, and in the opinion of the people in general, the taking of the relic was 'of infinitely more moment' than the taking of Keppetipola, Pilimatalawe and Madugalle.[13]

Dr John Davy, who attended on the governor and his wife throughout the whole period of the Kandyan War, made many expeditions into the hill country from Kandy, repeatedly with the British troops and again on his return journey to Colombo with the Brownriggs in 1818. He was therefore well placed to observe at first-hand the damage that had been done by the ravages of war to the 'Romantic valleys' of the hill country (which had been so much admired by John D'Oyly when he first crossed the frontier in 1815). The province of Uva, home of Keppetipola, the chieftain whose name had been most closely associated with the war, had been the special target of British troops who had been ordered, following the end of the rebellion, to burn the villages of the disaffected provinces. Revisiting Uva in 1818, Davy was to write with dismay of the deserted appearance of the surrounding country; – its cottages in ruins, its fields lying waste, its cattle destroyed, and its population fled, – all effects of the rebellion, of which this province was the principal theatre. Had the country never been inhabited, its desolate appearance would be little thought of; the wild beauty and untamed majesty of nature, which displays itself around, would occupy the mind with delight, instead of associations of every kind of human misery that war and famine can inflict.[14]

Brownrigg's grudging acceptance of D'Oyly's advice in relation to the rebels' claim to possess the Tooth Relic was an early sign that the governor's attitude towards his erstwhile 'obedient servant' and right-hand man was changing. After martial law was declared over the Kandyan provinces, D'Oyly's administration as Resident was constantly interfered with and interrupted, by military officials and by the governor himself. His efforts at conciliation were constantly misconstrued. During the 'anxious period' spent by Brownrigg and his party in the garrisoned town of Kandy, when apportioning blame for what had occurred gave the stranded visitors plenty to occupy their minds, D'Oyly was held responsible, openly or covertly, for much that happened.[15]

It is noticeable that D'Oyly's name ceases about this time to be mentioned with any kind of praise or approval in Governor Brownrigg's despatches to the home government. Vimalananda suggests that a possible loss of confidence in D'Oyly's abilities was at the root of Brownrigg's apparent reluctance to mention D'Oyly: 'It is evident from the commencement of the Insurrection that Brownrigg had ceased to consult D'Oyly in all matters of public affairs relating to the Kandyan Provinces'.[16]

Brownrigg went so far as to complain of D'Oyly to the Secretary of State, describing his erstwhile trusted lieutenant in deliberately ambiguous terms as 'a private Gentleman of very retired and unostentatious habits' who seldom left his chambers, and whom he had to personally 'arouse . . . into that energy of which he is so capable when the Occasion appears sufficiently interesting to require it'.[17]

Similarly, D'Oyly's name is mentioned only once in John Davy's *Account of the Interior of Ceylon*, even though the two men had many scientific interests in common. D'Oyly was, of course, Davy's senior by sixteen years, but they must have been brought into close daily contact during the thirteen months Davy spent as physician in attendance on Governor Sir Robert Brownrigg and Lady Brownrigg when the governor's party founded itself stranded in Kandy. This was a city which D'Oyly ruled in the capacity of British Resident, yet, although Davy would have owed much to the Resident's protection and hospitality during the whole of his sojourn in Kandy, D'Oyly's character and diplomatic record go unremarked by him. Instead, when listing his sources in the preface to his book, Davy excludes D'Oyly from the list of credits, claiming that his descriptions of the island's natural history are entirely 'the result of my own enquiries, enriched by the contributions of some medical friends'.

Chapters 4, 5 and 6 of Davy's book focus on the political condition of the interior, and on its system of government. Now, Davy was no expert speaker of Sinhala. D'Oyly, on the other hand, besides being an accomplished speaker and writer of the Sinhala language, not only was treated as a friend and confidant by the Kandyan chiefs, but had been making a detailed study of the constitution of the Kandyan kingdom. It seems that D'Oyly must have been the conduit through which Davy gained his information on Kandyan social custom and political practice, yet the Resident's assistance is nowhere acknowledged, though other government officials working in Sri Lanka at the time are mentioned.[18]

Davy provides a lively description of the events at the Kandyan court leading up to the capture of Kandy by the British and the signing of the Kandyan Convention on 2 March 1815. We know that D'Oyly masterminded the capture of Kandy, and Brownrigg, on whose instructions he did it, could have provided Davy with details of D'Oyly's contribution which, as we have seen, was crucial to its remarkable success. Not once, however, is D'Oyly mentioned by name. Instead, Davy insists that his findings are based entirely on

> native sources, principally from Kandyan chiefs high in office, and conversant with business, and who were constantly in attendance at the court of the dethroned monarch.[19]

Later, Davy gives details of the administration of Kandy between 1815 and 1817, describing the outbreak of the Kandyan War and the circumstances in which it was put down and the rebels punished. Although D'Oyly was very much in the eye of that particular storm, at no point is his assistance with information, or even an opinion, acknowledged.

The single mention by Davy of D'Oyly's name in his *Account* occurs in connection with a geological specimen that D'Oyly had shown him – and even then the name is mis-spelled:

Sulphur is extremely rare in Ceylon; indeed its occurrence is not yet demonstrated in a manner perfectly satisfactory. Till about three weeks before I left the island, I had no suspicion of its existence, having ascertained that most of the sulphur used by the natives was brought from the continent and introduced clandestinely, by pilgrims proceeding to Adam's Peak. At the time mentioned, a specimen of rock was shown to me by the Honourable the Resident in the Kandyan Provinces, John Doyley Esq., which he had picked up in Doombera, near Memoora, and which he suspected contained sulphur. I was favoured with a fragment of it for examination. The specimen was of sp. gr. 2.9; it contained a considerable portion of sulphur, with a little sulphat of iron, and slight traces of alum.[20]

The curious attack of amnesia suffered by Davy in regard to mentioning his obligations to 'the Honourable the Resident in the Kandyan Provinces' may be connected with the fact that the good doctor was the confidant of Brownrigg, to whom he also owed his position. It is difficult to avoid the conclusion that D'Oyly was, at this point in his Civil Service career, working determinedly on in an atmosphere so unpleasant that it amounted almost to ostracism. While men of Davy's temperament apparently resorted to silence, with others suspicion took the more vicious form of gossip, which was equally difficult to counteract.

D'Oyly's punctilious observance of traditional custom in the pursuit of his duties as Resident in Kandy had already led, as we saw in Chapter 8, to deep suspicion regarding his loyalty to the Christian faith. *'Was Mr D – a Budhite?'* Gossip in the British community, especially among the ignorant and uninformed, suggested that he was.[21] A respect for Buddhism, a philosophy known for its denial of an after-life and its failure to recognize the risen Christ as the saviour of mankind,[22] could only be judged as un-Christian, and worse, un-British.

Many of the missionaries who came to Ceylon in the early years seem in any case to have packed British class prejudices in their baggage along with their Bibles and prayer books. To some extent this was inevitable – the Church of England was not represented in the Ceylon mission field until much later on, and the Methodist Missionary Society, which was, had been reluctantly admitted to the island by the administration. The British government did not welcome 'interference' by missionaries in the delicate relationship which had to be maintained in the colonies between ruler and native. Civil servants, the agents of that government, were regarded by most nonconformist missionaries as arrogant, privileged, over-educated snobs, an attitude well exemplified in a warning the Methodist missionary Benjamin Clough transmitted to mission headquarters in 1814. The missionary in Ceylon, wrote Clough, had

> to mix with two Classes of people; the first is English Gentlemen all of whom have had a Classical education. And sometimes he will have to contend with a little fashionable D-ism, delivered in rather a pretty manner. The other Class is the Natives who though they are Strangers to the corruptions of Europe . . . have . . . received educations which he will find it his duty to counteract.

It would appear that the Resident's activities were being carefully observed by his colleagues and superiors. It was well known that D'Oyly had headed one of the most effective intelligence networks in the empire: what was the explanation, then, for his failure to detect, and duly report, the signs of rebellion before they appeared as full-scale war? D'Oyly's sympathy for his friends among the Kandyan nobility, several of whom had been condemned to death for their part in the 'troubles', added an extremely sinister shading to his unconventional conduct.

In such disheartening circumstances as these it must have been with mixed feelings that John D'Oyly received and read on 1 February 1818, a letter from his younger brother George. George D'Oyly had succeeded to their father's living and was now Rector of St Margaret's Church at Buxted. George had not written to his elder brother since the annexation of Kandy in 1815, and had evidently been inspired to recommence correspondence by a gift of £300 that D'Oyly had sent him.

> My circumstances being now improved [wrote George], the money
> will be placed in the funds to accumulate with your other remittances
> and I trust it will not be long before you return home to enjoy what
> you have so honourably earned.

George D'Oyly's letter reached Kandy at a time when D'Oyly was
being harried on all sides by administrative and military matters.
Personal issues complicated his situation further, in particular his
distress at the defection and disgrace of chiefs on whom he had formerly
relied for information and support, and whom he had gradually come
to regard as friends and colleagues. What could have provoked his
colleagues among the Chiefs to rebel? D'Oyly must have frequently
pondered this question, and arrived at the conclusion that it could only
have been resentment at the Crown's failure to observe the terms of
the treaty. At the heart of their resentment, as he well knew, would have
lain a tacit rejection of *himself* as a sympathetic, just official who had their
interests at heart.

D'Oyly was aware that Brownrigg, presumably in the grip of the
euphoria which followed the annexation of the Kandyan kingdom, had
recommended that a baronetcy be conferred upon him in recognition
of his services in the negotiations that had made conquest possible.
Lord Bathurst, through whom these moves had been made, had been
pleased with the suggestion and planned to recommend it to the Prince
Regent whenever he should be disposed to create baronets for civil
services. What were such recommendations, hopes and plans worth
now? D'Oyly, well aware that his intelligence system had broken down,
knew he was being personally blamed for neglecting to take a hard line
with the chiefs. He felt himself to be distrusted by both sides.

Ignorant of the turn affairs were taking in Ceylon, and happily
unconscious of the irony of his words, George D'Oyly went on in his
letter to compliment his brother on his continuing success:

> I most sincerely wish you joy of the credit you have obtained and of
> the lucrative station to which you have attained. I am most happy also
> to find that you enjoy good health in your residence in the interior.
> Great fears were entertained at home, that the interior country wd
> prove too unhealthy to admit of the permanent residence of
> Europeans. We shall be rejoiced when we hear that you are seriously

intending to return to England: I conjecture that you make yourself so useful in the island, that you cannot easily be spared.[24]

George's 'conjectures' on John's presumed indispensability to the government in Ceylon must have been read with ironic amusement by the Resident of Kandy.

News of the rebellion had been slow in reaching Sussex (or perhaps John's brothers had kept the worst of the news from Mrs D'Oyly). His mother's letters to John, which were always full of family and neighbourhood gossip, and teasing reminders that she would like to see him married as soon as possible,[25] changed their tone abruptly on 1 August 1818, when she wrote him an agitated letter, urging him to 'have nothing to do with this insurrection but live quietly at Kandy', or, better still, return home:

> Mr & Mrs Tolfrey returned here a few days ago he tells me he thinks [the insurrection] cannot last long that either the chiefs must give up or you must give up Kandy in the latter case I hope you will come home directly & not take any other situation & in case the chiefs give up I still hope you will return next year as in a letter I recd from you 2 years ago you said you would not stay more than 2 years.

He had now lived seventeen years in Ceylon, Mary D'Oyly reminded her son, and she saw no purpose whatever in his remaining any longer in the island:

> You will have enough to live very comfortably on in England & it is not worth your while to stay longer for the purpose of saveing & if you stay much longer you will be too old to think of marrying & settling comfortable.

'I shall expect & hope in your next letter you will say when you mean to return,' she urged him, and added petulantly:

> . . . or else I shall expect that you never will & believe what Mr Chase says that all Gentlemen who go to the East Indies have so much command & are made so much off & that when they return are nothing here that they do not like to come home I told him you must

be much altered if that is the case as I think you must have had enough of a busy life & will like to retire and live comfortably in the Country & have a farm.

Her anxious letter, followed by another in which she urged him to return with the Brownriggs when the governor's term of office ended, 'for their are young men enough who will be glad to take your Place', took seven months to reach her son. 'It is very likely that this Rebellion may last several years as they can hide themselves in the woods,' wrote a worried Mary D'Oyly in her second letter (of 15 October 1818), 'I much wonder that you should like to live with such a treacherous set of people.' She ended on a note of despondency and resignation: 'If you do not come with Genl. B. I do not expect ever to see you.'

His mother's letters reached John D'Oyly in 1819, by which time the insurrection was over and the Brownriggs were safely back in Colombo. The rebellion was suppressed ruthlessly, the rebels were punished and their lands confiscated or subjected to tax. Chiefs who had not joined the rebellion were appropriately rewarded, and the administration of the Kandyan provinces was reorganized. In the midst of all these changes D'Oyly, according to Hulugalle, was the only official who preserved his calmness of judgement and exercised some compassion.[26] He continued for three more years in service, years during which he was forced to watch Governor Brownrigg's successor, Edward Barnes, deliberately destroy the relationships between the Crown and the people that he had devoted years of his life to building up.

Of particular concern for D'Oyly would have been the public auction in London in 1820 of the Regalia and jewels of the King of Kandy, which he had given his word to Maha Adikaram Ehelepola on behalf of the Crown would never be sold, nor even gazed upon by unworthy eyes.[27] D'Oyly's state of mind at this low point in his career might well have resembled the bitterness felt by a European student disillusioned with his life at Hanwella, whose verses the Dutchman Johann Wolffgang Heydt recorded in 1744:

> Is this the lovely land? Is Adam buried here?
> Is this the Paradise that God's hand planted?
> Can any honest man quench here his thirst and hunger?

And live in happiness? It goes beyond my understanding
A nest of toads and snakes, with hills and valleys deep:
Leeches that suck the blood, Schagers that suck the gold
From sack and purse. And yet, even if one will pay
Nothing will one obtain, unless by favour given.
If this is Paradise, it is accursed of God:
To go from it one begs, beseeches and implores.[28]

During this period, D'Oyly's family appears to have launched a concerted effort to bring him home. On 17 December 1819, Thomas D'Oyly wrote to John that he had just put his name up for membership of the Travellers' Club, which had been formed during the summer of that year, and which Thomas believed John 'would find very agreeable in point of Society'. The Travellers', he wrote, had 'become much in vogue', and was a place where John would be able to renew 'old School & College connections'. His glowing description of the club's facilities was perhaps intended to reawaken memories in John of the social life to which he had formerly been accustomed, and convince his brother that a long spell of living abroad had not necessarily rendered him unfit to re-enter English society. It was surely not by accident that Thomas enquired in the same paragraph of his letter whether John had yet fixed on a date by which he might think of 'taking leave of Ceylon & returning home?'.

Mrs Mary D'Oyly, less patient than her eldest son and much less tactful, combined a direct tirade with emotional blackmail of a particularly unsubtle kind. On 5 February 1820, as if daring him to disprove her assertion, she told John she was convinced that he preferred Ceylon to England:

This shall be the last time I will Plague you about coming home both George & Henry think you like the life you live & have a pleasure in managing the affair – you do it very well & are beloved by the natives & that everybody would wish you to stay.

Aware that he had been sending Thomas D'Oyly regular remittances with instructions that the money should be spent on setting his mother up with her own carriage and helping his younger brother George tide over a difficult period, Mrs D'Oyly pointed out that John's generous

nature would never allow him to live 'in a grand stile', either in England
or in Ceylon: 'You are so very generous to every body'. But, she assured
John, his income would most certainly provide for a comfortable
bachelor life in England:

> Your income of six hundred with the 3 hundred interest you have
> from the money you have here will make 9 which as a single man you
> might live very well here that is a good Lodging in London with a
> Gig 2 Horses & man Servant & to visit your friends in the summer
> or if you like it better you might have a small house in the Country . . .

Her thoughts then moving with natural rapidity to marriage, Mrs
D'Oyly urged her son to marry quickly, and marry well:

> If you marry it will be your own fault if you do not marry a Lady of
> some fortune when you might do very well you ought to reculect
> that you are not a young man & that if you stay five or six years
> longer it will be too late to settle comfortably when you return . . .

John D'Oyly's younger brother George[29] had developed into a
worldly and pragmatic cleric, an individual very different in character,
it would seem, from his elder brother Thomas, who devoted most of
the space available in his letters to considering ways by which John's
scientific interests could be advanced. Thomas had married, according
to George, a 'handsome' young woman with a delicate constitution and
a negligible fortune. While Thomas D'Oyly was, at this very time,
negotiating tactfully with Brownrigg to recommend that a baronetcy
be conferred on his brother John, and firmly disclaiming any extension
of such an honour to himself or any other member of the family[30]
George D'Oyly had not allowed sentiment to get in the way of financial
profit. Offered two rectories, one of Lambeth, the other of Sundridge
in Kent, George had promptly given up his father's living of Buxted
and accepted both:

> I deem myself unusually fortunate in getting so large an income
> [wrote George D'Oyly to John]; & the situations of the livings give
> them an additional value to me. There is an excellent house at each:
> Lambeth will supply me with a town house, & Sundridge, distant

only 24 miles, with a country house in a particularly pleasant country. Of course, I feel it something of a drawback, that I have to resign the living of Buxted, with which our family has been so long connected; but I do not think it right to give way much to feelings of this kind, in a case where the advantages greatly preponderate in the other scale.

George D'Oyly now looked forward eagerly to leading the life of a gentleman of means with a house in town and another in the country. In a long letter to John D'Oyly of 30 June 1820, he stated his reasons for abandoning Buxted. 'You are aware,' wrote George D'Oyly,

that my father suffered the tithes to remain at a rate unusually low. It became my business on coming to the living to have them valued, & to set on them such a fair sum as it was fitting that they shd pay, & I receive. In doing this, I found the farmers a very troublesome and illconditioned race, who played tricks of every description, & in some instances have forced me to take their tithes in kind. All this is unpleasant, & of course, diminishes my regret at quitting the parish, particularly, as from knowing the characters of the people there, I am satisfied that there is little chance of it being otherwise than an unpleasant parish to deal with.

George D'Oyly's arguments might have struck home more sharply to John, and with much greater force, than he had ever intended. As the Crown's agent of revenue in what had been the Kandyan kingdom, John D'Oyly had daily dealings with a hardworking peasantry accustomed from ancient times to pay their taxes in kind, and he knew at first hand the hardships they endured. While George had been calculating ways and means of increasing his income by raising the rate of tithes that church-going farming families paid at Buxted, his brother John had been working out methods by which taxes could be made to fall with diminished weight on the people in the hill country districts who were least able to pay them. He, like George, had grown up in their father's parish of Buxted, and knew the Sussex farming families well. Yet it was possible for George, who was familiar with their difficulties, to dismiss the poor folk of Buxted easily as 'a very troublesome and illconditioned race, who played tricks of every description'.

By March 1821, when D'Oyly received George's letter, the difficulties of Kandyan farmers had greatly increased, following the wholesale destruction of their orchards and the burning of their homesteads by British troops during the Kandyan War. D'Oyly himself was still coming to terms with the implications of the rebellion, for himself as well as for 'the Kandyan Nation' on whose affection he had built such high hopes for the future of empire.

In the people of Kandy D'Oyly may have believed he had found the 'golden race' which (as he had prophesied several years previously in his poem 'Commercii Laus') would one day inherit the benefits of peace. But many people, including his family in England, thought D'Oyly had been shamefully betrayed by his friends among the chiefs. Were these, then, not a 'golden race' at all, but on the contrary, a society as 'troublesome and illconditioned' as the people of the 'unpleasant parish' of Buxted, whose honesty could not be relied on, and who deserved therefore to be abandoned?

In the last part of his letter, George D'Oyly passed on news of some of John's old Cambridge friends: 'I continually meet with your old friend Baugh Allen,' he wrote,

> he has lately married a Miss Romilly. Not long ago he invited me to dinner to meet Geo. Strachey, yr friend, who has lately returned from India. I have not seen for some time Sir Robt. Ainslie. From what I have heard I fear that he is a good deal lost to society. I have reason to think that he has formed a connexion with a woman to whom he is not married & has by her a large family. This of course throws him a good deal out of society.

Whether these varied approaches by members of his family were successful in convincing a disillusioned and disappointed John D'Oyly that he should indeed think seriously of a return to England, we may never know. On the other hand, it is certainly possible that George's letter, reaching D'Oyly at a time of crisis in his own affairs, worked against the family's dearest wishes. Robert Ainslie had been John D'Oyly's closest associate and companion at Cambridge, the boon companion of his undergraduate days.[31] The mercantile values which saturate George's letter, its piously moralizing tone, and its implicit condemnation of the playful and unconventional Ainslie, might well have brought home to D'Oyly a very clear impression of the closed and stifling society that would certainly engulf him if he were to return to England.

On 29 August 1821, John D'Oyly was created a baronet, with the title 'D'Oyly, of Kandy'. This, the highest honour conferred on any member of the Ceylon Civil Service throughout its long history,[32] was greeted joyfully by the D'Oyly family in England. Mrs Mary D'Oyly was particularly gratified: she took great pride thereafter in embellishing all the letters she sent subsequently to Ceylon with the superscription: 'Sir John D'Oyly Bart, Kandy, Island, Ceylon'.

D'Oyly's coat of arms was chosen for the new baronet by his elder brother Thomas, and displays the *fleurs-de-lis* of their ancestral France. Thomas had been particularly anxious, he wrote, that the new design should differ as little as possible from the old D'Oyly arms (represented in Burke as 'Or, two bendlets az'), and he sent his brother 'an emblasoned [*sic*] drawing from the Heralds office' as assurance that his

FIGURE 11 The dignity of a baronet

Sir John D'Oyly's coat of arms in St Peter's Church, Fort of Colombo. From a photograph by Nemone Boteju (Gooneratne Collection).

wishes had been carried out. Applied to by the Heralds for a motto for the new baronet's arms, Thomas D'Oyly had consulted friends, finally settling on one he believed to be 'a very good general sentiment' (and also thought, no doubt, especially applicable to an empire-building brother).[33] *Omne Solum Forti Patria* ('To a brave man his native land is the only thing that matters') was an original choice, having never, he assured John, 'been pre-occupied by any Peer or Baronet'.[34]

Writing from his rectory at Lambeth on 6 October 1822, this time to congratulate John on the honour he had received, George D'Oyly, now the prosperous father of five sons, gave his elder brother the benefit of his advice on personal matters and urged him strongly 'to turn your thoughts to marrying':

> I am quite certain that all your relations and friends will greatly regret, and none more than myself, that the distinction you have acquired shd not be continued in a family of your own. Pray consider this.

With the benefit of hindsight, we might justifiably speculate on the state of mind in which these honours and congratulations, so long awaited and so late in coming, found John D'Oyly. He had seen the Kandyan officials with whom he had worked closely, and whom he personally trusted, executed as traitors. He had seen the solemn promise he had made on behalf of the Crown regarding the protection of the Kandyan regalia subverted and betrayed. In these circumstances, a modern reading of the biblical passage chosen by Thomas D'Oyly for his brother's motto carries considerable ironic resonance for us in both its original and its imperial contexts:

> It is not because you fear God that he reprimands you and
> > brings you to trial.
> No, it is because you have sinned so much; it is because of
> > all the evil you do.
> To make your brother repay you the money he owed, you
> > took away his clothes and left him nothing to wear.
> You refused water to those who were tired, and refused to
> > feed those who were hungry.
> *You used your power and your position to take over the whole*
> > *land.*

Such a reading could be interpreted as condemning both D'Oyly and his imperial mission[35]. It is unlikely that such ironies and contradictions struck Thomas D'Oyly when he chose the motto, or John D'Oyly when he consented to its being added to his arms. The Authorized Version of the Bible, which was of course the one available to Thomas, is milder than our contemporary versions, and more accommodating to the ambiguities of imperial compromise.

A further source of concern for D'Oyly was the present situation and future fate of Ehelepola Maha Nilame. Fearing an attempt by the formerly powerful chieftain to take advantage of British reverses to seize power in the Kandyan provinces, the British government had placed him under arrest in Colombo for the duration of the Kandyan War. Ehelepola had answered all the charges made against him. He hoped, he said in a letter written in 1818 to George Lusignan, Secretary for the Kandyan Provinces, in which he rehearsed his services to the British Crown, that the governor would act justly towards him, 'avoiding partiality, malice, imprudence and timidity'.[36] Such action, it will be remembered, had been the duty, according to Kandyan tradition, of a just judge.[37]

Nothing was done, however, to alter the circumstances in which Ehelepola was eking out his days, and when Sir Edward Barnes succeeded Brownrigg as Governor of Ceylon, he found the chief still living a half-life in Colombo. Barnes doubtless felt that some action had to be taken in the matter, and on 13 May 1823 the British ship *Alexander* carried Ehelepola away from the island in which he had lived all his life, to another Indian Ocean island, that of Mauritius. In exile, Barnes had decided, the former Great Chieftain would be powerless to foment rebellion, although he put the decision in rather different terms. In Mauritius Ehelepola could be 'afforded a greater degree of personal liberty than he could enjoy in Ceylon'.

Mrs Mary D'Oyly's dream of a happily wedded John D'Oyly, father of several children, passing a comfortable retirement on a Sussex farm, was never to eventuate. As for Ehelepola, the exiled chieftain never saw Ceylon again. Until his death in Mauritius on 4 April 1829 at the age of 57, he lived a quiet existence, cared for by his Sinhalese major-domo and interpreter, Mohandiram Don Bastian, invited occasionally to the houses of island residents and returning their hospitality punctiliously 'in the English style'. For Edward Barnes's decision amounted to nothing less than a life sentence. And John D'Oyly would live for the remainder of his own life with the words of reproach Ehelepola had addressed to him personally when that sentence was pronounced:

> Sir, whence this conduct? 'Tis through me you gained possession of this pleasant country. Is this then my reward for victory won and enemies overthrown?[38]

CHAPTER ELEVEN

1822–1824: 'D'OYLY OF KANDY'

Into my heart an air that kills
From yon far country blows:
What are those blue remembered hills,
What spires, what farms are those?
That is the land of lost content
I see it shining plain,
The happy highways where I went
And cannot come again.

A.E. Housman

My embarkation from the jetty at Galle was a step
of cruel severance from scenes and associations, toils
and responsibilities, in which I had borne my part.
I had found scenes and associations of the purest and
most elevating sort among the beauties of nature and
the friendship of valued friends; the toils and
responsibilities I had, I hope, borne cheerfully; and
I had endeavoured to act rightly, according to my
judgment, in matters of importance. Now all was to
cease, and I was to be parted from *all*, to which I had
clung with so much devotion, and from the officers
of my department, to whom I was deeply indebted
for their zealous energetic activity, and for the
economy with which they carried out their work.

> In an hour this country, which had been my home
> for so many years, and where the energies of my
> whole manhood had been spent, would be for ever
> lost to sight, and I was to wake in the morning with
> the sense of having nothing further to do. Henceforth
> mine was to be a life of 'idleness', and an entire
> absence of public responsibility! Who that has taken a
> similar step will not have felt as I have done?

The writer of this emotional passage, expressive in many ways of the typical state of mind of a colonial officer at the close of a useful career, was not John D'Oyly, but one of his younger colleagues in Ceylon's government service, Major Thomas Skinner.[1] What D'Oyly's own thoughts were on the matter we are not in a position to know, but it is possible to go some way towards deducing them through a close reading of the letters he received from his family after 1818.

As in India after the Sepoy War of 1857, the atmosphere surrounding relations between the rulers and the ruled undoubtedly changed in Ceylon after 1818, following the Kandyan War and the terrible retribution visited by the British government on the chiefs and people of the Kandyan provinces.

A notable change of policy might be seen, for instance, in the fact that after 1818, the British government appears to have lost interest in encouraging its officers to learn the local languages. This lethargy did not pass unnoticed. At mid-century, Sinhalese nationalists were still urging the government to rethink its attitude to language:

> If nothing else prompt the European to study the native languages,
> the affairs at least of an important Colony like Ceylon, where the
> Singhalese constitute the great mass of its population, should rouse
> him from his inattention to the native language . . . Until the Civil
> Servant makes the Singhalese the instrument of conveying his
> sentiments to the natives, the latter can hardly fail of being
> misgoverned; their habits and feelings being but little understood, and
> their wants altogether unknown.[2]

It will be seen that D'Oyly's efforts to establish relationships of mutual friendship and trust between the 'Kandyan Nation' and the government in Colombo had come to nothing, the work he and Sawers had done in collaboration with the chiefs in collecting and codifying the customary laws of the Kandyans lay unpublished and neglected,[3] and a peaceful future for the island could no longer be taken for granted.

As a *Memorandum* presented subsequently by Major Skinner to the House of Commons was to indicate, a process had been set in motion that was to do lasting damage to the social fabric of the island. Skinner, who had arrived in Ceylon in 1819, and had worked closely with Governor Barnes to build the network of roads that criss-crossed the hill country, had had plenty of time and opportunity during his fifty years in the island to observe the gradual deterioration that set in during his period of service. He drew the attention of the House to the fact that by the 1840s

> intercourse between the European local public functionaries and the natives had become less frequent, while the native chiefs were placed in a position anomalous and invidious for some years past. A vague idea has prevailed that their influence and authority has been too great, and under an impression that it was necessarily subversive of the stability and efficiency of our own authority, the policy has been to allow it to decline, and without any avowed determination to destroy it we have practically discouraged and undermined it.[4]

Metaphors drawn from roads and railways came easily to Ceylon's great road- and railway-builder. They would probably not have come as easily to D'Oyly, but he would certainly have endorsed Skinner's view that

> the authority and influence of the European over the native, to be as general, effective, and beneficial as it ought to be, must necessarily descend, railway-like in an unbroken gradient from the governing through the various grades of the governed, rather than by abrupt leaps and disjointed falls. Masses of the machinery of the social order cannot be cast off and heedlessly strewed in the way without danger; but we have placed the chiefs and headmen (a most important fraction of that machinery) in a position in which they are in various degrees calculated to impede, rather than to facilitate, the progress of good Government; we have rendered them discontented, their respectability, and influence (for good) with the mass of the people is generally impaired, and they are becoming alienated in feeling from the Government.[5]

It can hardly be doubted that D'Oyly's appointment as Resident of Kandy placed him after 1818 in a situation of considerable personal difficulty. He found himself increasingly at odds with imperialist practice, and alienated, against his will, from the people he was called upon to rule as the king's representative.

Among matters that caused him disquiet was the requirement, after 1818, that he personally administer policies designed to repress and punish persons who had associated themselves with the Kandyan rebels. The government, anxious to make it clear to all concerned that just as treason had brought execution and disgrace to the rebels, loyalty to the Crown would bring immediate and tangible rewards in the form of lower taxes, sanctioned acts of favouritism to 'loyal' chiefs who had proved pliable for its purposes. This gave rise to divisions among the chieftains, and it was said that a new class of protected propertied persons, the 'D'Oyly aristocrats', had been created.[6]

Such policies were abhorrent to D'Oyly. Not only were they repressive in themselves, but they involved the breaking of commitments he had made on behalf of the British government to the Kandyan people in relation to their religion. Further, they undermined the traditional relationship between the chiefs and the people on which he, more than anyone else in the British administration, fully realized the integrity of Kandyan society depended.

To which must be added the destruction, which D'Oyly realized was now inevitable, of a social system that he had just been coming to know through the exercise of documenting its customary laws. There was no possibility, after 1818, that the British government would honour the terms of the Kandyan Convention which Brownrigg had signed jointly with the chiefs.

D'Oyly's role as Resident, involving him in such symbolic acts as the offering of flowers at 'pagan' shrines and temples, removing his shoes before entering such places, supervising arrangements at public ceremonies and processions, and making official donations to Buddhist institutions, inevitably caused him to appear to unsympathetic fellow countrymen as un-Christian and therefore un-British. At the same time, as we have seen, his failure to anticipate, and guard against, the outbreak of the Kandyan War of 1818 led to covert accusations within the Government ranks of inefficiency, and even of divided loyalty. He found his authority undermined, his performance criticized, his patriotism doubted, his day-to-day work shared (and no doubt secretly reported on) by other, newly appointed officials. His baronetcy was delayed till 1821.

Although he does not seem to have ever swerved from his stance of loyalty to his king and his country, it was natural, and probably inevitable, following the disillusionments that the Kandyan War had brought with it, that D'Oyly's thoughts should have begun to turn (as Leonard Woolf's were to do many years later, at the end of an equally exemplary career in the Civil Service) towards resignation and retirement from the Civil Service.

For the first time in the twenty years he had spent in Ceylon, John D'Oyly began to seriously consider returning to England. Nothing, it seemed, mattered more now to the Crown he had once been proud to serve than the making and saving of money and the control and exploitation (rather than the enlightenment and protection) of the native population.

It was in these years that the British government established taverns in the Kandyan districts which purveyed cheap liquor, the profits from which went to the Crown. Overlooking or ignoring the undertaking that had been given to the chiefs regarding the protection of Buddhist interests, the government permitted Christian missionaries to enter and work in the Kandyan districts. When the Methodists requested permission in 1820 to establish an English school at Kurunegala, they were informed by John D'Oyly as British Resident at Kandy on 14 October that the governor 'had no objections to the proposed measure provided that the Government is put to no Expence thereby'.[7]

For years D'Oyly had ignored or evaded his family's pleas that he had been resident long enough 'on Ceylon', and that it was time for him to come home. Now, however, the situation was very different from what it had been in 1814 when, aware that the Kandyan kingdom was weakened within by intrigue, he had known himself to be the master strategist who alone possessed the skills to win it for his country.

Although D'Oyly had acquired an estate at Gannoruwa,[8] which would seem to be an indication of his having intended to continue living in Ceylon, he now made discreet enquiries of his family regarding present conditions in England. He received a strongly positive response. 'You mentioned in one of your letters,' wrote Mrs Mary D'Oyly on 30 August 1821, 'that you did not know how you should like the society in

England you was 28 when you went and if you liked it then it is just the same now and I cannot think how you can dislike it now'.

His elder brother Thomas wrote with renewed enthusiasm to John on 20 July 1822 about 'our Travellers Club', which, he said,

> flourishes extremely; it occupies a large well-furnished House in Pall Mall which affords a coffee-room, dining-room, drawing-room, Library, newspaper-room, baths, billiard-room &c. & most of the foreign journals as well as the London Papers are taken in together with the other current publications of the day, & the Library is indeed by no means scanty & has constant additions made to it, both by purchase, & by presents from the Members; Besides the Coffee-room in which refreshments & meals may be had at any hour at a moderate price there is also provision made for giving a handsome dinner to such as choose to put down their names for that purpose at a fixed sum in a separate room; & the whole is managed by a Committee of the Members who overlook the accounts, regulate the servants &c. &c. Many Clubs have of late years been established in London upon a similar plan, but I think the Travellers is, just now, more in request than any other; & it is much resorted to by Foreigners, who, if of a respectable class, easily procure admission to it as honorary members.

To this encouragement Thomas added on 10 September 1822 the news that he had 'procured from Government a Letter which gives you the option of returning to England upon leave of absence'. This was a tactful move, inspired by Thomas's sensitivity to his younger brother's justifiable reluctance to give up altogether 'every connection & concern with a place which you have so long super-intended'. It was possible, after all, that John might 'prefer returning for some short time, after your visit here, to assist again in promoting the welfare of the colony, rather than remaining at home quite as an unemployed individual'.

The dilemma of the colonial officer who ends his term of office to return to Europe has frequently been canvassed in twentieth-century English fiction, notably by E.M. Forster in *A Passage to India* and by Paul Scott in *Staying On*. In the latter novel Tusker Smalley stays on in India because he has no intention of 'growing old in bloody Stevenage'. In William Knighton's novel *Forest-Life in Ceylon*, one of the characters, a coffee-planter named Hofer, examines the subject from a slightly different point of view:

There is much in Asiatic life generally that tends to unfit a man for active duties in England afterwards; here, and more especially on the continent of India, a man begins naturally to regard himself as one of the aristocracy, however humble his lot at home. He sees the great mass of the population beneath him, its chiefs solicitous for his friendship or notice, and a favoured few of the same rank and class with himself enjoying a monopoly of the advantages of life. It is therefore but natural that he should begin to esteem himself as a very different being from the common herd of humanity around him – as a portion of china amongst the earthenware of the world.[9]

Did D'Oyly see himself from Skinner's viewpoint, fearing, after a lifetime of unremitting work, to 'wake in the morning with the sense of having nothing further to do', resigning himself somehow to 'a life of "idleness"', and an entire absence of public responsibility'? Had the thought of a retirement spent in England, possibly at a seaside resort on the Sussex coast or managing the affairs of a farm, lost its attraction for the man who had once recalled with pleasure his youthful adventures in the Sussex woods? Or had the Civil Service spoiled him so much for ordinary life in England that he now saw himself as Knighton's character Hofer did, 'a portion of china amongst the earthenware of the world'?

Further – would his country welcome him back? After such a long absence, did he count for anything in England? Despite Brownrigg's efforts, and discreet urging by his brother Thomas of elderly noblemen who had the ear of the Prince Regent, D'Oyly's baronetcy had been six long years in coming to him. His brother George had commented a trifle waspishly on the long delay when he wrote to John D'Oyly from Lambeth Rectory on 20 September 1821

to wish you joy on having at last had a baronet's title conferred upon you. I confess I had my fears that the thing, which had been so long promised, wd never be performed; & the delay which took place is quite unaccountable on any ordinary principles. However it is satisfactory to have at last the honor bestowed, which all yr friends know to be so well deserved.

The reasons for that delay remained a mystery as far as D'Oyly's family in England was concerned but, rather than waste time enquiring what those reasons could have been, his mother and his brothers had begun to make preparations for John's expected visit on 'leave of absence'. Their plans were dashed in 1822, however, by the information that a new governor, Sir Edward Paget, had recently arrived in Ceylon, and required D'Oyly's experience and assistance to help him settle in. Mrs D'Oyly, predictably, was extremely annoyed.

'I do not wonder that Sir E. Paget wishes you to stay,' she wrote angrily to John on 30 September 1822, 'as it will save him a great deal of trouble.' Her irritation provoked a tirade, part of it directed at her son and part at the government that employed him:

> There will be no end to your staying there if you are to stay 2 or 3 years every time there comes a new governor . . . I cannot think the reason that you can like to live your whole life at Kandy it may be very well for a few years . . . If you come home next Spring you will not be older than your Brother when he married & I want you to do the same as to your title it must sink with you theirfore I cannot help very much wishing you to marry & have a son to succeed you . . . Government have not done anything for you except this Title which they were very long about theirfore you have no obligation to stay on their account.

Thomas D'Oyly was more temperate in his reaction to the news. He put into quiet, reasoned words the arguments that his brother had clearly been turning over in his own mind. On 21 March 1823, Thomas advised:

> I need not tell you that should you relinquish *altogether* your situation at Ceylon it could not be expected that you would obtain in England any post of active business, & it must remain for your decision, & for yours alone, whether at your time of Life you would like to retire altogether from scenes of efficient & active employment; I cannot forbear pointing out that in forming one's judgment in such a case one of the most weighty circumstances in my mind would be how far your residence at Kandy & the official duties of your office were, from climate & other matters favourable, or otherwise, to your health & constitutional strength, for to this main consideration one would

feel inclined to make most others give way; *You* also know best how far the actual Business, which engages you, is distasteful & irksome, or whether although no Business can be a matter of pleasure, yet on the whole it affords an interest & creates a zeal for the well-doing of the whole public concern.

Thomas was well aware of Mrs D'Oyly's annoyance. On 13 June 1823 he wrote diplomatically: 'My Mother expresses herself, I doubt not, strongly in her letters to you on the side of your leaving India, but her view of the matter is not, as you may suppose, a very enlarged one.' Thomas encouraged John to look on the bright side. The governor who was to succeed Paget was Sir Edward Barnes, who had already served a term in Ceylon. 'I have frequently seen & conversed with Sr E. B.,' wrote Thomas, '& he always expresses himself most friendly to you.'

Younger brother Henry D'Oyly also sent encouragement in his own way. In a lively and cheerful letter of 29 July 1823 Henry gave John a thumbnail sketch of Governor Barnes's vigorous and impulsive personality:

Sir E. Barnes I have seen frequently he engaged the Hercules to take him to Ceylon; she, in going round to Plymouth, got on shore & was damaged, It became necessary to land all the cargo, & this caused a delay of six weeks. In the mean time Sir Edward met at dinner a Miss Fawkes, daughter to a Yorkshire country Gentleman of large fortune, & it was settled in a few days that he was to marry her. About a week ago he left London for Yorkshire in order to be married, & was to cross over from thence with his wife to Plymouth & to embark immediately.

'I think', Henry continued, 'Sir Edward is now likely to continue your Governor for a long time, & he is a most excellent person.' With John's prospects and plans in mind he added: 'I do not know whether you remember Edward Parry Son of Mr Parry of Warfield; he went to India about the time you did, & has just returned with I believe a comfortable but not a large fortune & means to settle in England.'

The assurance Thomas had received from the government in London notwithstanding, the position in 1823 was that John D'Oyly's prospects of returning to Britain on leave would depend entirely on

Governor Barnes's good will and convenience. Since Barnes, unlike Paget, had prior experience of island affairs, Thomas felt he would be unlikely to hinder John's departure, whether that was to be temporary or permanent. However – and on this point the lawyer in Thomas D'Oyly[10] came to the fore – John would be well advised to get all arrangements with the governor in writing:

> But *specially*, let me exhort you . . . to allow no manner of doubt or uncertainty to exist in any arrangement which you make with Sir Edwd. Barnes on the part of Government, but to take particular care that everything is explicitly & distinctly understood with reference to your present & future situation; as very unpleasant embarrassments & disappointments frequently arise to parties from a want of sufficient accuracy in their intercourse with Government.

Thomas's letter was received in Kandy on 21 August 1824, too late for his brother to act on his kind advice, or even to read it. While on a circuit of duty in the Seven Korales, D'Oyly had suddenly been taken ill. Mrs D'Oyly (who enjoyed her occasional visits to the seaside resort of Brighton) had continually advised her son to leave Kandy and seek the sea air of a coastal station, but he had never done so, probably assuming that time and experience of 'oriental fevers' had rendered him immune. On 25 May 1824, John D'Oyly died in Kandy, of malarial fever.

Sir Edward Barnes wrote to Lord Bathurst at the Colonial Office in London, to inform him of the passing of this most 'zealous and able public servant':

The Right Hon'ble
> The Earl Bathurst K.G.
>> &c. —— &c. —— &c. ——
>> Colonial Office
>> London

>>> King's House
>>> Colombo, June 10, 1824.

My Lord,

It is under feelings of the greatest regret that I have by the present opportunity to report to Your Lordship the death of that eminent and distinguished member of the Civil Establishment of this Island Sir John Doyly, which took place at Kandy on the 25th ultimo after a severe and unremitting attack of fever for thirteen days, which he caught while visiting the Seven Korles on official duty. He had returned to Kandy in apparent health on the 9th May but the disease shewed itself three days after, and baffled by its violence the skill and attention of the medical Officers who attended him.

The eulogium of this zealous and able public servant had been so warmly given from Your Lordship's pen that any tribute on my part to the memory of the deceased, must lose vastly by the comparison with the praise bestowed by the Highest in authority. I shall therefore content myself with expressing my conviction that the loss which the Crown has sustained in this Island of a person so well calculated to administer the functions of Government to a people who had the greatest confidence in him, is not to be replaced. It therefore is not my intention to appoint any successor to Sir John Doyly whatever other changes it may be necessary to introduce into the state of the situations in Kandy in consequence of his Death.

The deceased left no Will. His property therefore falls under the official administration of the Registrar of the Supreme Court. I am not as yet able to state what the value may amount to (which it might be satisfactory to his relatives to learn from Your Lordship's Office) but shall as soon as possible convey to you certain information on the subject.

The enclosed sheet of the Ceylon Gazette contains a note of the manner in which the funeral of the distinguished officer of the Crown was conducted.

I have the honor to be &ca

(Signed) E. Barnes[11]

Governor Barnes's letter enclosed a printed account of D'Oyly's death and funeral that seems to have been of his own composition.

DIED.] At Kandy on the 25th instant at 1 o'clock A.M. of Remittent Fever caught on an Official Tour in the Seven Korles, The Honourable Sir JOHN D'OYLY Baronet, a Member of His Majesty's Council in Ceylon and Resident & First Commissioner of Government in the Kandyan Province.

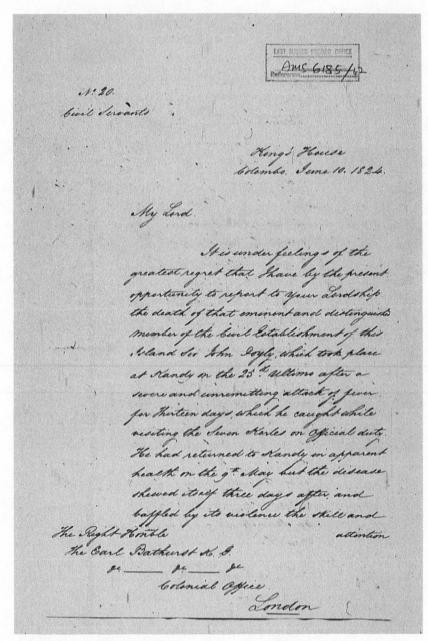

FIGURE 12 His worth as a man . . .

Governor Barnes announces the death of John D'Oyly. Letter from Governor Edward Barnes to the Rt. Hon. the Earl Bathurst, written from King's House, Colombo, 10 June 1824. (Source: East Sussex Record Office, AMS 6185/12.)

(Sgd) G. Barnes

His remains were removed from his late residence in the Palace for Interment in the Burial Ground of the Garrison on the morning of the 26th Inst. at 7 o'clock the troops of the Garrison lining the road from the Palace to the Burial Ground resting on their arms reversed, while Minute Guns were fired by the Royal Artillery in the Castle, as the Procession moved along in the following order.

The Korales & Aratchies of the Udaratte,
The Band of the Ceylon Regiment,
THE BODY,
Born by twelve European Soldiers of the 45th Regiment,
The Pall born by six Field Officers and Captains of the Garrison,
Chaplain The Rev. N. Garstin. Medical Attendant Surgeon Armstrong,
Lieut. Colonel L. Greenwell, S. Sawers, Esq., H. Wright, Esq., the Commissioners of the Board, as Chief Mourners,
Officers of the Garrison & Gentlemen of Kandy,
The Adigar of the Kandyan Provinces & Kandyan Chiefs,
Modliars, Mohandirams of the Residency, Clerks of the Public Offices, together with an immense concourse of Natives.

To all in Ceylon & every one in any way connected with this Island, no Eulogium on the character of Sir JOHN D'OYLY is necessary; and to those unacquainted with the deceased, Language must fail in conveying an adequate idea of his worth as a man & merit as a Public Servant.

His talents and acquirements were of the first order, and little doubt will be entertained on this head, when it is known that before he quitted Westminster he was particularly distinguished by the friendship of the late learned Head of that School Dr. VINCENT, with whom we have heard he maintained a correspondence till the death of the Reverend Doctor: The honorable and high feelings which were conspicuous in Sir JOHN D'OYLY's character, combined with an amiable gentleness of disposition, naturally produced a courteousness of manner which made his society much more desired by all who were acquainted with him, than his laborious zeal in the execution of his public duties would allow of their enjoying

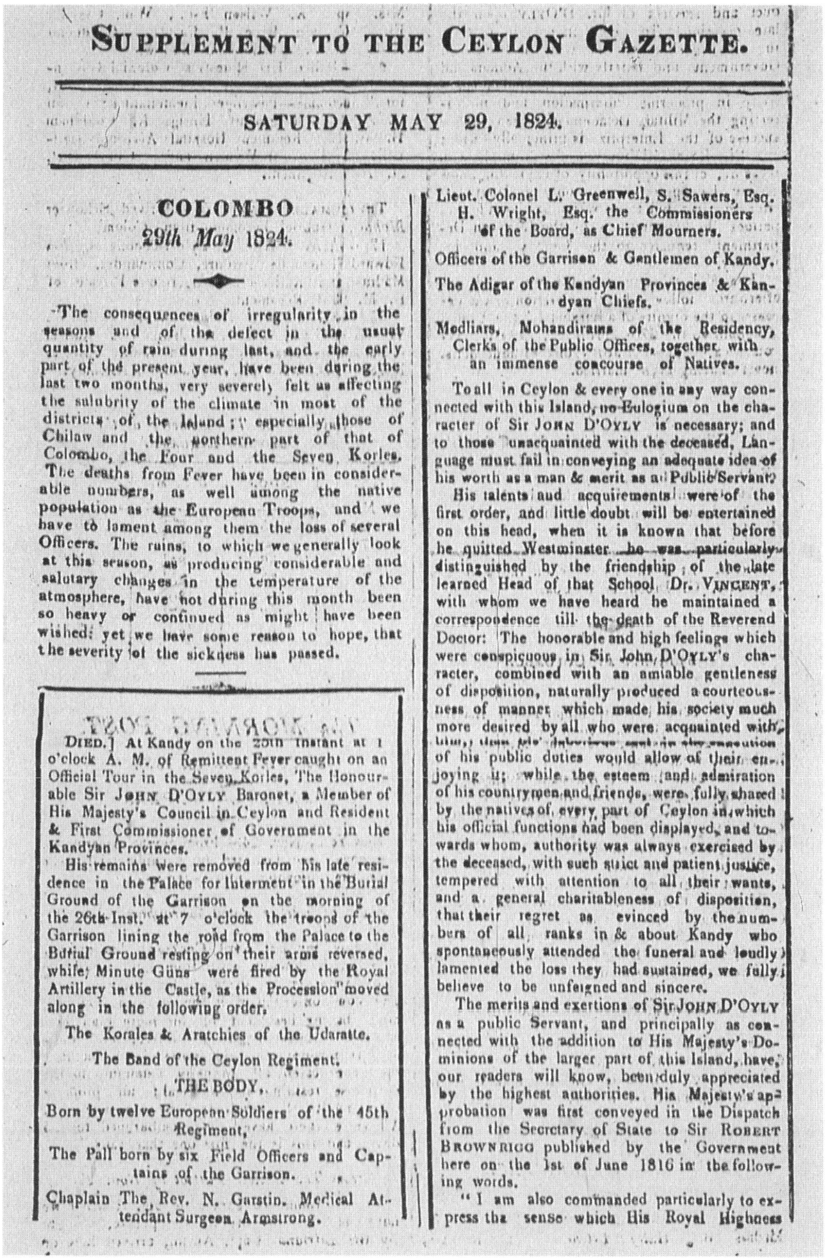

SUPPLEMENT TO THE CEYLON GAZETTE.

SATURDAY MAY 29, 1824.

COLOMBO

29th May 1824.

The consequences of irregularity in the seasons and of the defect in the usual quantity of rain during last, and the early part of the present year, have been during the last two months, very severely felt as affecting the salubrity of the climate in most of the districts of the Island; especially those of Chilaw and the northern part of that of Colombo, the Four and the Seven Korles. The deaths from Fever have been in considerable numbers, as well among the native population as the European Troops, and we have to lament among them the loss of several Officers. The rains, to which we generally look at this season, as producing considerable and salutary changes in the temperature of the atmosphere, have not during this month been so heavy or continued as might have been wished; yet we have some reason to hope, that the severity of the sickness has passed.

DIED.] At Kandy on the 25th Instant at 1 o'clock A. M. of Remittent Fever caught on an Official Tour in the Seven Korles, The Honourable Sir John D'Oyly Baronet, a Member of His Majesty's Council in Ceylon and Resident & First Commissioner of Government in the Kandyan Provinces.

His remains were removed from his late residence in the Palace for Interment in the Burial Ground of the Garrison on the morning of the 26th Inst. at 7 o'clock the troops of the Garrison lining the road from the Palace to the Burial Ground resting on their arms reversed, while Minute Guns were fired by the Royal Artillery in the Castle, as the Procession moved along in the following order.

The Korales & Aratchies of the Udaratte.

The Band of the Ceylon Regiment.

THE BODY,

Born by twelve European Soldiers of the 45th Regiment,

The Pall born by six Field Officers and Captains of the Garrison.

Chaplain The Rev. N. Garstin. Medical Attendant Surgeon Armstrong.

Lieut. Colonel L. Greenwell, S. Sawers, Esq. H. Wright, Esq. the Commissioners of the Board, as Chief Mourners.

Officers of the Garrison & Gentlemen of Kandy.

The Adigar of the Kandyan Provinces & Kandyan Chiefs.

Modliars, Mohandirams of the Residency, Clerks of the Public Offices, together with an immense concourse of Natives.

To all in Ceylon & every one in any way connected with this Island, no Eulogium on the character of Sir John D'Oyly is necessary; and to those unacquainted with the deceased, Language must fail in conveying an adequate idea of his worth as a man & merit as a Public Servant? His talents and acquirements were of the first order, and little doubt will be entertained on this head, when it is known that before he quitted Westminster he was particularly distinguished by the friendship of the late learned Head of that School, Dr. Vincent, with whom we have heard he maintained a correspondence till the death of the Reverend Doctor. The honorable and high feelings which were conspicuous in Sir John D'Oyly's character, combined with an amiable gentleness of disposition, naturally produced a courteousness of manner which made his society much more desired by all who were acquainted with him, than the interviews and in the execution of his public duties would allow of their enjoying it; while the esteem and admiration of his countrymen and friends, were fully shared by the natives of every part of Ceylon in which his official functions had been displayed, and towards whom, authority was always exercised by the deceased, with such strict and patient justice, tempered with attention to all their wants, and a general charitableness of disposition, that their regret as evinced by the numbers of all ranks in & about Kandy who spontaneously attended the funeral and loudly lamented the loss they had sustained, we fully believe to be unfeigned and sincere.

The merits and exertions of Sir John D'Oyly as a public Servant, and principally as connected with the addition to His Majesty's Dominions of the larger part of this Island, have, our readers will know, been duly appreciated by the highest authorities. His Majesty's approbation was first conveyed in the Dispatch from the Secretary of State to Sir Robert Brownrigg published by the Government here on the 1st of June 1816 in the following words.

" I am also commanded particularly to express the sense which His Royal Highness

FIGURE 13 . . . his merit as a public servant

Two-page supplement to the *Ceylon Gazette* of 29 May 1824, containing an account of the death and funeral of Sir John D'Oyly. (Source: East Sussex Record Office, AMS 6185/13.)

SUPPLEMENT TO THE CEYLON GAZETTE.

SATURDAY MAY 29, 1824.

COLOMBO
29th May 1824.

The consequences of irregularity in the seasons and of the defect in the usual quantity of rain during last, and the early part of the present year, have been during the last two months, very severely felt as affecting the salubrity of the climate in most of the districts of the Island; especially those of Chilaw and the southern part of that of Colombo, the Four and the Seven Korles. The deaths from Fever have been in considerable numbers, as well among the native population as the European Troops, and we have to lament among them the loss of several Officers. The rains, to which we generally look at this season, as producing considerable and salutary changes in the temperature of the atmosphere, have not during this month been so heavy or continued as might have been wished; yet we have some reason to hope, that the severity of the sickness has passed.

DIED.] At Kandy on the 20th Instant at 1 o'clock A. M. of Remittent Fever caught on an Official Tour in the Seven Korles, The Honourable Sir JOHN D'OYLY Baronet, a Member of His Majesty's Council in Ceylon and Resident & First Commissioner of Government in the Kandyan Provinces.

His remains were removed from his late residence in the Palace for Interment in the Burial Ground of the Garrison on the morning of the 26th Inst. at 7 o'clock the troop of the Garrison lining the road from the Palace to the Burial Ground resting on their arms reversed, while Minute Guns were fired by the Royal Artillery in the Castle, as the Procession moved along in the following order.

The Korales & Aratchies of the Udaratte.

The Band of the Ceylon Regiment.

THE BODY,

Born by twelve European Soldiers of the 45th Regiment.

The Pall born by six Field Officers and Captains of the Garrison.

Chaplain The Rev. N. Garstin. Medical Attendant Surgeon Armstrong.

Lieut. Colonel L. Greenwell, S. Sawers, Esq. H. Wright, Esq. the Commissioners of the Board, as Chief Mourners.

Officers of the Garrison & Gentlemen of Kandy.

The Adigar of the Kandyan Provinces & Kandyan Chiefs.

Modliars, Nohandirams of the Residency, Clerks of the Public Offices, together with an immense concourse of Natives.

To all in Ceylon & every one in any way connected with this Island, no Eulogium on the character of Sir JOHN D'OYLY is necessary; and to those unacquainted with the deceased, Language must fail in conveying an adequate idea of his worth as a man & merit as a Public Servant?

His talents and acquirements were of the first order, and little doubt will be entertained on this head, when it is known that before he quitted Westminster he was particularly distinguished by the friendship of the late learned Head of that School, Dr. VINCENT, with whom we have heard he maintained a correspondence till the death of the Reverend Doctor: The honorable and high feelings which were conspicuous in Sir John D'OYLY's character, combined with an amiable gentleness of disposition, naturally produced a courteousness of manner which made his society much more desired by all who were acquainted with him, than the interviews and in the execution of his public duties would allow of their enjoying it; while the esteem and admiration of his countrymen and friends, were fully shared by the natives of every part of Ceylon in which his official functions had been displayed, and towards whom, authority was always exercised by the deceased, with such strict and patient justice, tempered with attention to all their wants, and a general charitableness of disposition, that their regret as evinced by the numbers of all ranks in & about Kandy who spontaneously attended the funeral and loudly lamented the loss they had sustained, we fully believe to be unfeigned and sincere.

The merits and exertions of Sir JOHN D'OYLY as a public Servant, and principally as connected with the addition to His Majesty's Dominions of the larger part of this Island, have, our readers will know, been duly appreciated by the highest authorities. His Majesty's approbation was first conveyed in the Dispatch from the Secretary of State to Sir ROBERT BROWNRIGG published by the Government here on the 1st of June 1816 in the following words.

"I am also commanded particularly to express the sense which His Royal Highness it; while the esteem and admiration of his countrymen and friends, were fully shared by the natives of every part of Ceylon in which his official functions had been displayed, and towards whom, authority was always exercised by the deceased, with such strict and patient justice, tempered with attention to all their wants, and a general charitableness of disposition, that their regret as evinced by the numbers of all ranks in & about Kandy who spontaneously attended the funeral and loudly lamented the loss they had sustained, we fully believe to be unfeigned and sincere.

The merits and exertions of Sir JOHN D'OYLY as a public Servant, and principally as connected with the addition to His Majesty's Dominions of the larger part of this Island, have, our readers will know, been duly appreciated by the highest authorities. His Majesty's approbation was first conveyed in the Dispatch from the Secretary of State to Sir ROBERT BROWNRIGG published by the Government here on the 1st of June 1816 in the following words.

'I am also commanded particularly to express the sense which His Royal Highness entertains of the conduct and services of Mr. D'OYLY upon the late occasion. To his intelligence in conducting the negociations, first with the Kandyan Government and latterly with the Adikars and others who opposed it, to his indefatigable activity in procuring information and in directing the Military Detachments, the complete success of the Enterprize is principally owing; and His Royal Highness avails himself with pleasure, of this opportunity of expressing, how greatly he appreciates, not only Mr D'OYLY's later Services, but those which he has at former periods by his attention to the Kandyan Department, rendered to the Colony and his Country.'

His Majesty's approval thus expressed, was afterwards followed by the elevation of the deceased to the dignity of a Baronet of the United Kingdom on the 27th July 1821. This title becomes extinct, as Sir JOHN died without heirs, never having been married.[12]

Every British ex-colony in Asia has its graveyards, cemeteries and British-built churches, where granite tombstones and marble plaques mark the resting-places of men and women who died in the service of the empire. Sri Lanka is no exception. On such memorials, often in a state of neglect and half-obscured by weeds and tall grasses, the dates inscribed indicate how numerous were the British people who died within a season or two of 'coming out East'.[13]

The visitor may find in such places some unexpected names: Jane Austen's younger brother, Charles Austen, for example, died at sea off the east coast of Ceylon, and is buried in the Naval Cemetery of the port of Trincomalee. When the present writers visited Rear-Admiral Austen's grave in 1964, it was surrounded by an ornate iron railing, presumably to distinguish even in death the occupant, a senior officer, from the lesser ranks who served under his command. When we saw the grave again, in 1979, the iron railing had disappeared, presumably to be used as fencing by some enterprising keeper of goats, of whom a number were amiably grazing among the gravestones.[14]

Two monuments may still be seen in Sri Lanka that were raised in memory of 'D'Oyly of Kandy', and of his unique contribution to the island's history. Set into the wall of St Peter's Church in the Fort of Colombo is a marble plaque framed in oak surmounted by John D'Oyly's coat of arms and the motto Thomas had chosen on his brother's behalf: OMNE SOLUM FORTI PATRIA. Beneath the coat of arms are the words:

> In Memory of the Honourable Sir John D'Oyly Bart., Resident of the Kandyan Provinces and one of the members of His Majesty's Council of this Island, whose meritorious services to this Government from the year 1802 and his talents during the Kandyan War stand recorded in the archives of this Government and in the Office of the Secretary of State for the Colonies. Born June 11th 1774, died at Kandy aged 49 years. He was the 2d son of the Revd. Mathias D'Oyly, late Archdeacon of Lewes in Sussex, and this Memorial is erected by his three surviving Brothers.

The same words are inscribed on the pediment of a granite obelisk that stands in the Garrison Cemetery in Kandy. This, too, was erected in their brother's memory by Thomas, George and Henry D'Oyly.[15] Royston Ellis provides a description of John D'Oyly's last resting-place, and its location at the heart of the royal city he captured in 1815 and ruled for eight difficult years:

FIGURE 14 Omne Solum Forti Patria

Marble tablet erected in memory of Sir John D'Oyly in St Peter's Church, Fort of Colombo, by Thomas, George and Henry D'Oyly. From a photograph by Mr Decker of Studio Times (Gooneratne Collection).

FIGURE 15 He rests at the heart of a royal city

Granite obelisk erected in memory of Sir John D'Oyly in the Garrison Cemetery at Kandy, by Thomas, George and Henry D'Oyly. From a photograph by G. Godamunne (Gooneratne Collection).

Situated between Malabar Street and the Udawattekela Forest Reserve up a short, steep climb along a lane to the left beyond Kandy's National Museum, is the Garrison Cemetery. Not mentioned in the guide books but known to British visitors (especially those from Scotland) for the history buried within its confines, the Garrison Cemetery contains the remains of many pioneers of British involvement in Sri Lanka . . .

This small plot of land of less than an acre in area was registered as a cemetery in 1822. Entrance is through a gate. The caretaker inhabits a granite, cell-like building which was formerly the Chapel of Rest where coffins were kept before burial. The peak year for burials was 1824 when there were 168.

On May 25 it will be 170 years since one of the most illustrious Britons ever to settle [in Sri Lanka] was buried in the cemetery. Sir John D'Oyly rose from being a clerk in the civil service of the British administration to Resident and First Commissioner of Kandy in 1816. He was fluent in Sinhala and widely respected for his integrity and compassion.[16]

Sir John D'Oyly's body was buried in Kandy's Garrison Cemetery on 26 May 1824, very far from England and Sussex in terms of distance, but very near in spirit to the Oxfordshire church where his ancestor 'the Noble Knight' Sir Cope D'Oyly lies beneath an inscription dated 1633 that might have served equally well for 'D'Oyly of Kandy':

Ask not who is buried here
Go ask the Commons, ask the Shire,
Go ask the Church, They'll tell thee who,
As well as blubber'd Eyes can do;
Go ask the Heralds, ask the Poor,
Thine Ears shall hear enough to ask no more.
Then if thine Eye bedew this sacred Urn,
Each drop a Pearl will turn
To adorn his Tomb, or if thou canst not vent,
Thou bringst more Marble to his Monument.[17]

CHAPTER TWELVE

OMNE SOLUM
FORTI PATRIA

· Doubtless [they] are seeking ardently, as all thinking men do seek, to solve this strange enigma of a nineteenth-century world, with such lights and helps as Europe and Asia respectively can afford for that purpose.

William Knighton, *Forest-Life in Ceylon*

It might be appropriate, having related the 'story' of John D'Oyly's life and career as accurately as the facts we have allow, to attempt to take stock of those qualities of character and personality which mark him – quite apart from the part he played in that crucial event in Sri Lanka's history, the fall of the Kandyan kingdom – as a subject worthy of biography. This is a delicate and difficult task for any biographer because, as E.F.C. Ludowyk noted in his account of 'this inscrutable Englishman',

On the surface he appears to have been – right throughout his career from North's time till his death in 1823 [*sic*] – nothing more than the conscientious official engrossed in his duties and interested in Kandyan institutions. He had gained the goodwill of some of the Kandyan chieftains and one of them entrusted his family to his care. He was assiduous in his letter-writing – to the chiefs, and to the Governor – but hardly anywhere does he betray anything more than the feelings of the good Civil Servant.[1]

All attempts to assess D'Oyly's character and his unique contribution to Sri Lanka's history must begin with his rapidly acquired proficiency in Sinhala. Many well-educated, indeed erudite, men served the empire in the nineteenth century, and Sri Lanka was fortunate in that a good many of them spent several years of their lives working in the island as civil servants, military men, physicians, educationists and engineers. But D'Oyly's speedy acquisition of Sinhala and his ability to use it in the practice of diplomatic negotiation set him apart from, and above, the majority of his colleagues. From the time of his arrival in Ceylon he devoted himself to acquiring an intimate knowledge of the Sinhala language, mastering it eventually to a degree which had seldom or never been attained by any European.[2]

From that knowledge flowed not only D'Oyly's understanding of, and sympathy for, the people he governed on behalf of the British Crown between 1816 and 1824, but his achievement as a British colonial officer and administrator.

> He acquired [wrote one near-contemporary commentator] extraordinary influence over the natives by the opinion which prevailed of his integrity and upright views in settling and adjusting their disputes, insomuch that there was no person in whose decision they were at all times more ready to acquiesce.[3]

That D'Oyly was patient, tactful, diplomatic, and as tenacious 'as Wealden clay' we have seen well demonstrated in the way he conducted, first, negotiations to secure the release and return of Major Davie, and then negotiations with the ambitious and increasingly desperate Ehelepola, *maha adikaram* of Kandy. Most European negotiators lacked the patience to cope with the etiquette of the Kandyan court, according to which visitors were often kept waiting several days before they were admitted to an audience, were required to approach the king and retire from his presence on their knees, and were sprinkled with perfumes or served with sweetmeats that might not have been always to their taste. D'Oyly set himself to learn what was required by Kandyan custom, and in his own practice and personal conduct he punctiliously observed the rules: when he was visited by the chiefs, for example, white cloths were placed over the chairs in accordance with Sinhalese tradition, a courtesy unfailingly shown by Sinhalese hosts to visitors of high status.[4]

D'Oyly's intelligence and shrewdness require no proof. Ludowyk has observed that when Ehelepola kept sounding him as to what the British would be prepared to do to put an end to what he termed the 'injustices' of the king, he found D'Oyly 'sphinxlike and as ambiguous as the Delphic oracle'.[5] That D'Oyly was also quick-witted and resourceful in support of his country's reputation may be judged from his reaction, described in Chapter 8, when he belatedly discovered, on the occasion of the restoration of the Buddha's Tooth Relic to the Dalada Maligava at Kandy, that gifts were customary from dignitaries taking part in the ceremony. Most other Europeans caught in such a situation might have privately dismissed it as trivial, made a polite excuse, and hoped that the error would be overlooked. Although new to the task of government, D'Oyly grasped the significance of the occasion to the Kandyans he had been appointed to rule. Although taken by surprise, he contrived to present an acceptable gift on behalf of the British government to the great satisfaction of all present.[6]

D'Oyly's loyalty to the British Crown shines through all his correspondence with Sinhalese leaders. Making clear to them at every turn that he was unwilling on any account to compromise British interests and the reputation of the Crown for honesty and fair dealing, he won, very early in his career, the confidence of numerous Kandyan chiefs and the friendship of members of the Buddhist *sangha*. Such friendship, established – despite the divisive effects of colonialism – across the lines of race and political opposition, cannot be achieved without a high degree of respect and courtesy on both sides.

D'Oyly's courteous treatment of the fallen King of Kandy, his refusal to allow the king's humiliation at the hands of his vengeful ministers, and his insistence that the King and the rest of the royal family should be 'decently' attired, and escorted to Colombo with all proper marks of respect paid that were due to their rank and status, suggest too that high-mindedness was a consistent and integral part of his character, and was not merely assumed by him for political advantage.

D'Oyly's personal qualities of generosity and humanity were well known, and can easily be substantiated. In an age in which brutality to servants and domestic slaves was common in British households throughout the colonies, Governor Maitland described D'Oyly as humane, presumably drawing this conclusion from his observations of the officer's transactions with the native population. Although his mother, Mrs Mary D'Oyly, continually urged him to save his salary in order to live a gentleman's life on his return to England, D'Oyly sent generous gifts to his nephews and other members of his family, and was found on his death to have supported out of his own pocket 115 'indigent natives' to whom his payments amounted to 163 Rix-dollars a month. These included the orphaned children of British soldiers such as Major Davie, who had died in active service in Ceylon, or who had left the island.[7]

Maureen Seneviratne has remarked on D'Oyly's unshakeable discretion on the subject of his personal life and his inner feelings.[8] He might well have been naturally shy: indeed, in Oliver Goldsmith's play *She Stoops to Conquer*, the playwright (who was D'Oyly's contemporary) calls shyness 'the Englishman's disease'.[9] The diary D'Oyly kept while at Cambridge suggests that he might also have been repressed, especially in regard to his relations with women. There is certainly no mention of any serious romantic involvement in either of D'Oyly's diaries.

The failure of an obsessive diarist (such as John D'Oyly undoubtedly was) to record any personal details about himself is certainly striking, and merits some discussion here. It is possible, of course, that records containing such details did exist, and were deliberately suppressed or destroyed, either by D'Oyly's family in England or by the government in Colombo. This could well have happened, especially if they seemed to provide evidence of sexual or political contact across lines of race, religion, class or gender that was too controversial or close to be officially approved of by an imperial British government. D'Oyly's friendships with members of the Buddhist clergy had already made him suspect in regard to religion.

A personal record might also betray a deeper stain, the unnameable (because regarded at the time as unnatural) 'flaw' of homosexuality: for the possibility has not, naturally, escaped us that D'Oyly might have been homosexual. Following his poetic idyll in Matara and the death of Gajaman Nona herself in the December of 1814, was the loneliness of the scholarly British Resident living in isolation among the Kandyan hills alleviated by the presence of a beautiful youth or two? British officials in the East appear to have frequently consoled themselves in this way.[10] It is only the complete absence of any kind of corroborative evidence that discourages speculation of the kind which might otherwise have been fuelled by D'Oyly's apparent lack of interest in women of his own, or any other, class or race.[11]

Homosexual leanings might also help to explain D'Oyly's reluctance, as described in 1810 by Sir James Mackintosh, to participate actively in the social life of the colony. If D'Oyly were homosexual, however, his family does not seem to have been aware of the fact, for his mother pleads that he should marry, and his brothers urge him to do the same with a view to keeping his baronetcy in the family.[12]

The 'taint' of homosexuality, whether actual or merely suspected, might also go some way to explaining the seeming prejudice against D'Oyly among his fellow Britishers. Despite Brownrigg's enthusiastic recommendations, we have observed (as did the D'Oyly family, with understandable annoyance) that D'Oyly's baronetcy took six years in coming to him. If, indeed, he was homosexual, D'Oyly was fortunate that the honour came at all: imperial prudery (or hypocrisy) on the subject of homosexuality has been known to have obstructed and even prevented promotion (especially to a ministerial post), earned dismissal from the service, and even led to suicide, however deserving or talented the officer involved in the case might have been.[13]

The possibility that D'Oyly was either homosexual or suspected of being so might also explain the curious negligence displayed towards him by Dr John Davy that we have described in Chapter 10: Davy appears to have been anxious to give his readers the impression that he hardly knew D'Oyly. Perhaps the good doctor was playing (very) safe and keeping virtuously clear of homosexual 'scum', in shrewd anticipation of Rudyard Kipling, who was to write some years later to his son John at Wellington:

> I wanted to tell you a lot of things about keeping clear of any chap who is ever suspected of beastliness. There is no limit to the trouble possible if one goes about (however innocently) with swine of that type. Give them the widest of berths. Whatever their merits may be in the athletic line they are at heart only sweeps and scum and all friendship or acquaintance with them ends in sorrow and disgrace.[14]

It is also notable that the monuments erected on D'Oyly's death were put up by his brothers, not by the British government, and that his personal letters have never been archived or published.

In the absence of hard fact, however, all the possibilities listed or recapitulated above must remain speculation. The scraps of gossip about

D'Oyly that have survived focus, as we have seen, on a possible heterosexual relationship in his youth, on his 'orientalist' reclusiveness, and on his interest in Buddhism. They are not based on rumours of homosexual activity. We can hardly doubt that the British community in Sri Lanka would have seized gleefully on such rumours, had they existed.[15]

Even Brownrigg's despatches to Lord Bathurst following the Kandyan War of 1818, which are filled with complaints regarding D'Oyly, do not include references to sexual impropriety. We regard it as much more likely that Davy's failure to give adequate recognition to D'Oyly in his book stemmed from reluctance on the part of Governor Brownrigg's personal physician to be associated with an official whose sympathy for exotic and 'oriental' habits of living, and friendships with rebel Kandyan chieftains, had placed his patriotism in doubt, and who had, by 1818, fallen out of favour with Brownrigg himself.

Many questions remain, besides those relating to D'Oyly's sexuality, the answers to which we shall probably never know. Was he sincere when he promised the Kandyan chiefs that the royal regalia they entrusted to his safe-keeping would never be sold or even exposed to unworthy eyes? Was that promise given in good faith? What were his feelings when his promise was overridden by the British government, and the regalia auctioned in London in 1820? Was he disillusioned with empire? Or merely disappointed?

Why did D'Oyly never return to England? Could one reason have been that he knew he would never again fit comfortably into English society? There is no doubt that by immersing himself in 'oriental' ways of living and thinking, D'Oyly had made himself into an individual who would have been regarded in the England of his day as eccentric, un-English, an oddity. From an early period of his career in Sri Lanka (possibly from the time he came into close contact with his tutor, the Venerable Karatota, and observed the inner life of a temple), D'Oyly had become increasingly austere and simple in his habits and dress. As Resident in Kandy, it would have been easy for him to continue in this chosen way of life, perhaps adopting the customs of the Kandyan Buddhists in preferring a vegetarian diet.

But England in the early nineteenth century was a country in which, despite occasional crazes for *chinoiserie* and other oriental exotica, even tropical orchids and un-British cacti could displease many, and a liking for the exotic could be regarded as corrupt.[16] Mrs Mary D'Oyly could not understand why her son, having served his time in Ceylon, did not return home, to dwell amidst English comforts in health and prosperity, removing himself permanently from the dangers posed by tropical diseases and treacherous natives. Eventually even she seems to have resigned herself to an unwilling acceptance of the fact that her son had been profoundly changed by his life 'on Ceylon'. He *wanted* to stay on.

'It is a drawback in the Colonial Service,' Thomas Skinner was later to observe, 'that an officer is tempted and beguiled to remain on, from year to year, until his interest in a new country, in which he is made useful, overcomes the ardour of his zeal for his profession.'[17] Skinner could have been, and perhaps was, thinking of John D'Oyly as well as of himself when he wrote those words, the fruit of fifty years' experience in Ceylon. Mary D'Oyly would have heartily agreed. If premature death had not closed her son's innings after 22 years in the island, it is not unlikely that he would have equalled or outstripped Skinner's record half-century.

It is pleasant to contemplate the possibility – indeed, the likelihood – that D'Oyly not only had heard the East a-calling, but had become deeply attached to the island and its people. Most of his fellow colonialists would not have believed such a possibility, nor would they have shared his feelings. 'You cannot convince an English settler,' wrote Sir Samuel Baker, who established a little English colony in the hill country of Nuwara Eliya before moving on to Africa to explore the upper reaches of the Nile,

> that he will be abroad for an indefinite number of years . . . With his mind ever fixed upon his return, he does nothing for posterity in the colony. He rarely even plants a fruit-tree, hoping that his stay will not allow him to gather from it.[18]

It is possible, too, that in D'Oyly's devotion to Ceylon, a particular attachment to the environs of Kandy may have played a considerable part. No one who has lived there for any length of time could help speculating a little on that subject. Did he entertain any aesthetic feelings about the wooded glories of the Kandyan landscape, comparing it, for instance, to 'the forests and woodlands of Hampshire and Sussex' of which William Cobbett writes so vividly in *Rural Rides*?[19] D'Oyly grew up in the legend-haunted landscape of Sussex. Kipling in *Puck of Pook's Hill* evokes a Sussex countryside which calls up the English spirit of the earth, and Sussex legends which feature magic tokens such as leaves from ancient indigenous trees, oak, thorn and ash.[20] The Kandyan country was, and still is, rich in such ancient legends and beliefs.

Some interesting examples of the kind of information, part fact, part legend, that came the way of British government agents such as D'Oyly in the course of their everyday duties in rural districts of Sri Lanka have been unearthed by Wilfrid Jayasuriya in the diaries and official log-books that these officials kept of their travels 'on circuit'. Jayasuriya has found that the diaries kept by government agents in the Ratnapura district provide 'a record of the insights that the old administrators developed about the past and the future'.

> I was very glad to go out again to inspect the site of the old Kandyan dam across the Walaweganga and the old channel . . . Tradition seems [notes one government agent] that 700 Amunams were irrigated on each side of the river from this [old channel] in ancient times.

Jayasuriya notes that the 'tradition' referred to by the government agent quoted above is the legend recorded in Sinhala folktale of the Neelamaha Yodaya (the legendary Giant of Neelamaha) who had irrigated the Uggalkaltota paddy fields and made a heap of the paddy harvest so high that, standing on it, he could see the sea. But on the instruction of his avaricious wife who wanted her husband to perform still greater feats of irrigation and cultivation, their son had complained that the sea could not be seen from the top of the heap. Enraged, the Neelamaha Yodaya had kicked the heap of paddy and broken the ancient anicut across the river. After that, according to legend, the land lay bare and barren.[21]

Another legend recorded by a government agent and noted by Jayasuriya is that of the 'Porch of Penitence' at Kurunegala. Overlooking the Kaltota plain is the Kurunegala shrine which is sacred to Muslims as the resting place of a saint who had come there to seek solace in meditation and find the gateway to eternity. The government agent commented:

> The place has been sacred for ages, and owes its original sanctity perhaps to its singular character and its suitability as a place of

meditation . . . The story is that at Pataliputra, which is, if I remember right, one of the many ancient cities in the neighbourhood of Delhi, he first tried in vain to seduce the wife of a holy man; then violated her and murdered her husband. She was pregnant and bore in due course a son who when he came of age vowed to avenge his father. The murderer meanwhile had repented of his crimes and taken up his abode in Kurunegala. Here the avenger came upon him at night and after a desperate struggle killed him and disappeared. In the morning the curious who climbed the hill to satisfy themselves as to the cause of the hideous noises heard by them overnight found nothing but a heap of ashes, the smouldering remains of the hermit . . . The Mohammedans say that if our eyes were morally clear we should see in this rock and its cavernous shaft and galleries the gateways of heaven and hell.[22]

His prolonged residence in a landscape instinct with such legends as these meant that D'Oyly, brought up on the ideas of the sublime, the beautiful and the picturesque popularized by Edmund Burke and William Gilpin, could hardly have failed to encounter in the central hills of Ceylon splendid examples of the 'sublime' as beauty tinged with terror.[23] Nature certainly cannot be seen in the Kandyan provinces as 'a prettily arranged prospect, subject to man's domination'.[24] What the vocabulary of English aesthetics described as a 'wilderness', a 'heath', a 'thicket', or a 'dell', sublime in their combination of the delightful with the 'horrid', the 'vast' and the 'obscure', even what was to be found in the rugged magnificence of Scotland as described by Sir Walter Scott, would have seemed to D'Oyly's eyes like the orderly arrangements of an eighteenth-century quincunx in a country-house garden when compared with the wild sublimity of Sri Lanka's mountain landscape, replete with mystery and myth.

The beauty and stillness of the 'wilderness' around Kandy would have made, in addition, a clear contrast with the industrializing Britain that the country-bred D'Oyly had left. Foliage, morning mists, ravines, torrents, the fields, the people in their tidy villages were to impress and deeply move Dr John Davy, another observer at the same period. Kandy was whole, it was healthy. By contrast, the England William Blake knew and wrote of must have seemed increasingly unattractive. At the same time Kandy provided a background of haunting beauty against which had been recently projected certain sordid and macabre events, the details of which none knew better than D'Oyly himself. There could have developed in his mind the idea, attractive to an Archdeacon's son, that he might be of some use, of some purpose to humankind, by continuing to serve in Kandy.

In 'Alastor, or, The Spirit of Solitude', which Shelley composed near Windsor Park in the autumn of 1815, and published in March 1816 as the title-piece of a volume of poems, the hero is presented as wandering the world, traversing all kinds of landscapes, among them some which strikingly resemble those which, during his travels in the interior of Sri Lanka, became intimately known to D'Oyly:

> On every side now rose
> Rocks, which, in unimaginable forms,
> Lifted their black and barren pinnacles
> In the light of evening, and its precipice
> Obscuring the ravine, disclosed above,
> Mid toppling stones, black gulfs and yawning caves,
> Whose windings gave ten thousand varying tongues
> To the loud stream. Lo! where the pass expands
> Its stony jaws, the abrupt mountain breaks,
> And seems, with its accumulated crags,
> To overhang the world . . .

Plunged unexpectedly into intimate contact with oriental culture and aesthetics during the years he spent in Sri Lanka, did D'Oyly perceive 'among the ruined temples there / Stupendous columns, and wild images / Of more than man', what Shelley terms 'the thrilling secrets of the birth of time'?[25] Did he come near to entering, as did the government agent of a later day, 'the gateways of heaven and hell'? We do not learn from his diaries that D'Oyly was overly imaginative, or that he had any artistic inclinations, but an education in aesthetics was an essential part of the training usual among men and women of his class and background.

Finally, how did D'Oyly perceive his own role in the administration of the island? We know that he was a loyal servant of the Crown, and that he placed his country's interests before his own or the interests of any other individual. But was he tempted, even momentarily, to stretch his powers as Resident to the point at which he could play the *Raja-Deviyo* (God-King)? The established customs of the country encouraged, indeed at times even required him to do so.

Leonard Woolf, a British civil servant of a later date who served in Ceylon from 1904 to 1911, wrote of his first official encounter with the Sinhalese people of the Kandyan hill country as an 'extraordinary' experience:

> The headman & villagers met me in procession ½ a mile from the village & brought me in with tom-toms & dancers. Then . . . each member of the crowd came & prostrated himself or herself & touched the ground with his forehead.[26]

What Woolf regarded as 'extraordinary' because in his eyes it resembled an act of religious worship was simply a sign of veneration: he was being treated with the respect that was traditionally accorded to a Kandyan chief. D'Oyly would have received precisely similar honours wherever he went in the Kandyan country. It was part of a Resident's or government agent's role as inheritor of the chieftain's office that he should respond to such courtesies with at least equal grace.

Several interpretations are possible of D'Oyly's grant of an entire village in the Southern Province to the poet Gajaman (if, indeed, he made such a grant).[27] He could have been carrying out his duties as an agent of revenue at Matara empowered to make good injustices perpetrated by the previous (Dutch) regime against the people. He could also be seen as adapting to a colonial situation the famous advice offered in the sixteenth century by Niccolo Machiavelli that a prince who wished to gain reputation should 'show himself a lover of merit, give preferment to the able, and honour those who excel in every art'.[28] Finally, the role of a noble patron of the arts would have neatly combined traditions established by D'Oyly's own aristocratic ancestors with the time-honoured and well-known practice of Sinhalese kings.

Wilfrid Jayasuriya makes a point that illuminates not only D'Oyly's perceptive understanding of the status attached to his position as British Resident in the Kandyan provinces, but his capacity to enter with imagination and sympathy into the duties and responsibilities of a chief of chieftains:

The Government Agent of Sabaragamuwa Province was expected to climb Sri Pada once a year during the pilgrim season and see for himself that the route was well preserved and the pilgrims well looked after. From the times of [King] Nissanka Malla it had been a function of the rulers to look to their welfare in this respect. *The Government Agent by performing this annual pilgrimage not only asserted the right of the British sovereign to succeed to the power of the Sinhalese kingdom. In his own locality where he was all-powerful he asserted his right of succession to the Kandyan adigars who had preceded him.*[29]

The narrative of empire had been constructed in terms of uniformity. The view of most Colonial Secretaries was that a more objective (and therefore more enlightened) view could be had of any colonial problem from the metropolitan centre of Westminster, than from the men on the spot. The building of government residences, the establishment of rules regarding protocol, the drawing up of laws and constitutions were all done with the empire as a whole in mind, rather than a particular or distinctive part of it.

This was, of course, an approach natural to an age which believed, with Pope, that beauty and order lay, not in particular parts but in a unified whole.

When John D'Oyly began his enquiries into the customary laws of the Kandyan kingdom, the chances are that he began with the intention of uncovering a solid structure, on the basis of which the society that had produced it could be more efficiently and knowledgeably governed. But there might well have been another motive, one of which D'Oyly himself may have not been consciously aware: that of preserving for the future, uncorrupted by time and human error, a unique society in the form that the British had found it.

Which motive preceded which? D'Oyly, conservative by nature and training, with friends among the chiefs, would probably have inclined towards the second. His own poem 'Commercii Laus' had looked forward with youthful confidence to the time when, after a period of trial and suffering,

a reign of Saturn will return with happy auspices; when Peace, firmly settled for all living creatures, will have brought happiness to their cultured generations and, arms set aside, a golden race will inhabit the earth.

Perhaps his *Sketch of the Constitution of the Kandyan Kingdom* was viewed by D'Oyly as a means of bringing about in Sri Lanka that hoped-for return to a golden age.

The Kandyan War of 1818 effectively dashed such hopes, if, indeed, he had entertained them. The value to his masters of the manuscript and notes he left behind him would rest in what it could teach them of ways in which the chieftains' powers could be pruned and their influence reduced, so that no rebellion like that of 1818 would ever recur in any part of the island. When D'Oyly died in 1824, there died with him all attempts to resist change.

To Dr John Davy, riding through the devastated Uva Province in 1818, it came as a profound shock to realize that the colonial experience, which was believed in his own time and D'Oyly's to be the agent of universal improvement and modernization, could damage and destroy. Englishmen who had not served overseas and witnessed 'empire' in action could never, probably, have regarded imperial activity as anything but beneficial to the non-English societies which superior British arms had welded into a whole. And even an individual as intelligent and uniquely sensitive as John D'Oyly could not possibly have shared in his own lifetime the post-colonial outlook of a modern Welsh poet such as R.S. Thomas, who meditates in 'Reservoirs' on the destruction by imperialists of a subject nation's culture:

> There are places in Wales I don't go
> Reservoirs that are the subconscious of a people . . .
> There are the hills,
> Too; gardens gone under the scum
> Of the forests; and the smashed faces
> Of the farms with the stone trickle
> Of the tears down the hills' side.
>
> Where can I go, then, from the smell
> Of decay, from the putrefying of a dead
> Nation? I have walked the shore
> For an hour and seen the English
> Scavenging among the remains
> Of our culture, covering the sand
> Like the tide and, with the roughness
> Of the tide, elbowing our language
> Into the grave that we have dug for it.[30]

It is certainly possible – and indeed, the personal decisions that he was to take in the later years of his career are firm evidence of it – that, in one way or another, as a result of his experience in Sri Lanka, D'Oyly's mind and spirit grew beyond the confines of his education and training.

Is this a true assessment? Is it possible to stop in mid-career, reconsider one's position, and move, without compromising oneself or betraying others, in a completely different direction? A hundred years later, another sensitive and erudite Englishman of a background and education similar to D'Oyly's, Leonard Woolf, served the British Crown for seven years (1904–1911) as an agent of government. He too, like D'Oyly, developed a close relationship with the island:

> I fell in love with the country, the people, and the way of life which were entirely different from everything in London and Cambridge to which I had been born and bred . . . I did not idealize or romanticize the people or the country; I just liked them aesthetically and humanly and socially . . . I became completely immersed, not only in my work, but in the life of the people.[31]

But at the end of his first term of office, Woolf returned to England, and resigned from the colonial service. He had made up his mind that imperialism was not for him.[32] It is evident that the empire, what it stood for, and what it was doing in the colonies had changed so much over a hundred years that Woolf preferred to distance himself from it.

Such a decision D'Oyly either could not contemplate, or was prevented from taking by his premature death in 1824. He remained to the end of his life an enigma to his family, to his colleagues, and to his numerous beneficiaries. For readers who encounter him in the post-colonial years of the twentieth century, that enigmatic quality remains, resisting explanation on any but the most extraordinary terms.

For us, as his biographers, he remains 'this inscrutable Englishman', an example unique even to the Raj which bred so many remarkable men, of an individual intensively trained in the outlook of his age and the ambitions of his class, educated in the political and material aims of nineteenth-century imperial England, who maintained to the end a life of dedicated service to the people he had been appointed to rule.

APPENDIX 1

Lineage of Sir John D'Oyly, Baronet, as set out in Burke's *Extinct and Dormant Baronetcies of England, Ireland, and Scotland* (1841), p. 167:

Thomas D'Oyly, D.D. (descended from Edward D'Oyly, Esq., of Littlemarsh, in the parish of Stone, Bucks), Archdeacon of Lewes, in Sussex, Chancellor of the diocese of Chichester, and prebendary of Ely, m. February 1744 Henrietta-Maria, second daughter of Robert Godfrey, Esq. of London (by Elizabeth, sister of Mathias Mawson, Bishop of Ely). They both died on the same day, 27th January, 1770, leaving issue three sons,

    I. MATTHIAS, of whom hereafter,

    II. Thomas, vicar of Walton-upon-Thames, and chaplain-in-ordinary to the king, b. 2nd April 1745, m. March 1772, Susanna, daughter of Barham Rushbrooke, Esq. of Westowe, county of Suffolk, and died October 1816, without issue,

    III. Francis, lieut.-general and colonel of the 67th foot, married Anne, daughter of Hugh Thomas, D.D., Dean of Ely, and Master of Christ's College, Cambridge, and died in 1803, without issue.

The eldest son,

REV. MATTHIAS D'OYLY, rector of Uckfield, in Sussex, Archdeacon of Lewes, and prebendary of Ely, born 23rd November 1743, married Mary, daughter of George Poughfer, Esq. of Leicester, and died November 1815, having had issue,

    i. Thomas, D.C.L. and sergeant-at-law, born 16th November 1772, married 4th January 1820, Elizabeth, daughter of the Rev. Nicholas Simons, of Canterbury, and has one son, Thomas.

    ii. John, of whom presently.

    iii. Francis (Sir), K.C.B., lieut.-colonel in the 1st Guards, slain at Waterloo, unmarried.

iv. George, D.D., rector of Lambeth and of Sundridge, born 31st October 1778, married 9th August 1813, Maria-Frances, daughter of William Bruene, Esq. of London, and has issue,

Francis, born 27th November 1815,

George-Henry, born 27th June 1817,

Henry-Thomas, born 3rd April 1819,

Charles-John, born 31st July, 1820.

v. Henry, captain in the 1st Guards, born 21st April 1780.

vi. Henrietta, died unmarried 1804.

The second son, **SIR JOHN D'OYLY**, official Resident at Kandy, in the island of Ceylon, b. 6th June 1774, was created a baronet in 1821, but dying unm. in three years after, the title became EXTINCT.

Arms: Or, two fleurs-de-lis in bend, sable, between as many bendlets, azure.

APPENDIX 2

The Latin ode by John D'Oyly which obtained for him the Sir William Browne's Medal in 1795, as preserved at the Registry, University of Cambridge:

Commercii Laus

En! Sol laborans lampadis aureae
Celavit ignes – Conscia luridos
     Fert Luna vultus, et micanti
          Astra ruunt labefacta caelo!

Heu! signa luctus! – Vidimus impias
Saevire caedes: Terra tumultibus
     Belloque devastata Reges
          Terruit attonitasque gentes;

Ne nos nocentes tristia saecula
Damni et timoris plena reviserent,
    Cum turba foedis Barbarorum
        Mersa diu tenebris jaceret;

Cum saeva nondum foedere mutuo
Pacis coissent pectora, cum scelus
    Interque bellorum rapinas
        Jura, Fides, Pietas silerent:

Tunc omne Nautis aequor inhospitum
Infesta passim littora, et accolis
    Non tuta Tellus. Nunc sed Artes,
        Musa, refer melioris aevi,

Ex quo in marinas caesa jugis aquas
Descendit Arbor, Tiphyos et manum
    Experta Rectoris, liquentes
        Ausa vias homini negatas,

Portansque robur Pubis Achaicae,
Cum parta magno vellera poscerent
    Phryxaea, per rupes et atras
        Vorticibus volitavit undas.

Post haec relictis Navita fortior
In vasta ripis prosiluit freta,
    Aususque Neptunum polumque
        Nil nisi sidereum tueri;

Vosque O! benignum Tyndaridae vagis
Numen carinis, sollicita invocans
    In vota, non Austri furorem
        Extimuit celeresve nimbos.

Hinc illa fructus gens didicit novos,
Aurumque et usus repperit, hinc sinu
    Quascunque foecundo teneret
        Colchis opes, Priamique regna.

At te, O Dearum Diva Scientia,
Mater bonarum nobilis Artium,
    Qua parte terrarum, vel ex quo
        Fonte canam potuisse nasci?

Sive in remotae finibus Indiae
Ortam, recepit frugiferis agris,
    Seu terra Memphitis vetusto
        Indigenam tulit ipsa Nilo,

Omnes ad oras hinc tibi pervii
Reclusa porta est Oceani: Procul
    Ablata ventorum volasti
        Praepetibus super alta pennis,

Divina circum spargere lumina
Quaerens vel agros divitis Inachi,
    Vel regna Phoenices, adustas
        Flamma velut populans aristas –

Tu prima onustis classibus enites
Spectanda Sidon. O! Tyros Urbium
    Regina, an ex omni per orbem
        Ultimum opes Oriente dicam

Mercesque missas? Heu! nimium tuis
Confisa demens divitiis, ruis,
    Tactaeque divino superbae
        Fulmine procubuere turres!

Majorne prisci gloria nominis
Deflendae an Urbis casus erat? – Tamen
    Te magna Carthago recisam
        Filia candidior parentem

Siccis renasci jussit in Africae
Campis, gubernans aequora navibus
    Impleta; dum Victrix crematas
        Roma ferox spoliarit Arces,

Unumque junctis gentibus in sinum
Diversa terrae dona coegerit,
    Forti, sed haud aequo per omnem
        Imperio dominata mundum –

Nos, multa duxit quae melior dies,
Cessamus ultro muneribus frui?
    Queis, quicquid humanos in usus
        Attalicae Cypriaeque merces

Donent, quot herbas utraque sidere
Ridens sub almo proferat India,
      Portus in optatos Sorores
            Aequoreae Zephyrique mittunt.

Gaudete Gentes! – Ni furor hosticus
Bellique tantam spem rabies vetent,
      Mox regna Saturni secundis
            Auspiciis reditura cerno;

Cum fixa cunctis Pax animalibus
Mollita cultu saecla beaverit,
      Armisque securum repostis
            Aurea gens habitabit orbem.

O! laeta Tellus, si sua noscerent
Humana recte gens bona! – Purior
      Tu, casta Libertas, novemque
            Phoebe, venis, comitate Musis.

Doctrina ab omni littore navibus
Advecta, vivos hic latices Dea
      Dicavit, hic Praeses colendas
            Supplicibus, sibi legit Arces:

Quales in alti culmina Pieri
Nascuntur, ipsis nubibus aemulae,
      Clivosque convallesque pinus
            Suppositos foliis obumbrant,

Qualis sacratas Aonidum specus
Rivo sonanti praefluit, et tuos,
      Parnasse, secessus amoenos
            Castalii rigat unda fontis.

Mortalis illas Mens licet excolat,
Has cura magni servet Apollinis,
      Non vestra concedet vetusto
            Pieridum Domus Alma luco –

Source: P.E. Pieris (ed.) *Letters to Ceylon*, pp. 136–8.

The following note on the young poet's performance has been kindly provided by Professor J.J. Nicholls, together with a literal translation of D'Oyly's 'Ode':

> The first five stanzas are a conventional account (like that in *Lucretius* Book V) of the supposed early brutish state of mankind; stanzas 6 and 7 refer to the Argonauts (Tiphys was their helmsman), then follow stanzas devoted to the development of trade, from Phoenicia to Carthage and finally Rome. In stanzas 20–21 the 'Sea Sisters' may be supposed to be sea nymphs. Stanzas 25 to the end are allusive. The towers and the living springs consecrated here by Learning probably refer to Academe, and more particularly to Cambridge.
>
> The metre is Alcaic, as Horace used it, and is handled with great skill.

IN PRAISE OF TRADE

Lo! the waning sun has hidden the fires of his golden torch – his accomplice moon shows her wan ghostly face and the stars in flight rush down the flickering sky!

Alas! signs of grief! we have seen foul slaughter rage: Earth devastated by tumult and war has brought terror to princes and affrighted peoples;

may we not suffer again the gloomy centuries filled with loss and fear when the horde of Barbarians lay sunk in shameful darkness;

when our savage hearts had not yet come together in a common bond of Peace, and when, amidst wrongdoing and the rapine of war, Justice, Good Faith and Piety went unheard.

In those days every sea was unwelcoming to sailors, everywhere were hostile shores and the earth was not safe for settlers. But now, O Muse, bring back the arts of a happier age,

from the time when the tree, cut down on mountain ridges, came down into the waters of the sea and, submitting to the hand of helmsman Tiphys, braved watery paths forbidden to man,

bearing the flower of the youth of Achaia, when they sought the fleece of Phryxus, won at great price, and flew between rocky crags and through waters black with whirlpools.

After these days the sailor, with greater boldness, leaped out into the expanses of the sea, forsaking the shores of the land, braving Neptune and daring to heed nothing but the Pole Star;

and You, O children of Tyndareus, gods of comfort to wandering ships. Calling on you in his troubled prayers, he had no fear of the fury of the south wind or of the scudding rain clouds.

From this activity that race of men learned new products, discovered gold and the uses of gold; from this activity they discovered all the wealth that Colchis, and Priam's kingdom held in its teeming bosom.

But you, O Knowledge, divine one amongst goddesses, noble mother of the worthy arts, in what part of the lands, from what source shall I sing that you were born?

Whether the earth received you in her fertile fields after a birth in the confines of distant India, or whether Egypt's land bore you, a native daughter near the ancient Nile,

in every direction, from your birth, the portals of Ocean, now ready for you to travel, were thrown open to you: carried far on high you flew on the swift wings of the wind,

seeking everywhere to scatter divine lights or the fields of rich Inachus or the kingdoms of Phoenicia, like a flame ravaging parched ears of corn –

You, splendid Sidon, were the first to gain eminence from your loaded argosies. O! Tyre, queen of cities, or am I rather to say that wealth and merchandise were sent throughout the farthest parts of the world from all the cities of the East?

Alas! trusting, in your madness, too much to your own wealth, you are come to ruin, your proud towers have fallen, struck by the god's thunderbolt!

Is the glory of your former name or the destruction of your city the greater cause for grief? Still mighty Carthage, a daughter more fair, bade her stricken parent to come to new birth on the arid plains of Africa, ruling seas filled with ships; until fierce, victorious Rome burnt and destroyed her towers

and, by uniting the nations, gathered the diverse blessings of the earth into one embrace, lording it over the whole world with a powerful, but unjust sway. –

But we, why are we reluctant to enjoy the many good things which a better age has produced? For to us the Sea Sisters and the West Winds bring into harbours of our choice whatever merchandise Pergamene and Cypriote offer for mankind's use, all the spices that both Indies produce beneath their kindly skies.

Rejoice, ye nations! unless the fury of an enemy or the madness of war forbid such high hopes, I see that soon a reign of Saturn will return with happy auspices; when Peace, firmly settled for all living creatures, will have brought happiness to their cultured generations and, arms set aside, a golden race will inhabit the earth.

O! happy Earth, if mankind rightly recognizes its blessings, You, chaste Liberty and you, Phoebus, accompanied by the nine Muses, come in a purer light.

The Goddess Learning, brought in by sea from every shore, has consecrated here her living springs, here, as presiding spirit she has chosen for herself towers to be tended by her suppliants,

towers such as come into being on the peaks of lofty Pierus, rivalling the very clouds, and pine trees cast a shadow over slopes and valleys under a canopy of leaves,

like the sacred caves of the Muses which the waters of the Castalian spring lave with melodious flood, and lave too, O Parnassus, your pleasant nooks.

The mind of man may tend these towers; the forethought of mighty Apollo may preserve them; your nurturing House will not yield place to the ancient grove of the Muses.

APPENDIX 3

The royal regalia of Kandy

P.E. Pieris (*Tri Sinhala*, p. 130) prints a letter from John D'Oyly to Sir Robert Brownrigg, dated Kandy, 2 November 1816:

Kandy, Nov. 2nd, 1816.

My dear Sir,

I have much satisfaction in acquainting Your Excellency that the unrecovered Regalia are safely delivered into my possession.

Ehelepola to whom I sent a message on Wednesday, excused himself that day on account of sickness and attended yesterday. He informed me that the articles had been brought, and that the Dissave of Uva would wait upon me with them in the evening. He added that certain persons had ruined them by calumnies in the King's time and would do so now, if it were not for the goodness of the officers in authority, who do not give credit to them without inquiring nor act precipitately, that he is guilty of no infidelity towards the English Government, and that I should learn further from the Dissave of Uva.

The Dissave of Uva came late in the evening with the following articles . . .

A Sword with Gold hilt studded with small red stones and a diamond at the end.

Sheath of wood covered with blue velvet very much worn, with some Gold work.

Red velvet band with Gold embroidery.

Three cloths enfolding it.

A Gold four-cornered Cap or Crown with carved work at top. The four faces and four corners studded with stones, principally red – a few emeralds and blue sapphires. The centre ruby is fallen from one face, but in the box.

A large brocade cloth.

A Gold crest or top-knot.

A four-cornered black beaver hat, Gold laced, surmounted with white feather all round the brim.

Two cloths.

The Dissave in answer to my enquiry after the band or belt studded with precious stones which is said to belong to the Sword, stated that the band was not in the box, that there were 11 or 12 *peti* or plates set with precious stones, which are sometimes attached to the band, but sometimes not, and those plates he believed were amongst the valuables delivered up by Ehelepola to Your Excellency. He stated further that these Regalia were found deposited in a case in the forest between Uva and Kotmale, and were under the charge of Agale Kumbure Sattamby, who was half inclined not to produce them, and the Dissave discovered them by means of other persons.

The Dissave renewed his expressions of fidelity to the British Government on the part of Ehelepola and himself and stated their request that the Regalia which they hold in great respect, should not be exposed to sale or exhibited to common persons, or to those Chiefs who under the King's Government were never admitted to see them. I promised that they would not be exposed to sale and in general terms that they should be treated with every respect by the British Government.

I propose with Your Excellency's permission to notify to the Kandyan Chiefs the recovery of these valuables and assure them that the Government is well aware of the high honour and estimation in which they are held by the Nation, and that having become the property of the king of Great Britain, they will be preserved with the same respect as the Regalia of the British Crown.

I have, etc.,
J. D'Oyly.

P.E. Pieris (*Tri Sinhala*, p. 131) prints an extract from *The Gazette* of 13 November 1816, as follows:

It is not we believe known to our readers that the ancient Royal Crown and Sword of State of the Kandyan Government had until lately remained secreted and that every endeavour to recover them had long proved ineffectual. A Golden Crown was indeed found and a Sword mounted with Gold, but neither proved to be of the Regalia used on occasions of public solemnity. The latter were held by the Priests, Chiefs and people in great veneration and considered as symbolical of the Sovereign Power. We have therefore much pleasure in stating that the zeal and fidelity of certain Chiefs have by much pains and enquiry discovered the place in which these Insignia were concealed and that they are now safe in the possession of the Resident.

On 3 March 1818, Ehelepola Maha Nilame was arrested.

P.E. Pieris (*Tri Sinhala*, pp. 131–3), prints Brownrigg's Despatch 299 of 24 July 1818. CO 54/71.

In addition to the above are articles mentioned in the enclosed list which on the day subsequent to Ehelepola Maha Nilame's arrest (3rd March 1818) were taken by the guard at Gonarua Ferry on a person of his establishment, attempting to carry them into the Four Korles for concealment. This circumstance naturally attracted suspicion and they were detained in the treasury here and lately exhibited to the First Adikar (Molligoda) who declared they were jewels which with the exception of those numbered 4 in the list, no wife of a subject could possess or wear, and that they were the Queen's jewels which had been long searched for in vain. Their value I have no means of judging of but should estimate them at about 2,000 pounds. In Ehelepola's baggage which was sent from this the day after his arrest was a large assortment of most valuable jewels which he was in the habit of wearing since the establishment of the British Government, although the greater part never, according to the Customs of the country, could have been exhibited by him during the former administration of the deposed King.

Annexed . . .

A list of property belonging to Ehelylepola [*sic*] Maha Nilame taken from Pehenne Rala who was removing the same by desire of Henwittiponne Mohottala to conceal in the Four Korles.

1. 1 ornament consisting of 25 Gold Balls strung on black cord and ended by one large Gold tassel cup and three small do. Weighing 100 pagodas, at rxd 6½ a pagoa, rxd. 650.

2. 1 ornament consisting of 25 balls, 1 large tassel cup and 4 small. 75 Star pagodas at 7 rxd . . . 525.

3. 1 necklace of large coral and Gold beads of 25 each, 1 necklace, smaller, 21 Gold and 22 coral, 1 necklace, smaller, 19 Gold and 20 coral. Total weight 175 pagodas at 7 rxd . . . 1,400.

4. 1 necklace of 27 Gold beads, 1 Gold worked chain, weight 52 pagodas at — rxd . . . 312.

5. 1 pair bird bracelets richly set with rubies, 5 rose diamonds and 2 small emeralds in each . . . rxd. 2,500.

[216] 6. 1 pair of three-ribbed Gold bracelets richly set with emeralds and rubies and 3 table diamonds to each . . . 1,000.

7. 1 pair of serpentine Gold lights with clasps set with emeralds, rubies, catseyes, etc. . . . 750.

8. 1 necklace of Gold beads and pearls, four rows, pearls about size of a peppercorn, 1 necklace of Gold beads and pearls. Value rxd. 2,500.

9. 2 rich head ornaments representing the sun and moon entirely studded with rubies, emeralds, table diamonds and pearls, 2 rich head ornaments but much smaller and inferior in value. Value rxd 1,000.

10. 1 rich bandeau for the head richly studded with rubies and a few table diamonds and emeralds and pearls . . . 600.

11. 1 armlet set with rubies, emeralds and few diamonds . . . 350.

12. A necklace consisting of a string of small Gold beads ending in 4 large Gold and coral beads and a small Pedegam consisting of rubies and rose diamonds. A necklace of glass beads and Gold (20) beads set with rubies.

13. 13 coral and 1 Gold bead . . . rxd. 50.

14. A Royal whip set with Gold and some precious stones, crystal knob.

Geo. Lusignan,
Secretary,
Kandyan Board.

N.B. – No.14 was found among Eheylepola's property in his house and immediately recognised as the whip the King used.

The values are added from Barnes' Despatch 57 of 3rd January 1821. There is a *Note*: 'recognised to be the King's property by the Kandyan Chiefs'.

Jewels taken from Ehelepola after his imprisonment and declared to be the King's 'as being of a quality no subject could wear':

Gold Box, 280 Star pagodas at 6 rxd	1,680
Gold Chain, 128 Star pagodas at 7 rxd . . .	896
Gold Padecum set with precious stones with a Gold chain . . .	3,000
Do do do do . . .	1,300
Gold Buckle, with rubies and sapphires . . .	190
16 Gold Buttons, emeralds . . .	400
20 Gold Buttons, rubies . . .	1,100
[217] 1 large Dagger, velvet scabbard . . .	640
1 Gold Handled Dagger, set with rubies . . .	750
1 Do do do do . . .	950
1 Ornament for the top of a Cap . . .	50

CO 54/78

P.E. Pieris prints (*Tri Sinhala*, p. 133) a sale catalogue preserved at Downing Street, a copy of which was supplied to him by the Colonial Office:

Regalia of the King of Kandy.

A CATALOGUE

of

A Splendid and Valuable Collection of Jewellery forming the

Regalia of the King of Kandy,

The whole of the purest massive Gold comprising the Crown, a complete Suit of Embossed Armour, a great variety of armlets, bracelets, breast ornaments (*called Paddakums*), plumes of jewels for the head, chains for the neck, particularly one 23½ feet in length, a magnificent dagger, and various other costly articles of regal decoration, all of them of elaborate workmanship and richly studded with diamonds, emeralds, rubies, sapphires, pearls, etc., many of which are of an extraordinary size and beauty; a catseye of matchless grandeur, an immense mass of ruby in the rough, etc., presented by His Majesty to the captors for whose benefit they will be sold without the slightest reservation by Mr King, at his great room, 38, King Street, Covent Garden, on Tuesday, the 13th day of June, 1820, very punctually at one o'clock.

May be viewed on Monday, 5th June, till within two days preceding the sale in their present state, after which they will be unset and lotted out. Catalogues, price *2s.6d* without which no person will be admitted may be had at the Auction Room.

Conditions of Sale

Which must be rigidly observed

First, Each person bidding to advance one shilling per oz. for the Gold, and one shilling per carat for the jewels.

Second, A deposit made by each purchaser (without distinction of persons) of 25 pounds per cent. in Bank of England Notes, or cash, and each purchaser to give his real name and place of abode.

[218] Third. Every article purchased, to be paid for the [*sic*] taken away within three days from after the sale, or the deposit

money forfeited, and the lots re-sold at the Buyer's expense who must make good the deficiency, if any.

Fourth. It is believed that each article (not otherwise mentioned) is of the purest gold, and the jewels all of them real; but the purchaser must exercise his own judgment, as all faults and errors of description, T. King will not be responsible for.

Such gentlemen, as cannot attend the sale, may have their commissions faithfully executed, and free of expense by their obedient humble servant

Thomas King.

5 July 1820. A memorandum quoted by Pieris in *Letters to Ceylon*, p. 129, refers to purchases made on D'Oyly's behalf by Alexander Cadell 'at the Sale held at the General Treasury, Colombo, on 3 July'. These included '1 Silver "Banna Book" at rds. 1355, 1 lot of Elephant Tusks at rds 133.3, 1 Firelock inlaid with Silver and Gilt at rds 410, and 1 Ditto at 100 rds.' (The Book would have been a collection of the Buddha's teachings, inscribed either on silver sheets, or on strips of palm leaf held between silver covers.) Pieris presumes that these items came 'from the Sinhalese King's Treasure', and it is possible that a collection of objects, not part of the regalia sent for auction in London on 5 June 1820, was retained in Colombo by the British government and put on sale at the General Treasury in Colombo.

APPENDIX 4

Twelve verses addressed by Cornelia Isabella Perumal (Gajaman Nona) to John D'Oyly. Adapted from a literal translation by Lakshmi de Silva from the Sinhala of Bandusena Gunasekare (ed.), *Gajaman Nonage Kavi: Seepada [Gajaman Nona's Verse Compositions]* (Colombo 1991):

(1) Placing my head at your feet, I pay my respects to you, noble John D'Oyly, Lord of this District,

Whose equal not having been born in the world's womb, are equalled in glory and fame by none but the King of the Gods,

Possessed of majesty and power in the four directions, you gladden the hearts of your subjects as the mild moon causes night-flowering *kumudu* blossoms to bloom,

And humble the pride of your enemies as the lion vanquishes hosts of hostile, maddened elephants.

(2) Are you not a mother, treating as your children the folk who dwell within this Lanka?

Is not your right hand, which gladdens the hearts of the poor, a branch of the shining Divine Tree?

Are you not a second radiant wish-fulfilling Gem, fulfilling the wishes of many folk in an instant?

Are you not a Bodhisatva of magnanimous merit whose path to Buddhahood lies clear before you?

(3) Like Eros himself, handsome above all others, are you O noble John D'Oyly, Lord of this District,

Like the Moon itself, you light up a whole city with the gentle radiance of your virtues,

Like Lord Ganeshvara himself in the range and depth of your wit, you grasp the intricate meanings of poets' linked verses and phrases,

And like the Divine Tree itself your shining right hand rewards with gifts their hopes and desires.

(4) Aware that Fortune finds a constant dwelling on your broad shoulders, hearing the rumours of your generosity that resound in all directions,

Seeing that Heaven is kept within this noble city by the gem-radiance of your kindness,

Knowing that sweet speech fills your mouth, like the fragrance of lotuses, O Lord of this District,

I place my head at your feet and, with my children, beseech your help.

(5) John D'Oyly of spotless virtue, Lord of this District,

Sent here from England, a land blessed with boundless fortune, shining in glory and majesty, glowing in comfort and ease,

I who own nothing, possessing neither pearls nor jewels, flowers nor grain, land nor villages,

Bow at your lotus-like feet: help us in the name of the divine gods!

(6) He is indeed like the full moon, brimming with soft radiance,

He is indeed the five-arrowed Eros, inspiring love by his beauty,

He is indeed, in the matter of giving, divine in his limitless benevolence,

He is indeed great and noble in spirit, possessing all glory and prosperity.

(7) In wit and intellect resembling Lord Ganeshvara, God of Wisdom,

Guided in all things by the Ten Kingly Rules that are constant as the moon,

Possessing speech that pleases the mind and is like ambrosia to the ear,

His fame is as luminous and constant as the radiance of the moon.

(8) Shining, as I have described him, in virtue, wisdom, glory and wealth,

Famed throughout the world for the radiance of his meritorious deeds,

To the pleasing John D'Oyly, handsome Lord of this District,

I pay my respects and show my sorrows at this time.

(9) Having thus come before you, my hands on my head in worship,

I speak to you of the state in which I live,

The sons to whom I am bound in love

Wander everywhere, crying 'Give rice! Give rice!' like beggars.

(10) There is not rice enough to keep in life and health for the space of even one day

The children I once fed and cherished, bringing them up in noble fashion.

To John D'Oyly of gentle birth and sound virtue, Lord of this District,

I pay my respects, and speak of these sorrows in order to obtain succour.

(11) Lord, equipped with virtues, descended from a lordly line,

If, for the sake of your merit, I should obtain help according to my wishes,

The noble rays of those goodly virtues

Would please the gods, and win applause in Heaven.

(12) Vishnu, Sakra, Vishvakarma, the divine teacher Sikura, Chandra, Nosanda, Surya, and Lord Shiva who wears a shawl of skin and serpent,

I pray by the beneficial grace of these powerful Gods

That you, John D'Oyly, fertile in merit, noble Lord of this District,

May live enjoying ease and such happiness as will reach as high as Mount Maha Meru, and as wide as the limits of earth and sky.

NOTES

Introduction

1 Ravi Vyas, 'Between Lies and Silences', *Hindu Magazine Literary Review*, Sunday 2 February 1997, p. ix.

2 Geoffrey Powell, *The Kandyan Wars* (London and Colombo 1973), p. 13.

3 V. Woolf, 'Walter Sickert: A Conversation' (1934), new edn introduced by Richard Shone (London 1992), p. 23.

4 Venerable Maedauyangoda Vimalakirti Thera's *Matara Sahitya Yugaya* (The Matara Literary Era) (Peliyagoda 1953), p. 93, cited in Lakshmi de Silva, 'Cornelia Perumal (Gajaman Nona): Her Life and Writings' (1997).

5 Cf. J.P. Lewis, *List of Inscriptions on Tombstones and Monuments in Ceylon of Historical and Local Interest with an Obituary of Persons Uncommemorated* (Colombo 1913), p. 299.

6 Stanza from a poem addressed by the Sri Lankan poet Gajaman Nona to John D'Oyly while he was Agent of Revenue in Matara in the early 1800s; see Chapter 5 and Appendix 4.

7 Quoted by K.O. Longley, 'Fabricating Otherness: Demidenko and Exoticism', *Westerly* 42/1 (Autumn 1997), p. 36.

8 Edward Said, *Orientalism* (London 1978), p. 40.

9 See Chapters 8 and 9.

10 Cf. L.F. Liesching, who, in *A Brief Account of Ceylon* (Jaffna 1861), pp. 136–7, rests his praise of Western institutions upon the plank of Victorian anti-intellectualism: 'Do not trouble yourselves to refute [the Nya'ya, the Sa'nkaya and the Veda'ntic systems]. They may be very transcendental, and very learned, but they are worthless: for all they can do, is to unfit a man to be a man . . . Whatever differences there may be between these systems of philosophy, they all agree in regarding whatever is practical, as unworthy the attention of the philosopher, nay even opposed to the attainment of future happiness; if mere freedom from suffering can be so called. A philosophy of such a character is fatal to progress. A nation that possesses a Baconian, must ever be ahead of one that possesses a purely speculative philosophy.'

11 Cf. Yasmine Gooneratne, *English Literature in Ceylon 1815–1878* (Dehiwela 1968), pp. 1–39, for an account of English education in Sri Lanka's nineteenth-century schools.

12 Cf. Arnold Wright (ed.), *Twentieth Century Impressions of Ceylon: Its History, People, Commerce, Industries, and Resources* (London 1907), a good example of this kind of thoroughgoing classification.

13 John Ferguson, *Ceylon in the 'Jubilee Year'* (London 1887), p. 2.

14 Ibid., pp. 2, 6.

15 B. Clough to Dr Clark, 27 September 1814, MMS/IA/1814–1817.

16 R.S. Hardy to the Methodist Missionary Society Committee, Colpetty, 14 February 1865, MMS/VIII/1863–1867.

17 Longley, 'Fabricating Otherness'.

18 Cf. Ferguson, *Ceylon in the 'Jubilee Year'*, pp. 14–15.

19 W.G.A. Ormsby Gore, foreword to P.E. Pieris (ed.), *Letters to Ceylon 1814–1824* (Cambridge 1938), p. vii.

20 Pieris, ibid. (hereafter cited as *D'Oyly Family Letters*), pp. 1–2.

21 Powell, *Kandyan Wars*, p. 219.

22 H.A.J. Hulugalle, *Ceylon of the Early Travellers*, 2nd edn (Colombo 1969), pp. 121, 116.

23 Cf. Philip Denwood, introduction to *Brian Houghton Hodgson* (New Delhi 1972). We are obliged to Peter H. Roberts for this reference, and for research generously shared into the work of Brian Houghton Hodgson.

24 E.F.C. Ludowyk, *The Story of Ceylon* (London 1962) (hereafter cited as Ludowyk).

25 William Cobbett, *Rural Rides* (1822).

26 S.D. Saparamadu, introduction to D'Oyly, *Constitution*, pp. vii–viii.

27 T. Vimalananda, 'D'Oyly, the Crown's Crafty Agent', *Ceylon Daily News*, 2 March 1972.

28 T. Vimalananda, *The Great Rebellion of 1818: The Story of the First War of Independence and Betrayal of the Nation* (Colombo 1970), p. lii.

29 L.S. Dewaraja, *The Kandyan Kingdom of Sri Lanka 1707–1782* (Colombo 1988), pp. 17, 18.

30 In H.A.I. Goonetileke, *A Bibliography of Ceylon* (Zug, Switzerland 1970), vol. II, p. 413.

31 Cf. Appendix 3 of this book for documents relating to the recovery and sale of the royal regalia of the Kandyan kingdom.

32 Cf. Roger W. Oliver, '*L'umorismo* and the Theater', in *Dreams of Passion: The Theater of Luigi Pirandello* (New York 1979), p. 14.

33 Cf. *Letters of Leonard Woolf*, ed. F. Spotts (New York 1992), p. 62, for a note relating to the papers of a British CCS officer of a later period. According to Spotts, 'official correspondence by or about Woolf as an agent of the Ceylon government was destroyed in accordance with administrative practice'. Woolf's letter of resignation and related Colonial Office comments – which belong to a period following his departure from the island – are, however, preserved in the Public Record Office.

34 Hulugalle, *Ceylon of the Early Travellers*, p. 123.

35 Ludowyk, *Story of Ceylon*, pp. 149–50.

Chapter One
'Cultured Generations'

1 Cf. *The AA Illustrated Guide to Britain* (London 1971), pp. 104–6.

2 Cf. *D'Oyly Family Letters*, p. 3. Hastings's trial began in 1788 and ended in his acquittal before the House of Lords on 23 April 1795.

3 Maurice Shellim, foreword to *Patchwork to the Great Pagoda: India and British Painters* (Calcutta 1973).

4 Shellim, *Patchwork*, p. 61.

5 'Elephant Kraal of 1809', John D'Oyly to Thomas D'Oyly, letter written from Colombo, dated 18 June 1809, printed in *JRASCB*, 34/91 (1938), pp. 240, 253.

6 Cf. extracts from the *London Post and Public Advertiser*, printed in the *Elizabethan*, 6, p. 247, and 12, p. 324, quoted in G.F.R. Barth and A.H. Stenning, *Record of Old Westminsters* (London 1928), vol. I, p. 282.

7 Robert Southey, *Mr Rowlandson's England*, with illustrations by Thomas Rowlandson (1807), ed. John Steel (Woodbridge 1985), p. 135.

8 Cf. Nicholas T. Parsons, *The Joy of Bad Verse* (Cambridge 1988), p. 42.

9 Cf. ibid., pp. 23–59. Pye published his 'major' poem *Alfred: An Epic Poem in Six Books*, in 1801.

10 Quoted in Parsons, *Joy of Bad Verse*, p. 57.

11 It is possible that an eighteenth-century Latin poem by an unidentified author on the subject of cricket found among the D'Oyly family papers might have been from his hand. East Sussex Record Office AMS 6185/134.

12 It may be of interest to note that the family background of the English novelist Jane Austen (1776–1816), who was almost an exact contemporary of John D'Oyly, resembled his in many respects. She, too, grew up in the country as the child

of an Anglican ecclesiastical family with noble and wealthy connections, one of her brothers took orders, and two others fought for their country during the Napoleonic wars (though they did so in the Royal Navy, and not as army officers). In her novel *Mansfield Park* (1814), Jane Austen included among her characters a stately English baronet, Sir Thomas Bertram, whose wealth (as displayed in the magnificent house from which the novel takes its name, and the idle, materialistic lives led by his wife and three of his four children) is founded on the sugar plantations he owns in Antigua. The Bertrams' connection with church and state is clear: the elder son of Sir Thomas and Lady Bertram is destined to sit in Parliament, and their younger son seeks ordination in the Church of England.

13 From about 1834 the English East India Company was merely a managing agency for the British government of India. It was deprived of this sphere of activity after the Sepoy War of 1857. The company ceased to exist as a legal entity in 1873.

14 Professor J.J. Nicholls has provided the following note to the structure of D'Oyly's ode, 'Commercii Laus': 'The first five stanzas are a conventional account (like that in *Lucretius* Book V) of the supposed early brutish state of mankind; stanzas 6 and 7 refer to the Argonauts (Tiphys was their helmsman), then follow stanzas devoted to the development of trade, from Phoenicia to Carthage and finally Rome. In stanzas 20–21 the 'Sea Sisters' may be supposed to be sea nymphs. Stanzas 25 to the end are allusive. The towers and the living springs consecrated here by Learning probably refer to Academe, and more particularly to Cambridge.
  The metre is Alcaic, as Horace used it, and is handled with great skill.'

15 D'Oyly's Cambridge diary, hereafter cited as *D'Oyly, CD*.

16 Cf. L. Patton and P. Mann (eds), *Lectures (1795) on Politics and Religion*, in *Collected Works of S.T. Coleridge* (Princeton 1971), pp. 225–6.

17 Not only, writes Sheridan's biographer Stanley Ayling, were all the playwright's friends embracing him in raptures of joy and exultation, but 'the whole House, the members, peers and strangers, involuntarily joined in a tumult of applause'. Even the 'great shout' which had gone up in Drury Lane when the screen fell to reveal Lady Teazle was nothing to this. Cf. Stanley Ayling, *A Portrait of Sheridan* (London 1985), pp. 111–25.

18 See n. 2 above. Warren Hastings died in 1818 at the age of 86.

19 Niccolo Machiavelli, *The Prince* (1513), trans. Luigi Ricci (Oxford 1961), pp. 82–3. All subsequent quotations from *The Prince* are taken from this edition.

20 Cf. Paul Johnson, *The Birth of the Modern: World Society 1815–1830* (1991), p. 350.

21 Stuart Cary Welch, *Room for Wonder: Indian Painting during the British Period 1760–1880* (New York 1978), p. 183.

22 Benjamin Disraeli, *Tancred* (1847), bk. 2, ch. 10.

Chapter Two
'Harbours of Our Choice'

1 Elizabeth J. Harris, *The Gaze of the Coloniser. British Views on Local Women in 19th Century Sri Lanka* (Colombo 1994), pp. 1–3.

2 Joseph Conrad, *Youth* (1902), Penguin edn (Harmondsworth 1976), pp. 148–9.

3 Charles Wentworth Dilke, *Greater Britain: A Record of Travel in English-Speaking Countries during 1866 and 1867* (London 1872), p. 404.

4 Ibid., pp. 408–9.

5 Ibid., preface, p. vii.

6 William Knighton, *Forest-Life in Ceylon*, 2 vols (London 1854), vol. I, pp. 7–8 (our italics).

7 David Fitzpatrick, Macquarie University essay (1994), p. 1.

8 See Gooneratne, *English Literature in Ceylon*, pp. 164–86, for a detailed analysis of William Knighton's novel *Forest-Life in Ceylon*.

9 James Cordiner, *A Description of Ceylon* (1807), 1983 edn, vol. II, pp. 37–8.

10 John Davy, *An Account of the Interior of Ceylon* (London 1821), hereafter cited as *Davy*.

11 Richard Boyle, 'The Jewel of the Deep', Part 2 of a 3-part article 'Of Pearls and Pearl Fisheries', *Sunday Times*, 18 May 1997.

12 Cf. Brendon Gooneratne, *From Governor's Residence to President's House: Being an Account of the Building Formerly Known as 'Queen's House', Colombo, and of Some of the Personalities Associated with It* (Colombo 1981) (hereafter cited as *President's House*), pp. 5–7.

13 Samuel Tolfrey's son Edward, who had proceeded to Ceylon with him, succeeded D'Oyly as Auditor-General on 15 March 1815, and died at Kandy in 1821, three years before D'Oyly.

14 Cf. A.L. Lowell, *Colonial Civil Service* (New York 1900), pp. 3–112, 233–346.

15 Cf. Welch, *Room for Wonder*, p. 15.

16 Dr John Davy (1790–1868) was the brother of Sir Humphry Davy (b. 1778). It is said that the younger Davy considered a career in the natural sciences with his brother, but decided against it, studied medicine instead and joined the army. The major portion of his life was spent in the Royal Army Medical Corps (RAMC), in which service he was stationed in Ceylon, the Ionian islands, the West Indies, and in England. His *Account of the Interior of Ceylon*, published in 1821, and reprinted in Sri Lanka in 1969. It is hereafter cited as *Davy*, all quotations

being from the 1969 edition; cf. *Davy* on local literature, pp. 238–40. See also pp. 83–4 on cobras and snake-charmers, pp. 102–5 on leeches, and the best methods of dealing with them, p. 359 for pictures of elephant-hunting and a view of the southern town of Matara. See also n. 10 above.

17 Joseph de Joinville, 'On the Religion and Manners of the People of Ceylon', *Asiatic Researches*, 7(1803), pp. 307–444.

18 Quoted in R.K. de Silva, *Early Prints of Ceylon (Sri Lanka) 1800–1900* (London 1985), p. 42.

Chapter Three
1801–1805: 'Enjoying the Good Things of the Age'

1 Welch, *Room for Wonder*, p. 15.

2 Cordiner, *Description of Ceylon*, vol. I, pp. 81–2.

3 Fanny Parks, *The Wanderings of a Pilgrim in Search of the Picturesque during Four-and-Twenty Years in the East* (1850, reprinted Lahore 1975), vol. I, pp. 209–10.

4 Plate 8 of Charles Doyley's collection of drawings, *The European in India* (London 1813), is titled 'An English Family at Table, under a Punkah, or Fan, kept in Motion by a Khelassy'.

5 William Knighton makes entertaining fictional use of a punkah in his novel *Forest-Life in Ceylon*, vol. I, p. 65. Though superseded in our own times by electric fans and air-conditioning, punkahs may still be seen today in the old-fashioned *walauwas* or manor-houses of Colombo and Galle.

6 Cf. Welch, *Room for Wonder*, pp. 30–1.

7 The information on taxes in nineteenth-century Britain given here has been condensed from Ian Fullerton's comprehensive account in his paper 'Trade, Finance and Tax in Jane Austen's Time', *Sensibilities* 12 (1996), pp. 31–44.

8 Cf. E.V. Downs and G.L. Davies (eds), *Selections from Macaulay: Letters, Prose, Speeches and Poetry* (London 1932), p. 59.

9 Cf. *Davy*, p. 483.

10 Welch, *Room for Wonder*, pl. 45. See also Daniel Pool, *What Jane Austen Ate and Charles Dickens Knew* (1993), pp. 216–218, for an account of Englishmen's clothing in nineteenth-century England.

11 Cf. Welch, *Room for Wonder*, pp. 15, 28.

12 Situated between Malabar Street and the Udawattekele Forest Reserve, up a short, steep climb along a lane to the left beyond the National Museum in Kandy, the Garrison Cemetery was registered as a cemetery in 1822. It contains the graves of some 300 British people, many of them pioneers of British involvement in Sri Lanka. An early death from 'jungle fever' (malaria) seems to have been the fate of many, according to the decaying headstones marking the graves. The caretaker today inhabits a granite, cell-like building which was formerly the Chapel of Rest where coffins were kept before burial. Cf. Royston Ellis, 'Buried History', *Sunday Times*, 24 April 1994, p. 13. Ellis notes that the peak year for burials was 1824, when 168 British people (including John D'Oyly) died and were buried in Kandy.

13 Cf. *D'Oyly Family Letters*, pp. 4–11, for a detailed picture of the 'full and merry life' John D'Oyly led as a Cambridge undergraduate.

14 H.A.J. Hulugalle, *British Governors of Ceylon* (Colombo 1963) (hereafter cited as *Hulugalle*), pp. 10–12.

15 Cf. *President's House*, pp. 4–7.

16 G. Valentia, *Voyages and Travels to India, Ceylon, the Red Sea, Abyssinia & Egypt in the Years 1802, 1803, 1804, 1805 & 1806*, vol. I, pp. 316–17.

17 Cordiner, *Description of Ceylon*, p. 308.

18 Cf. Welch, *Room for Wonder*, p. 27.

19 Cf. ibid., pp. 108–9, 153. Sir David Ochterlony (1758–1825) arrived in India at the age of 19, and died in Meerut.

Chapter Four
1801–1805, 'Proud Towers' – The Road to Kandy

1 Robert Knox, *An Account of the Island of Ceylon* ... (London 1681).

2 Cf. Captain Arthur Johnston, *Expedition to Candy* (1810), and A.A. de Alwis, 'The Secret Pass of One Thousand Steps' (1997) for detailed accounts of this adventure. Johnston, who had received his commission at the age of fifteen, arrived in Ceylon with his regiment in 1796, and was attached to Governor North's staff. On his return to England, Johnston transferred to a Ranger Battalion, was promoted to the rank of Lieutenant-Colonel, and was appointed to command the Senior Wing of the Royal Military Academy. A.A. de Alwis notes that a memorial to Johnston with highlights of his 'Expedition to Candy' is found on a tablet in the parish church of Shalden near Alton in Hampshire.

3 Cf. *Tri Sinhala*, pp. 13–20.

4 Robert Percival, *Account of the Island of Ceylon* (1803; Dehiwela 1975), p. 401.

5 Cf. ibid. See also *President's House*, pp. 4–5, 82.

6 Cordiner, *Description of Ceylon*, p. 309.

7 Ibid., pp. 82–3.

8 Cf. Woolf's letter to Lytton Strachey of 25 August 1907, from Kandy, in Woolf, *Letters*, p. 131.

9 Thomas Skinner, 'Memorandum with reference to the Past and Present Social Condition of the Native Population of Ceylon ... referred to in ... Evidence, before a Select Committee of the House of Commons, July 1849'. Reprinted in T. Skinner, *Fifty Years in Ceylon: An Autobiography*,

ed. Annie Skinner (London 1891), pp. 214–36, 233.

10 Cf. Kumari Jayawardena, *Feminism and Nationalism in the Third World* (Colombo 1986), p. 117.

11 Maureen Seneviratne, 'Memorial to an Eccentric Englishman', *Sunday Times*, 23 May 1993. See also Chapter 8, for Sir James Mackintosh's impressions of D'Oyly when he met him in 1810.

12 Cf. *D'Oyly Family Letters*, pp. 6–8.

13 Knighton, *Forest-Life in Ceylon*, vol. II, p. 249.

14 Letter from the Governor-General in Council to North, 28 May 1800, quoted in *Tri Sinhala*, p. 20.

15 *Ludowyk*, p. 148.

16 Conrad, *Youth*, p. 148.

Chapter Five
1805–1810: 'The Noblest Chace in the World'

1 Cf. Ronald Hyam, *Empire and Sexuality: The British Experience* (1990), p. 57. See also Kenneth Ballhatchet, *Race, Sex and Class under the Raj: Imperial Attitudes and Politics and their Critics* (London 1980), in particular the chapter 'Low Life and Racial Prestige', pp. 123–43.

2 R.G. Davies, 'Leonard Woolf: The Making of a Feminist' (MA thesis, University of Western Australia 1996); see also Hyam, *Empire and Sexuality*.

3 Pl. 19 in Doyley, *European in India*.

4 Cf. *D'Oyly, CD*, p. 11.

5 Hugh Boyd, *Miscellaneous Works* (1800), vol. I, p. 54.

6 See Ch. 2, p. 53, for de Joinville's description of the graceful dress of the rural women of 'Candy'.

7 Lt. William Lyttleton's notes to 'The King's Palace at Kandy', quoted in R.K. de Silva, *Early Prints of Ceylon 1800–1900* (1985), p. 46.

8 Letter from John D'Oyly to Thomas D'Oyly, written from Colombo on 18 June 1809, printed in *JRASCB* 34/91 (1938), p. 255.

9 Born in August 1737, while the Dutch were in control of the Maritime Provinces of the island, the office and rank of 'Gajaman Arachchi' had been conferred on Don Francisco by the Dutch governor of the time. On 5 February 1758 the young *arachchi* married Francina Grero, the daughter of Jacinto Grero, Registrar of Milagiriya Church and headmaster of a Dutch Presbyterian parish school in Colombo. The couple had three children, of whom the eldest, a daughter, was born on 30 October 1758 and was baptized at St Paul's Church, Milagiriya on 30 July 1759, receiving the name of Dona Isabella Cornelia Perumal. A son, Louis Senaratna Perumal, later to become Gajaman Mohandiram in his own right, was born in December 1759, and a second daughter, Maria, was born in October 1761.

Descendants and near relations of Dona Isabella Cornelia Perumal ('Gajaman Nona') include Don Andrayas Panditha Gunawardena, Mohandiram; Venerable Pelene Sri Vajiragnana of Bambalapitiya; Scholar-pundit Dharmaratne, the founder and editor of *Lakmini Pahana*; R.L. Pereira, QC; Dr Cassius Perera (Bhikku Kassapa); H.J.C. Pereira and others. (Information supplied by L.S.J. Medis, together with details of Gajaman's ancestry, copied from a Dutch parish or school *thombo* (or register) held in Sri Lanka National Archives, vol. 1/3985, p. 18.)

10 Gajaman's poem written in memory of her father has attracted the following comment from a Sinhala critic: 'Her technique of using subtle words which have multiple meanings (is) perfected here. Alliteration and clever use of soft sounds make it a rhythmic as well as a very popular poem. Technique is not perfected at the risk of losing clarity of meaning.' 'Valli', 'Gajaman Nona', *Times of Ceylon Annual*, 1962.

11 Cf. James de Alwis, Introduction to *The Sidat Sangarava* (Colombo 1852), 2nd edn 1966, pp. ccxv–ccxvi.

12 R.S. Hardy, *Eastern Monachism* (London 1850), p. 21. James de Alwis quoted this passage in *Sidat Sangarava*, op cit., p. ccxvi, in order to counter contemporary criticisms of Sinhala literature.

13 Other women poets in the Matara district at this period included Dona Cornelia's younger sister Dona Arnolia Perumal; her daughter, Dona Katerina; Attaragama Kumarihamy, the daughter of a *disave* and Dissanayake Lamatani. Exchanges among the poets of Matara, male and female, could be hard-hitting and occasionally very earthy: Dr Lakshmi de Silva has kindly provided us with the text of a verse attributed to Dona Cornelia that was apparently a retort to malicious local gossip about her family life: 'Why are you concerned if I sleep with my son-in-law / When my daughter is not troubled about it? / I'm merely helping the poor darling to cope – / She's been complaining that she's feeling sore!' (personal communication of 7 March 1992).

14 Cf. de Alwis, *Sidat Sangarava*, pp. ccxvi–ccxviii.

15 Ibid., pp. clv, lxv.

16 Verses attributed to Gajaman were collected and printed many years after the poet's death, twelve of which are addressed to John D'Oyly. Since eight of these appear to form her petition to the English agent of revenue, and four to have been composed in gratitude for gifts received, they have been presented in this form in Appendix 4. It is, of course, quite possible that the twelve verses are part of a single work in which the poet praises and thanks her prospective patron in anticipation of gifts she hoped to receive.

17 The verse given here is an adaptation by the authors of stanza 3 in Dr Lakshmi de Silva's literal translation of Gajaman Nona's verses to D'Oyly in Appendix 4. Gajaman pays a high compliment to D'Oyly's literary skill in the third line when she compares him to Lord Ganeshvara in the range and depth of his wit, and his ability to grasp the intricate meanings of the linked verses and phrases of poetic language. Lord Ganeshvara, the Hindu God of Wisdom, officiated as scribe when the poet Vyasa composed the Indian epic *Mahabharata*. Dr de Silva notes that Gajaman Nona frequently displays her own erudition in her Sinhala verse, on one notable occasion employing a phrase that is capable of 31 different interpretations.

18 The two stanzas given here have been adapted from translations in D.B. Kappagoda, 'Gajaman Nona: The Songstress of Ruhuna', *Island* (n.d.), and Henry Wijetilaka. 'Nightingale of Sri Lanka', *Ceylon News*, 30 January 1975.

19 Cf. K.D.G. Wimalaratne, 'Did D'Oyly Grant Land to Gajaman Nona?', *Sunday Observer*, 4 December 1983; Wimalaratne asserts that an agent of revenue at Matara in the period 1804–1806 did not possess authority to grant land to natives for any purpose whatsoever without the prior permission of the governor and his advisory council. Wimalaratne also notes that although evidence exists that D'Oyly sought permission from the governor 'on various matters, including the repair of rest houses at Beliatta and Matara, and also for felling timber in the province', no records exist of a request made by D'Oyly to the governor, nor of permission granted by the Governor to D'Oyly, in relation to land granted to Gajaman Nona.

20 Cf. 'Valli', 'Gajaman Nona'.

21 Though not, apparently, known 'to be ardent in matters of the heart' (Wimalaratne, 'Did D'Oyly Grant Land?'), humanity, charity and generosity are notes that are frequently sounded in contemporary descriptions of D'Oyly. Governor Sir Thomas Maitland found D'Oyly to be 'one of the best informed and humane men

under Government'. Maitland to Castlereagh, 25 January 1809. CO 54/31, quoted in *Tri Sinhala*, p. 52. See Chapter 7 for a description of D'Oyly's sympathetic and courteous treatment of the fallen King of Kandy. Cf. Lewis, *Tombstones and Monuments*, p. 299: 'It was found on [D'Oyly's] death that there were 115 indigent natives who were monthly recipients of his bounty, and that his payments to them amounted to 163 Rix-dollars a month. Among them was a natural son of Major Davie [the British officer who had died in captivity in the Kandyan kingdom despite D'Oyly's efforts to rescue him]'. See also Chapter 11 for a reference in an obituary (probably written by Sir Edward Barnes) to D'Oyly's 'general charitableness of disposition', a character trait for which he was apparently well known in the island.

22 Compare with the grant made by D'Oyly to Gajaman the gift of 'a small village, in free tenure' made by Warren Hastings to that great traveller, the Indian fakir Purana Puri, who had delivered to him dispatches from the Dalai Lama in Tibet. 'One wonders', notes Welch in recording this incident, 'if [the fakir] was not employed by Warren Hastings as an intelligence agent'. Cf. Welch, *Room for Wonder*, p. 81.

23 Hyam, *Empire and Sexuality*, p. 2.

24 Good deeds performed in the service of the local people by British colonial officers were not infrequently celebrated, both in India and Sri Lanka, in popular ballads; cf. a Punjabi ballad, purportedly sung in honour of Captain Popham Young, Colonising Officer of the Chenab Canal Colony, and published in the *Gazetteer of the Chenab Colony* (1904) quoted by Sanjay Srivastava in 'The Management of Water: Modernity, Technocracy, and the Citizen at the Doon School', *South Asia*, (1993), pp. 63–4: 'There at Wazirabad / Where the whirlpools churn, / A weir has been made and the

river dammed, / Young Sahib has peopled the land . . .
'The English have measured the whole land, / Here a Patwari, there a Patwari, / Zilladars galore and mighty Munshis, / To them has been given the authority, / Water where they will they give,
'Young Sahib, etc.'

25 Maureen Seneviratne writes of the relationship of D'Oyly and Gajaman as an 'affaire d'amour', 'Memorial to an Eccentric Englishman', *Sunday Times* 23 May 1993; Dayananda Gunawardena's play *The Gajaman Story* (Colombo 1991) features a key scene which begins with Dona Cornelia being offered wine by the Resident at their interview and ends as she swoons into his arms. These interpretations are contested, however, by Wimalaratne, 'Did D'Oyly Grant Land' (1983), who states that the poet 'was never a mistress of any chieftain, [nor did she have] any unholy relationship with D'Oyly'. See also Yasmine Gooneratne's novel, *The Pleasures of Conquest* (New Delhi 1995, Sydney 1996), in which some of the possibilities canvassed in this chapter regarding the D'Oyly–Gajaman relationship have been explored through fiction.

26 Cf. Machiavelli, *The Prince*, pp. 87–8. Certain other advice offered by Machiavelli is equally relevant in this context: 'A prince must . . . show himself a lover of merit, give preferment to the able, and honour those who excel in every art', pp. 112–13.

27 See Ch. 3, and n. 19 there.

28 Ballhatchet, *Race, Sex and Class*, p. 9.

29 These attitudes could surface in some unexpected and amusing ways. Cf. Margaret Drabble, *A Writer's Britain: Landscape in Literature* (London 1979), p. 113, who perceives in the prejudice of some English writers against certain kinds of flowers 'a deep preoccupation with notions of

natural goodness and original sin'. Drabble provides some fascinating instances of middle-class British prejudice against the 'exotic' in nature, e.g. 'Exotic orchids and un-British cacti displease many.' She notes that Angus Wilson writes wittily in *The Middle Age of Mrs Eliot* of snobbish contempt for 'the vulgar calceolaria'.

30 Cf. Yasmine Gooneratne, 'Australia and her Postcolonial World', *Australian–Canadian Studies* 10/2 (1992), pp. 118–26, where the two illustrations in Cook's *Atlas* are discussed in some detail.

31 Cf. Mary D'Oyly's letter to John D'Oyly, 29 August 1815, received in Kandy 17 June 1816. *D'Oyly Family Letters*, pp. 24–6.

32 Edward Said has suggested (in connection with W.M. Thackeray's novel *Vanity Fair*) that Josh Sedley is always affiliated with India and later of course with Becky Sharp, as if, despite Sedley's colonial wealth, Thackeray wished to underline Josh's moral and social unacceptability in polite English society. Similarly, Edward Rochester's wife Bertha Morris (in Charlotte Bronte's *Jane Eyre*) is a West Indian, a fact, Said suggests, that is clearly linked to her bestiality: she must be exorcised (or controlled) before Rochester can marry Jane. In Said's view, this is Bronte's way of telling the reader that denizens of the outlying empire are useful as a source of wealth or as a moral ordeal for English men and women to experience, but never can they become persons acceptable into the heart of metropolitan society.

Applying these views to a discussion of Jean Rhys's novel *The Wide Sargasso Sea*, the pattern, says Said, is repeated frequently in British writing. Cf. 'Islam, Philology and French Culture', in *The World, the Text and the Critic*, p. 273.

33 In *Tombstones and Monuments*, p. 299, Lewis mentions translations of Sinhala poems (presumably by his own hand) sent home to England by D'Oyly. It seems unlikely that such translations would have included examples of erotic verse. On the other hand, the rectory family would certainly have been interested in what Lewis describes as still 'extant' in 1913, the 'set of verses addressed to [D'Oyly] by Gajaman Nona, the Matara poetess' while he was holding the office of Agent of Revenue and Commerce for the Districts of Matara and Galle in 1805.

34 See, in this context, a point made by Margaret Drabble, *Writers Britain*, p. 129: that the practice of seeing a landscape with 'organic vision', i.e. in terms of sexual imagery – hollow caverns, gushing water, secret approaches, tufted trees – was 'inaccessible to Thomas Gray (1716–1771) and his contemporaries, even though Milton uses plenty of it. Womb of waters, genial moisture, heaving mountains, shaggy hills, bushes with frizzled hair and hills with 'hairie sides' are among the examples Drabble cites from Milton. D'Oyly would probably have inherited Gray's way of regarding natural phenomena, since it was much too early in 1805 for him to have been influenced by Byron, and even, probably, by the *Lyrical Ballads* of Wordsworth and Coleridge.

35 'Valli', 'Gajaman Nona'.

36 Cf. T.M.G. Samat, 'Gajaman Nona: The Well-Known Poetess', *Ceylon Daily News*, 6 November 1975. Samat considers Gajaman's 50 verses addressed to Mudaliyar Tillekeratne to have been a feat for any poet, her lyric on the Nuga tree at Weligama, its metrical form (never having been used by any of her predecessors) being rich and unique. Samat provides the following literal translation of this poem:

'O friend, behold at Denipitiya the great Banyan tree, glorious as the azure sky. It is enchanting, alluring to all beholders. Surrounded by the perennial greenery of other trees, it stands by the river casting an ample shade that resembles a dark blue cloud. Amidst its leaves that flutter in the breeze, chant mating birds. Under the shade of its foliage, passers-by rest comfortably, easing the fatigue of their bodies as branches stretching out in ten directions ward off the intense heat of the sun.'

See also Wijetilaka, 'Nightingale of Sri Lanka'.

37 Lakshmi de Silva, author of the translation cited in this chapter, personal communication; cf. J.B. Dissanayaka, 'The Romantic Life of a Beautiful Poetess', *Island*, 25 February 1992. This Sinhala literary critic notes that Lakshmi de Silva's verse translation of 'The Banyan Tree at Denipitiya' captures 'not only the sense but also the rhythm of the Sinhala verse'.

38 An example of the poet's knowledge of popular elephant lore. The shell of the *divul* fruit or woodapple swallowed by the elephant is frequently found in elephant dung empty of the edible parts but seemingly whole and unbroken. The scientific explanation of this phenomenon is, that a small beetle that has penetrated into the *divul* fruit eats the soft pulp inside, leaving the shell intact, creating the illusion that the elephant's body absorbs the pulp through the hard shell of the fruit.

39 Jayawardena, *Feminism and Nationalism*, p. 117. It is significant, says Jayawardena of the women poets writing at this time, that all of them came from families of local officials who worked for the Dutch administration. For assessments of Gajaman's writing as well as various comments from different points of view on her relationship with John D'Oyly, see also the following: de Alwis, *Sidat Sangarava*, p. ccxvi; de Silva, 'Cornelia Perumal'; and Seneviratne, 'Memorial'.

40 The Sinhala verses given here and elsewhere in this chapter in English translation have been adapted from versions composed by Lakshmi de Silva, J.B. Disanayake, T.M.G. Samat, 'Valli', H. Wijetilake and other critics cited in this chapter.

41 By the 'five fruits', the poet refers to the five stages of spiritual evolution, and by 'grand alms' he hints at favours granted by Gajaman Nona to another priest.

42 Cf. 'Valli', 'Gajaman Nona': 'The "you" in the poem is the second person used to address menials, and the verb for "giving birth" is a very earthy one.'

43 'An European Gentleman with his Moonshee, or Native Professor of Languages', pl. 1 in Doyley, *European in India*, provides an intimate and delightful view of just such a language lesson.

44 'Elephant Kraal of 1809', John D'Oyly to Thomas D'Oyly, letter written from Colombo and dated 18 June 1809, printed in *JRASCB*, 34/91 (1938), pp. 240, 253.

45 Samuel Purchas, *Purchas His Pilgrimage, or Relations of the World and the Religions Observed in All Ages and Places Discovered, from the Creation unto This Present. In Four Partes* (London 1613), p. 458.

46 Captain Thomas Williamson, commentary to pl. 20 in Doyley, *European in India*. The English artist Charles Doyley recorded an occasion on which Marquis Wellesley and his suite had been entertained at breakfast by the Nawab of Oudh with 'an Elephant-Fight' (viewed, naturally, from the safety and comfort of a luxuriously equipped pavilion). Williamson, who provided an arch commentary to Doyley's drawings when they were published as a volume of engravings in 1813, remarked in connection with this particular drawing that 'the late Nabob of Lucknow, *Asoph al Dowlah* [*sic*], whose intellects were as heavy as his enormous head, derived much pleasure from such spectacles'. See Welch, *Room for Wonder*, p. 92, for a

note on 'Nawab Asaf-ud-daula (ruler of Oudh from 1775 to 1797) [who,] convinced by the British that their troops guaranteed security, devoted himself to a life of pleasure. He transferred his court from Faizabad to Lucknow, where he spent huge sums on palaces, mosques and shrines, determined to make it more splendid than Hyderabad, the Nizam's capital in the Deccan. If one regards the late Mughal period in Oudh as a phase of decline, 1775 marks the beginning of the end.'

47 Another picture by Andrasy, no less revolting in the tale it tells of callousness and cruelty, shows the European hunter, again with a gun-bearer in attendance, and 'Eight elephants killed in a heap, and a little one captured' to his credit, preparing to shoot a ninth elephant that is approaching from a distance.

48 North to Secret Committee, 19 May 1800; to Mornington, 30 May 1800. Quoted in *Tri Sinhala*, p. 18.

49 De Alwis, *Sidat Sangarava*, p. ccli, urging British civil servants to study Sinhala.

50 Captain Arthur Johnston, *Expedition to Candy* (London 1810), pp. 99–100.

51 D'Oyly's letter to Moratota, dated 5 September 1805. Enclosure to Most Secret Despatch. Maitland to Camden, 19 October 1805. CO 54/18. Quoted in *Tri Sinhala*, p. 52.

52 Cf. Khushwant Singh, *Delhi* (New Delhi 1989), p. 169.

Chapter Six
1811–1815: Obedient Servant

1 T. Vimalananda, 'The Kandyan Convention: Its Significance', pt. I, *Ceylon Daily News*, 2 March 1972.

2 John Wilson to the Earl of Liverpool, Secretary of State for the War and Colonial Department. From Jaffnapatam, 11 September 1811. CO 54/40.

3 Johnston, *Expedition to Candy*, pp. 15–16.

4 John Wilson to the King of Kandy. From King's House, Colombo, 29 September 1811. CO 54/40.

5 Cf. *Epic Struggle*, p. 4, on Portuguese commanders who employed, among other weapons of psychological warfare against the Sinhalese, the device of delivering 'one of the local people to the Kaffir soldiers who cut him up before the eyes of his wife and children and shared him among themselves for food'. For more detail, see Major R. Raven-Hart, *The Dutch Wars with Kandy, 1764–1766* (Colombo 1966).

6 Brownrigg to the Earl of Liverpool. From King's House, 29 March 1812. CO 54/42.

7 See Ch. 4, nn. 4, 5.

8 Reported by Brownrigg to the Earl of Liverpool, King's House, Colombo, 29 March 1812. CO 54/43, no. 2.

9 Davie to D'Oyly, n.d., received by him 6 January 1812, copy enclosed with D'Oyly to Ehelepola (as n. 12 below).

10 Cf. Percival, *Island of Ceylon*, ch. 12.

11 Ehelepola to D'Oyly, n.d., received 18 March 1812, fair copy enclosed with Wilson to King of Kandy (as n. 4 above).

12 D'Oyly to Ehelepola, Colombo 22 March 1812, fair copy enclosed with Wilson to King of Kandy (as n. 4 above).

13 *Tri Sinhala*, p. 64.

14 Lord Liverpool to Brownrigg, 31 March 1812. CO 54/43, no. 11.

15 See Brownrigg's letter to Lord Liverpool, King's House, Colombo, 12 June 1812. CO 54/43, no. 13, enclosing a copy of his letter to the King of Kandy, CO 54/43.

16 Brownrigg to Lord Liverpool (Secret and Confidential), King's House, Colombo, 3 November 1812. CO 54/44, no. 23.

17 Brownrigg to the Earl of Bathurst (Private and Confidential), King's House, Colombo, 15 March 1813. CO 54/47, no. 35.

18 See Johnson, *Birth of the Modern*, pp. 444–51.

19 See letters addressed to the Home Government from 1811 to 1815 by Major-General John Wilson and Lieutenant-General Robert Brownrigg, Governor of Ceylon, in T. Vimalananda (ed.) *Sri Wickrema, Brownrigg and Ehelepola* (Colombo 1984).

20 Johnson, *Birth of the Modern*.

21 See Thomas Roe, *The Embassy of Sir Thomas Roe to the Court of the Great Mogul 1615–1619*, ed. William Foster (1899) (Delhi 1990).

22 Cf. Welch, *Room for Wonder*, p. 87. Rumours of well-populated oriental harems very naturally engendered imitation, and 'an international cast of Westerners, magnetized by Lucknow's giddy reputation, flocked there during the late eighteenth century,' writes Welch. Plates 34 and 36 in his volume show European gentlemen being entertained privately by nautch dancers in Lucknow.

23 The portrait described in Ch. 3, of Sir David Ochterlony and his household, appears as pl. 46 in Welch, *Room for Wonder*, p. 108.

24 Vimalananda, 'The Kandyan Convention, pt. II: D'Oyly, the Crown's Crafty Agent', Part II. See also S.D. Saparamadu, Introduction to D'Oyly, *Constitution*, p. viii: 'D'Oyly set out deliberately to subvert the chiefs of the country against their legitimate king. He established a large cohort of paid spies who were sent inside Kandy in the guise of bhikkus, traders etc., and little of importance occurred in the kingdom without it coming to his notice. Chiefs and officials were usually bribed by rich presents, imported goods, medicines and copious flattery.'

25 Vimalananda, 'The Kandyan Convention'.

26 Sri Vikrama Rajasinha, the last king of Kandy, ruled the Kandyan kingdom for seventeen years until he was taken prisoner by the British on 19 February 1815, and deported to India, where he died on 30 January 1832 at Fort Vellore. The 37-acre lake in the heart of the town of Kandy, and the *patirippuwa* (octagon) adorning the *Dalada Maligava*, were works undertaken by the last king. The *patirippuwa* was designed by Unamboowe Nilame and constructed by the royal artisan Devendra Moolachari.

27 See A. Ratnasinghe, 'Tyranny Held Sway under Last King of Kandy', *Island*, 9 December 1984.

28 Cf. *Davy*, pp. 232–3.

29 See de Silva, *Early Prints of Ceylon*, pp. 53–8, for a commentary on Lyttleton's picture which includes a detailed account of the palace complex 'embracing courtyards, audience and music halls, Queens' palace and baths, residential quarters for court officials and soldiers, together with various stores; also, the hallowed grounds with the Temple of the Tooth and the three devales – all these being required for the complicated formalities of the Kandyan Court'.

30 See Ch. 1, n. 1.

31 Cf. Henry Marshall, *Ceylon: A General Description of the Island and Its Inhabitants* (London 1846; Dehiwela 1969), pp. 124–5.

32 Vimalananda, 'The Kandyan Convention', pt. III: Last Days of the Kingdom'.

33 John D'Oyly's diary was discovered in the Kandy *kachcheri* and published in 1917 with an introduction and notes by H.W. Codrington. Hereafter cited as *D'Oyly, SLD*.

34 Report by D'Oyly. Enclosed with Despatch 71, dated Aripo, 20 March 1814. CO 54/52, quoted *Tri Sinhala*, p. 76.

35 Pilimatalawe, Mattamagoda and others banished to Mauritius following the Kandyan War of 1817–1818. Petition to the Prince Regent. Encl. to Governor Barnes's Despatch of 18 August 1820. CO 54/77, quoted *Tri Sinhala*, p. 83.

36 Davy's spelling of Sinhala proper names has been modernized and regularized in this retelling. See also *Tri Sinhala*, pp. 239–41: the evidence for a particularly harrowing detail in the story of the execution of Ehelepola's wife and family – the forcing of the mother to pound the heads of her children – has been reviewed by P.E. Pieris in an appendix to *Tri Sinhala* and found unconvincing: this instance of inhumanity had frequently been used to illustrate the cruelty of Portuguese, Dutch and Sinhalese commanders of earlier times. See also *Ludowyk*, pp. 150–1, who notes that something like this story was picked up by Robert Knox in the 17th century, when it was repeated of Rajasinha II. 'The sexual fantasy lurking in it', adds Ludowyk, 'could have given pleasure to a psychopath. But Sri Vikrama Rajasinha was no psychopath. Quite apart from various practical difficulties in the story – such as the unusual size of the mortar which would have been required – its gory trimmings are more likely to have been corroborative detail familiar in folk belief about the activities of *yakkhas* (demons) than the sadism of any human being.'

37 In his discussion of the situation and the events that flowed from it, Sir Paul Pieris presents them from the standpoint of Kandyan law.
'Ehelepola's offence was of a peculiarly aggravated nature; his immediate predecessor's fate had ceased to teach its lesson and twice before the King's clemency had saved him from the death which by his offences he had merited. Now he had placed himself beyond reach of his Master's power, and abandoned his hostages, and the Law was that they must bear the penalty. His blood was attainted and could not be permitted to infect the race any further. The King pronounced the terrible sentence that his family was to be wiped out. The children, one said to have been an infant in arms, were put to the sword, and their bodies dragged through the streets to be thrown away, for burial was denied to those suffering capital punishment. Their mother, with three others, were led by female palace slaves to the brink of the lake at Bogambara, where their hands and feet were bound and a large stone secured round the neck of each, after which they were thrown into the water, the method of execution adopted in the very rare cases where a King of Ceylon sentenced a woman to death: they were spared the more terrible punishment of being consigned to the Rodi, the untouchables who according to the social scheme of the Sinhalese, were considered the vilest of the human race.
At the Solemnity of the Investiture of a Sinhalese King with the Sword of State representatives of the three castes poured water on his head exhorting him to rule in accordance with the Ten Royal Virtues, but at the same time imprecating a curse on him should he be found wanting – he was the source of Justice, which he had to administer to his subjects according to Law without affection or ill-will, ignorance or fear, and to that ideal Sri Vikrama continued steadfastly loyal. "The Kandyan laws are well known . . . Did I make those laws?" That is Sri Vikrama's answer to the malignant libels of interested traducers.' (*Tri Sinhala*, p. 84, quoting Granville's Journal in the penultimate sentence.)

38 The words are those of John D'Oyly's famous contemporary, Jane Austen. Cf. *Mansfield Park* (1814), vol. III, ch. 3: 'Shakespeare one gets acquainted with without knowing how [said Henry Crawford]. It is a part of an Englishman's constitution. His thoughts and beauties are so spread

abroad that one touches them every where, one is intimate with him by instinct . . .'

'[Shakespeare's] celebrated passages are quoted by everybody [replied Edmund Bertram]; they are in half the books we open, and we all talk Shakespeare, use his similies, and describe with his descriptions.'

39 M.B. Dassanayake, 'The Day 2539 Years of Freedom Ended', *Weekend*, 1 March 1987.

Chapter Seven
'The Portals Thrown Open'

1 Cf. K.M. de Silva, *A History of Sri Lanka* (Oxford 1981), pp. 228–9.

2 Skinner, *Fifty Years in Ceylon*, p. 4. See also W.I. Jennings, *The Kandy Road*, ed. H.A.I. Goonetileke (1993), pp. 12–13.

3 Captain Johnston's narrative, published in 1810 'in the hope of . . . giving to officers, who may hereafter be employed in the interior of the island, that information which they may not have had the means of obtaining', was reprinted in 1854. Its 'lessons learned' are judged by Lt. Colonel A.A. de Alwis of the Sri Lanka Military Academy to 'have relevance even today in the command and control of forces in a wartime scenario', cf. de Alwis, 'Secret Pass'.

4 Powell, *Kandyan Wars*, p. 219.

5 *D'Oyly, SLD*, p. 195.

6 Ibid., p. 202.

7 Johnston, *Expedition to Candy*, p. 65.

8 See Ch. 5, n. 8.

9 Kappagoda, 'Last King of Kandy'.

10 Cf. *Hulugalle*, p. 116.

11 Cf. *President's House*, p. 14.

12 Calladine was born in Leicestershire in 1793. His father was a gardener. Calladine enlisted in the Derbyshire militia and in June 1814, after service in England, he sailed for Ceylon and remained there until 1820. Ignorant of rhetoric and innocent of ethnic or moral scruples, this ranker took a Kandyan woman (Dingiri Menika) as his mistress, and claimed in his *Memoirs* that his regiment probably left behind more children than any other regiment serving in Sri Lanka. His diary, edited by Major M.L. Ferrar, 'late The Green Howards', was published as *The Diary of Colour-Serjeant George Calladine 19th Foot 1793–1837*, in London in 1922. All page references are to this first edition, hereafter cited as *Calladine*.

13 *Calladine*, p. 39.

14 *D'Oyly, SLD*, p. 212.

15 'Part of this Palace is now used as a barrack; it serves also for the residence of the chief civil and military officers and for several offices.' Captain L. de Bussche, *Letters on Ceylon* (London 1826), p. 82.

16 *D'Oyly, SLD*, p. 213.

17 See Appendix 3 for details of the 1820 auction, as given by Sir Paul Pieris. See also Ch. 7.

18 In his account of the princely families of India, Clark Worswick relates an anecdote concerning the famous Koh-i-Noor diamond:

A year after the British East India Company annexed the Punjab in 1849, the [Koh-i-Noor diamond] was "presented" to Queen Victoria. With regal insensitivity, the Queen invited Dhuleep Singh, the deposed heir of the now defunct kingdom of the Punjab, to visit her at Windsor Castle to view the diamond which had been further diminished to a lean 106 carats. When asked if he recognized the fragment of the (then) largest diamond in the world, the prince took the stone over to a window and studied it for fifteen minutes; he then handed it back to Her Majesty, expressing "deep pleasure at being able to place it in her hands". Thereafter, the prince allegedly referred to Her Majesty privately as "Mrs Fagin", saying, "She is really the receiver of stolen property. She had no more right to that diamond than I have to Windsor Castle."' Clark Worswick, *Princely India* (New York 1980), p. 11.

19 Cf. Shellim, *Patchwork*, an illustrated account of the work of Thomas and William Daniell, Sir Charles Doyley, William Hodges, Robert Home and other British artists who painted in India. See also Welch, *Room for Wonder*, de Silva, *Early Prints of Ceylon*, privately published (London 1985); and the entries on Thomas Daniell and his nephews William and Samuel Daniell (brothers) in the *Dictionary of National Biography*.

20 There is no reason to doubt that most of the illustrations in Caunter's book are the work of one or other of the Daniell family. The Daniells seem, however, to have been painters of picturesque landscapes and buildings, rather than of portraits. Also, despite Caunter's identification of William Daniell as the painter of the queen's portrait, he is not known to have ever visited Sri Lanka though his younger brother Samuel lived and worked in the island for several years. Contributions to the debate concerning the identity of the artist include J.T. Rutnam, 'Kandy Queen's Picture Starts a Debate', *Ceylon Daily News*, 16 February 1982; 'The riddle of the "Queen of Candy"', an unsigned article, *Ceylon Daily News*, 5 January 1983; S. Suraweera, 'Who Painted Her?', *Ceylon News*, 15 June 1978; and G.H. de Soysa, '"The Queen of Candy" – Painted in Colombo!', *Ceylon Daily News*, 26 January 1983. The drawing has been referred to by a number of writers. James de Alwis's unpublished history of Ceylon (1872) states that the portrait was painted in India and engraved in England many years after the weddings, which he describes in detail. In 1917 Dr Andreas Nell, writing in the *Royal Asiatic Journal*, doubted the accuracy of Revd Caunter's account. In 1978 Stanley Suraweera asked whether the picture could have been painted in Vellore, after the king and queens and their retinue were taken there by the British.

It is possible that the original drawing might have been made by Samuel Daniell, who frequently sent samples of his work to Thomas and William Daniell. When he could have made it, and where, remains a mystery. But if the portrait was indeed from his pencil, his work might, in this case, have been confused by Caunter with the work of William Daniell. This theory does not, however, support Caunter's claim that the portrait was executed during his own stay in Kandy. Samuel Daniell died in 1811, and cannot therefore be the painter reported to have painted the queen's portrait at Maligakande in 1815 (see n. 28 below).

21 The painting itself seems to be generally accepted as a portrait by an unknown European artist of Sri Vikrama Rajasinha's youngest queen. Her childlike appearance, the mountain peaks and lush hill-country foliage in the background, and the depiction by the artist of what seems to be the parapet surrounding the lake at Kandy (one of the lasting public works undertaken by King Sri Vikrama Rajasinha before his removal from his kingdom) all give support to this identification. The original drawing has long been lost, but copies of this portrait were hung in many nationalist Sri Lankan homes throughout the twentieth century as a mark of silent protest against the British regime.

22 The queen's blouse, stained with the blood that dripped from her ear lobes as her captors tore the earrings from her ears, may still be seen in the Kandy National Museum, formerly the queens' palace at Kandy.

23 Hobart Caunter, *The Oriental Annual, or, Scenes in India. Comprising 25 Engravings from Original Drawings by William Daniell, RA, and a Descriptive Account by the Rev. Hobart Caunter, BD* (London 1834), pp. 84–5.

24 See Ch. 4 for details of the elaborate escort provided when

General Hay Macdowall travelled to Kandy as Governor Frederick North's Ambassador Extraordinary and Commissioner Plenipotentiary in 1805. The Kandyan court's insistence on such pomp was inflexible, and always had been.

25 It will be noted that Caunter does not actually claim to have *seen* the queen; he could be reporting the painter's impression of the lady. His manner of writing, however, implies that he did see her, and was welcomed into her presence.

26 Roger Hudson, *The Grand Tour 1592–1796* (London 1993), p. 251.

27 Possibly a reference to dressmakers and seamstresses of Dutch (Burgher) descent, members of Colombo's European community.

28 Cf. de Soysa, '"The Queen of Candy"', who cites a reference to a special supplement of the *Government Gazette* published in 1824 in connection with the death of Maha Mudaliyar Adrian de Abrew Rajapakse. Later, according to the same report, this unidentified painter and his wife resided for some time at the *walauwa*, painting the portraits of the *maha mudaliyar* and a physician monk who treated the governor and the chief justice. If this report is accurate, the controversial portrait was painted in 1815, in the months preceding the queen's exile to Vellore with the other members of the royal family.

29 G. T. Wickremasinghe, 'The King Observes Table Manners', *Island,* 27 December 1981, quotes Granville's *Journal*. King Sri Vikrama Rajasinha is believed to have been survived by two daughters, Rajanachchiyar Devi and Rajalaximi Devi. His only son Rajadhi died in 1842 without issue. Cf. Ariyadasa Ratnasinghe, 'Destiny of Lanka's Last king', *Sri Lanka News*, 2 February 1984.

30 The situation of Sri Vikrama Rajasinha in exile may perhaps be compared with that of Bahadur Shah II, who ruled in Delhi from 1837 to 1858. The mutiny ended with most of his sons shot; but he himself was merely exiled, after a humiliating trial. Accompanied by his wife, his youngest son and a few servants, the last Mughal emperor was taken to Rangoon in Burma, where he wrote melancholy poetry until his death in 1862. To quote a verse that has been ascribed to him:

'On seeing me no eye lights up, no heart near me finds solace; serving no use or purpose, I am but a handful of dust.' Quoted in Welch, *Room for Wonder*, p. 118.

31 On 2 March the Kandyan Convention was signed, ceding the kingdom to the British Crown. See *Davy*, pp. 369–88, for Appendices in which are contained the complete text of the Official Bulletin (issued from British Headquarters, Kandy, on 2 March 1815 and signed by James Sutherland, Deputy Secretary), and the Official Declaration of the Settlement of the Kandyan Provinces, including the Proclamation, dated Kandy, 3 March 1815.

On 18 March, according to D'Oyly's own account, three other chiefs signed the convention: Ehelepola, Galagoda and Pilimatalawa. There is some doubt, as a result, whether Ehelepola ever did sign the document. For several reasons, including D'Oyly's expertise in both Sinhala and Tamil and the fact that the document remained in his keeping from 2 to 18 March, also the disillusioned state of Ehelepola's mind by 18 March, the fact that Ehelepola's signature on the document is in Tamil letters though his personal seal bore Sinhala letters, and that he habitually signed his name in Sinhala, the suggestion has been made (notably by L. B. Senaratne, 'Were the Signatures Forged?' *Island International*, 11 March 1992) that Ehelepola's signature might have been forged, presumably by the 'orientalist' D'Oyly.

32 See Dassanayake, 'Kandyan Convention'.

33 Gajaman died in Matara. The Thero was to die twelve years later, in 1827. There are two conflicting traditions regarding Gajaman Nona's grave. According to the first, it is located in Nonage-gama, the village near Hambantota said to have been granted to her by D'Oyly, its ruins being beneath a Nuga tree by the tank. The second tradition claims that the grave lies close to that of Karatota Thera, whose funeral pyre had been erected nearby. See Chs 4 and 5 for accounts of D'Oyly's relationships with these two literary personalities.

34 Thomas D'Oyly to John D'Oyly, 2 July 1815, received in Kandy January 1816. *D'Oyly Family Letters*, p. 19.

35 Thomas D'Oyly to John D'Oyly, 5 August 1815, received in Kandy 16 August 1816. Ibid., p. 21.

36 Mary D'Oyly to John D'Oyly, 18 August 1815, received in Kandy 2 June 1816. Ibid., pp. 21–2.

37 Mary D'Oyly to John D'Oyly, 29 August 1815, received in Kandy 17 June 1816. Ibid., pp. 24–6.

Chapter Eight
1815: 'A Common Bond of Peace'

1 'Official Declaration of the Settlement of the Kandyan Provinces', 3 March 1815, reprinted in *Davy*, pp 369–75. Hereafter cited as *D'Oyly, SKP*.

2 Vimalananda, 'Kandyan Convention', pt II: 'D'Oyly, the Crown's Crafty Agent'. To Vimalananda's shortlist of successful spymasters comparable with D'Oyly might be added the name of Markus Wolf, former Head of Intelligence in the German Democratic Republic.

3 Marshall, *Ceylon*, p. 123.

4 Cf. T. Vimalananda, 'Kandyan Convention', pt III: Last Days of the Kingdom'.

5 Marshall, *Ceylon*, pp. 130–1.

6 For the text of the Act of Settlement and the document that accompanied it, cf. *D'Oyly, SKP.*

7 *Travellers*, p. 121.

8 Benjamin Clough to Dr Clark, 27 September 1814, MMS/1A/1814–1817).

9 Vimalananda, 'Kandyan Convention', pt III: Last Days of the Kingdom'. See *Davy*, pp. 369–88 for appendices in which are contained the complete text of the Official Bulletin (issued from British Headquarters, Kandy, on 2 March 1815 and signed by James Sutherland, Deputy Secretary), the Official Declaration of the Settlement of the Kandyan Provinces, including the proclamation, dated Kandy, 3 March 1815; and the proclamation given out by Governor Brownrigg on 21 November 1818 following the conclusion of the Kandyan War.

10 Edmund Burke, *Reflections on the Revolution in France* (1790), p. 286.

11 Woods was Commissioner of Revenue in Kandy in 1810.

12 R.J. Mackintosh (ed.), *Memoirs of the Life of the Rt. Honourable Sir James Mackintosh*, 2 vols (London 1835), vol. II, p. 6.

13 Barbara Strachey, *The Strachey Line: An English Family in America, India and at Home from 1570–1902.* (London 1986), quoted in M. FitzHerbert, 'A Parti-Coloured Pedigree', *Times Literary Supplement*, 7 February 1986, p. 135. See also Gooneratne, 'Historical "Truths" and Literary "Fictions"', pp. 5–6.

14 Cf. Michael Cox (ed.), *The Cream of Noel Coward.* London 1996, pp. 39–41.

15 See David Weeks and Jamie James, to whose book *Eccentrics* (1995) our attention was drawn by Barry Oakes in an *Australian Magazine* article (10–11 June 1995). Research by Weeks and James reveals 'a great outburst of eccentricity beginning around 1725', especially among the aristocracy and landed gentry. The examples they give include Jack Mytton (1796–1834), who drank five bottles of port a day,

had more than 1,000 hats and 3,000 shirts, and once appeared at one of his own dinner parties in full hunting costume, mounted on his bear. 'In the ensuing panic, while his friends jumped out of windows or got behind chairs, Mytton called out "tally-ho" and spurred his mount, which turned impatient and ate part of his leg.' The scientist Henry Cavendish (1731–1810) was so shy that he developed an elaborate system of double doors in his house to avoid personal contact with his servants. Lord Monboddo (1714–1799), the Scottish jurist, never rode in a carriage, believing it an affront to human dignity to ride behind a horse rather than on top of one. Dame Edith Sitwell's matchless book *English Eccentrics* (1933) is, of course, a rich source of similar information.

16 Careme (1783–1833), quoted by Anne Willan in *Great Cooks and their Recipes: from Taillevent to Escoffier* (Harmondsworth 1993). Once chef to Talleyrand, Napoleon's foreign minister and the founder of *haute cuisine*, Careme crossed the English Channel in 1815 and for two years cooked in England for the Prince Regent.

17 Cf. Seneviratne, 'Memorial'.

18 *The Memoirs of a Highland Lady during her Three Weeks' Stay at Colombo*, quoted in *Hulugalle*, pp. 44–5.

19 Governor Barnes, in an obituary published in the *Government Gazette* after D'Oyly's death in 1824. Extract from the *Ceylon Gazette* of 29 May 1824. East Sussex Record Office, AMS 6185/13.

20 These Provincial Courts were supervised by the *disaves* till 1818, and after that by government agents.

21 Cf. *Hulugalle*, p. 122.

22 Sir Paul Pieris, who reproduces this drawing as the frontispiece to *Tri Sinhala*, states that no other likeness of the Sinhalese chiefs exists to his knowledge, 'and even of D'Oyly the

only portraits available are those taken when he was a little child'.

23 Cf. *Hulugalle*, pp. 117–18.

24 *Asiatic Journal* (1816), p. 91.

25 *Hulugalle*, p. 122.

26 Quoted in Drabble, *Writer's Britain*, p. 124.

27 George Osborne to J. Benson, Trincomalee, 4 March 1818. MMS/IIA/1817–1836.

Chapter Nine
1816–1817: Translating the Nation

1 Chris Berry, 'Dead or Alive: Reflections on Translating Non-Western Literature', in W. Ommundsen and M. Boreland (eds) *Refractions: Asian/Australian Writing* (special issue) Rubicon 1/2 (1995), pp. 3–4.

2 Henry Marshall, *Ceylon*, p. 175. See Ch. 8 for a more detailed account of Marshall's views on the subject.

3 Southey, *Mr Rowlandson's England*, p. 84.

4 Cf. Rosane Rocher, *Orientalism, Poetry and the Millennium: The Checkered Life of Nathaniel Brassey-Halhed, 1751–1830* (Delhi 1983), p. 48. Rocher notes that Halhed also published *A Grammar of Bengali* in 1780.

5 Simon Sawers, a civil servant, arrived in Sri Lanka in 1811, and eventually became Judicial Commissioner in Kandy.

6 *D'Oyly Family Letters*, p. 12.

7 Ibid., pp. 15–16, 29–30.

8 Cited as *D'Oyly, Constitution*.

9 The palace became John D'Oyly's residence and, subsequently, the residence of the government agents of Kandy. Cf. N. Karunaratne, *From Governor's Pavilion to President's Pavilion* (Sri Lanka n.d.), p. 4.

10 See Ch. 7 for the text of D'Oyly's letter to Brownrigg of 6 March 1815.

11 Cf. *Hulugalle*, pp. 117–18.

12 Cf. *D'Oyly, Constitution*, pp. 141–2.

13 Cf. Harris, *Gaze of the Coloniser*. It was not until 1882 that Englishwomen could retain control over property owned by them at the time of marriage; cf. Jayawardena, *Feminism and Nationalism*.

14 *Hulugalle*, p. 122.

15 Talipot: the broad leaf of the talipot palm was routinely used in Sri Lanka as protection against sun and rain. Captain Johnston noted in 1810 that 'a leaf of the talipot tree, an extensive umbrella', was part of the lightweight equipment of every Kandyan fighting man, since it 'serves to protect him from the heat of the sun during the day, and two men, by placing the broad end of their leaves together, may form a tent that will completely defend them against the rains or dews, by night'. *Expedition to Candy*, pp. 8–9.

16 D'Oyly, *Constitution*, p. 195.

17 T. Vimalananda, 'Kandyan Convention', pt III: 'Last Days of the Kingdom'.

18 *Davy*, pp. 266–7.

19 Ibid., pp. 265–6.

20 Machiavelli, *The Prince*, pp. 49–50.

21 See Ch. 8.

Chapter Ten
'Madness of War'

1 As will be gathered from the tone of this description of Keppetipola's execution, the story of the chieftain's end has now entered the area of national epic. The account given here has been adapted from the work of a modern Sri Lankan writer, S.M. Nanayakkara, 'Martyrdom of Keppetipola and Madugalle: Heroes of the 1817–1818 Uva Rebellion', *Sunday Observer*, 27 March 1994. See also Elmo Jayawardene, 'Ihagama: A Forgotten Hero of Sinhale', *Island*, 26 April 1998, for an account of a priestly 'revolutionary' who was exiled to Mauritius with 25 other leaders of the rebellion.

2 The similarity of Marshall's action to that perpetrated by British 'scientists' in Tasmania in relation to the skulls of murdered Aboriginals is difficult to overlook. Keppetipola's skull has since been returned to Sri Lanka.

3 *The Diary of Colour-Sergeant George Calladine 19th Foot*, ed. M.L. Ferrar (London 1922). Hereafter cited as *Calladine*.

4 Ibid., pp. 55–7.

5 Major McDonald, 19th Regiment, commanded a flying camp at this period. On a hill half a mile from the fort called after his name, he made a remarkable stand during the rebellion, against the whole forces of the country, assembled under the command of Keppetipola. On this hill of gentle ascent, with the advantage only of not being commanded, the gallant officer, with a party composed of 60 rank and file, for eight days in succession stood and repelled the attacks of about seven or eight thousand Kandians. *Calladine*, p. 64.

6 Ibid., pp. 63–4.

7 Ibid., pp. 73–4.

8 Ibid., p. 72.

9 'Dingy', Calladine's affectionate diminutive for 'Dingiri Menike', a name common among women of the Kandyan villages.

10 *Calladine*, p. 75.

11 Calladine died at Derby on 3 August 1876, aged 83, his wife Ann having predeceased him on 31 October 1846. Of their thirteen children eleven died in infancy. His son George died at Derby in 1871 aged 40, and Thomas, born 7 January 1838, survived him. Ibid., p. 210.

12 Ibid., p. 77.

13 Our source here is Powell, *Kandyan Wars*, pp. 259–65.

14 *Davy*, p. 302.

15 Cf. *Hulugalle*, p. 123.

16 Cf. Vimalananda, *Great Rebellion*, pp. lii, lxvii–lxviii. Vimalananda explores the evidence for Brownrigg's

neglect of D'Oyly, and the decline of D'Oyly's influence and authority.

17 CO 54/61, Brownrigg to Bathurst, 5 September 1816; CO 54/66, Brownrigg to Bathurst, 25 September 1817, cited in Powell, *Kandyan Wars* p. 238.

18 Cf. *Davy*: among those mentioned are Dr Farrell, Deputy Inspector of Hospitals (p. xxiii), Lieutenant-Colonel Hardy, Deputy Quarter-master-General (pp. xxiii–xxiv), Maha Mudaliyar de Saram (p. xxiv), and the 'Dissave of Welassey, Malawa', to whom in particular Davy states he owes the historical sketch he provides in ch. 10 of his book.

19 Cf. *Davy*, p. xxii.

20 Ibid., p. 21.

21 Cf. letter from George Osborne to J. Benson, Trincomalee, 4 March 1818, MMS/IIA/1817–1836, quoted at the end of Ch. 8.

22 'I lately conversed with some Kandians, who *laughed heartily* at the idea of knowing what was to become of them after death; & whose mirth seemed no way allayed on the intimation of a method by which they might be saved from their sins.' William Bridgnell to the Methodist Missionary Society Committee, Kurunegala, 26 August 1828, MMS/V/1829.

23 Clough to Dr Clark, 27 September 1814, MMS/1A/1814–1817.

24 George D'Oyly to John D'Oyly, Lambeth Palace, 16 April 1817, received in Kandy on 1 February 1818.

25 Mrs Mary D'Oyly wrote to John D'Oyly from Brighton on 28 March 1817, describing the Miss Hares, 'good humoured young Ladies', and said of a Mr Hodgson, a former associate of John's at Bene't, that 'he has made good use of his time & he may have a 4th she is a very pleasing woman neace to Dr Pemberton . . .

26 Cf. *Hulugalle*, p. 123.

27 See Appendix 3.

28 In R. Raven-Hart (trans.), *Heydt's Ceylon: Being the Relevant Sections of the 'Allerneuester Geographisch- und Topographischer Schau-Platz von Africa und Ost-Indien etc. etc.'* (Colombo 1952), pp. 14–15.

29 George D'Oyly graduated BA as second wrangler from Corpus Christi College, Cambridge, and followed his father into the Church. Ordained deacon in 1802 by the Bishop of Chichester, and priest in 1803 by the Bishop of Gloucester, he acted as curate to his father for a few months in 1803, and in 1804 became curate of Wrotham in Kent. From 1806 to 1809 he was moderator at Cambridge University, and was a select preacher to the university in 1809, 1810 and 1811. In 1813 he was appointed domestic chaplain to the Archbishop of Canterbury, and married Maria Frances Bruere, the daughter of a former principal secretary to the Government of India.

30 Thomas D'Oyly to John D'Oyly, 10–23 July 1820.

31 Cf. note in *D'Oyly Family Letters*, p. 128.

32 Cf. *Hulugalle*, p. 123.

33 Dr Sonia Hall has suggested that, in his search for a suitable motto, Thomas D'Oyly may have turned for inspiration to the Bible, that source familiar above all others to a clergyman's son. In a personal communication (10 March 1997) she traces the motto to a possible biblical source in the Authorized (King James) Version, Job 22: 8: 'But as for the mighty man, he had the earth; and the honourable man dwelt in it.'

The similarity of the source to the motto becomes, as she notes, even more striking in the version presented in the New English Bible: 'Is the earth, then, the preserve of the strong and a domain for the favoured few?'

It is interesting that the context does not congratulate Job, reproaching him instead for his sinfulness and selfishness.

34 Thomas D'Oyly to John D'Oyly, 23 December 1821, *D'Oyly Family Letters,* p. 89.

35 The Good News Bible (1976), Job 22: 4–8.

29 Cf. A.A. de Alwis, 'Island Exile', *Sunday Observer Magazine,* 13 August 1995, p. 21, and Elmo Jayawardene, 'In Search of Ehelepola's Tomb', *Daily News,* 2 April 1994. De Alwis cites 'Mrs Bartram's delightful journal entitled "Recollections of Seven Years Residence in Mauritius"' as containing many anecdotes concerning Ehelepola's stay in Mauritius, but provides no date of publication or other details. Jayawardene, 'Ihagama', records that Ihagama Thera, who shared Ehelepola's exile in Mauritius, established a small temple in Pamplemousse and practised ayurvedic medicine there, specializing in the field of opticals.

37 Cf. Ch. 9.

38 Ehelepola's last words to John D'Oyly, as given in T.B. Pohath Kehelpannala, *Life of Ehelepola,* quoted in de Alwis, 'Island Exile'; see also Ehelepola Maha Nilame, *Representations to His Majesty's Commissioners of Enquiry* (1829) in *Ceylon Literary Register,* Vol. 2 (1932), nos. 8, 9, 10.

Chapter Eleven
1822–1824: 'D'Oyly of Kandy'

1 Thomas Skinner, *Fifty Years in Ceylon,* ed. Annie Skinner (London 1891) (cited hereafter as *Skinner*), p. 187. Major Thomas Skinner came to Ceylon in 1819 at the age of fourteen, was made a lieutenant in the army, and within a few weeks of his arrival in Trincomalee was given the responsibility of marching a detachment of soldiers of the Ceylon Rifles regiment from Trincomalee overland to Colombo. In late 1819 the country was seeing the final stages of the Kandyan War. His 200-mile march took him through some of the areas which only a few weeks before had been in violent rebellion against the British.

When Governor Barnes first commenced his policy of road construction he entrusted this work to the young military officer. After Barnes departed, Skinner remained in Ceylon as a road-builder and it was largely under his direction that the vast network of roads which criss-crossed the Kandyan kingdom was continued in the next fifty years. His autobiography, written after his retirement from the colonial government's service in 1867, is the story of the development of the road system in Ceylon. This autobiography was not published during his lifetime, and was edited and printed in 1891 by his daughter Annie Skinner.

2 De Alwis, *Sidat Sangarava,* Introduction, p. cclii.

3 John D'Oyly's 'Sketch of the Constitution of the Kandyan Kingdom' was communicated by Sir Alexander Johnstone (Chief Justice of Ceylon, 1811–1820) to the Royal Asiatic Society, read at a meeting on 7 May 1831, and printed in the RAS *Transactions,* vol. III, pt II. It was later published under the title *A Sketch of the Constitution of the Kandyan Kingdom (1832) and other relevant papers, collated under the orders of Government,* ed. L.J.B. Turner (Colombo 1929); 2nd edn ed. S.D. Saparamadu (Dehiwela 1975).

4 *Skinner,* pp. 139–40. Cf. S.D. Saparamadu's introduction to the reprint of Skinner's autobiography, *Fifty Years in Ceylon* (1891) (Dehiwela 1974), pp. vii–viii.

5 *Skinner,* p. 140.

6 'Wayfarer', '1815 and the "D'Oyly Aristocrats"', *Times of Ceylon,* 2 March 1965.

7 MMS/IIA/1819–1820.

8 After D'Oyly's death in 1824, the estate was bought by Sir Edward Barnes, who began to cultivate coffee on it. Cf. Karunaratne, *Governor's Pavilion to President's Pavilion,* p. 36.

9 Knighton, *Forest-Life in Ceylon*, vol. II, p. 361.

10 Thomas D'Oyly described himself as a Barrister at Law and a Fellow of All Souls, Oxford *c.* 1815 (East Sussex Record Office, AMS 6185/85–6). By 1819 he had been promoted to the office of Serjeant at Law (AMS 6185/18). His office was at 4 Kings Bench Walks, Temple, but glimpses of his work on circuit and on the County Bench can be detected in these and other MSS held by the East Sussex Record Office. He is noted as a circuit judge in 1816 (AMS 6185/47), as a magistrate on the East Sussex Bench in 1825 (LAN 199), and as an assize judge in Lewes in 1828 (LAN 292). His family connections and properties in West Sussex ensured him a position in that county and in 1834 his work as Chairman of the Western Sessions earned him the warm appreciation of Lord Egremont at Petworth House (AMS 6185/34). In 1836 his opinion was consulted by the Commissioners of Lewes and Laughton Levels re vandalism to the sea wall, and in 1842 he acted as Enclosure Commissioner for the Manor of Warningore in Chailey (SRA6/14/20; QDD/6/E21). Thomas D'Oyly kept houses both in London and in Sussex at Brighton and at Rottingdean. He also stayed from time to time at Buxted, where his younger brother George had succeeded their father as rector (see Ch. 10, n. 29). His position in society is indicated by King George IV's invitation for D'Oyly to dine with him, presumably at the Brighton Pavilion, in 1835 (AMS 6185/35). Thomas D'Oyly died in 1855. The Earl of Chichester at Stanmer House had been among D'Oyly's associates, and was named as an executor of his will. Several items in the East Sussex Record Office collection indicate Thomas D'Oyly's keen interest in history and antiquities.

11 East Sussex Record Office, AMS 6185/12. Letter from Governor Edward Barnes to the Earl of Bathurst dated 10 June 1824.

12 East Sussex Record Office, AMS 6185/13. Extract from the *Ceylon Gazette* of 29 May 1824.

13 Cf. Lewis, *Tombstones and Monuments*.

14 Cf. Yasmine Gooneratne, 'Desire, Death and the Jewels of the Orient: Rear-Admiral Charles Austen and Sir John D'Oyly, Baronet', *Sensibilities* 12 (June 1996), p. 13.

15 Cf. 'Autobiography of a Periya Durai' (n.d.), quoted in Lewis, *Tombstones and Monuments*, p. 295, for a description of 'this lonely spot', the Old Garrison Cemetery at Kandy.

16 Ellis, 'Buried History', p. 13. In 1998 it was reported that Kandy's Garrison Cemetery is now transformed, thanks to the efforts of the British Ministry of Defence, the British High Commission in Sri Lanka and the Trustees of St Paul's Church, Kandy: 'Complete re-fencing, the removal of . . . top soil, new run-off drains, rebuilding of some of the tombs, and turfing has made this cemetery the quiet, beautiful place it always was', Carl Muller, 'Re-opening of Kandy's Garrison Cemetery', *Sunday Times*, 4 October 1998, p. 6.

17 Cf. *Burke's Extinct and Dormant Baronetcies of England, Ireland, and Scotland* (1841).

Chapter Twelve
Omne Solum Forti Patria

1 *Ludowyk*, pp. 149–50.

2 Cf. Lewis, *Tombstones and Monuments*, p. 299.

3 Quoted in Lewis, ibid.

4 See the frontispiece, showing John D'Oyly in conference with three Kandyan chieftains. The men are all seated on chairs which are covered with white cloth.

5 *Ludowyk*, p. 150.

6 See also in this connection the shrewd advice given by D'Oyly to

Brownrigg relating to Keppetipola's claim to hold the relic of the Buddha's Tooth, Ch. 10.

7 Cf. Lewis, *Tombstones and Monuments*, pp. 298–9; cf. also *Calladine*, who 'suppose[d] the 19th Regiment left more children [behind in Sri Lanka] than any regiment leaving the country before', p. 77.

8 Seneviratne, 'Memorial'.

9 Oliver Goldsmith, *She Stoops to Conquer, or, The Mistakes of a Night* (1773), in J.M. Morrell (ed.), *Four English Comedies of the 17th and 18th Centuries* (Harmondsworth 1974), Act II, p. 251.

10 Cf. Hyam, *Empire and Sexuality*, ch. 2, for numerous instances of such involvement on the part of officers of the Raj in India and Sri Lanka. 'Fierce Peshawar', according to Captain Kenneth Searight (p. 131), was 'An Asiatic stronghold where each flower / Of boyhood planted in its restless soil / Is – *ipso facto* – ready to despoil / (Or be despoiled by) someone else . . .' See also n. 13 below.

11 Which rather surprised Sir Paul Pieris, who published extracts from the diary D'Oyly kept as an undergraduate at Cambridge. D'Oyly did record occasional visits, in the company of other male friends, to the houses of the Cambridge *demi-monde*, but did not dwell on them as, for instance, James Boswell did in his journals at a comparable age.

12 On 28 March 1817, Mrs D'Oyly wrote to John D'Oyly from the seaside resort town of Brighton, describing the Miss Hares, 'good humoured young Ladies', and mentioning a Mr Hodgson, a former associate of John's at Bene't College, as having 'made good use of his time & he may have a 4th she is a very pleasing woman neace to Dr Pemberton'. Though he received many such letters from members of his family, urging him to return home and in any case to marry, D'Oyly failed to do either, and on his death in Kandy in 1824 his baronetcy became extinct.

13 Information on this subject is hard to find: cf. Ronald Hyam, *Empire and Sexuality*, who notes that 'historians writing about the empire remain extremely shy about putting sex on their agenda' (p. 4). See in particular pp. 32–5, for a detailed account of the case of Sir Hector Macdonald (1853–1903), Commander-in-Chief in Ceylon in 1902, rumours of whose homosexual involvement with a group of Sri Lankan boys led to a summons home, the threat of court-martial and Macdonald's suicide. See Woolf, *Letters*, pp. 103–4, for a reference, in a letter Woolf wrote to Lytton Strachey dated 16 October 1905, to Macdonald and his 'reputation' in the colony. Spotts relates a story, still circulating in the 1980s and doing further damage to Macdonald's name by adding the stigma of treachery to the 'taint' of homosexuality, which maintains that 'Fighting Mac' faked the suicide, defected to the Germans, took the identity of Field Marshal Mackensen, who had purportedly just died of cancer, and during World War I led German troops on the Eastern Front. Family connections and social class almost certainly made a difference in the official attitudes adopted in such matters: it is unlikely that an English civil servant with aristocratic connections would have received the treatment that was meted out to Macdonald, a Scottish crofter's son who became a draper's apprentice before enlisting in the British Army in 1870.

14 E.L. Gilbert (ed.), *'O Beloved Kids': Rudyard Kipling's Letters to his Children* (London 1983), p. 78, quoted in Hyam, *Empire and Sexuality*, p. 67.

15 It was that tiny community's taste for scandal and gossip which led to charges being laid by schoolmasters and clergymen against Sir Hector Macdonald, and ultimately to his death. See n. 13 above; also T. Royle, *Death Before Dishonour: The True Story of 'Fighting Mac'* (London 1982).

16 See Drabble, *Writer's Britain,*
p.113, for some interesting instances of
middle-class British prejudice against
the 'exotic' in nature. She notes that
Angus Wilson writes in *The Middle Age
of Mrs Eliot* of snobbish contempt for
'the vulgar calceolaria'. Drabble sees in
the feelings of some English writers
prejudiced against certain kinds of
flowers 'a deep preoccupation with
notions of natural goodness and
original sin'.

17 *Skinner*, p. 249.

18 Sir Samuel Baker, *Eight Years'
Wanderings in Ceylon* (London 1855),
pp. 98–9.

19 Cobbett, quoted in Drabble,
Writer's Britain, p. 78.

20 Rudyard Kipling, quoted in
Drabble, ibid., p. 257.

21 Wilfrid Jayasuriya, 'The Ratnapura
Diaries' (4 pp.), a research paper, part
of a larger work, later published,
pp. 1–2. The Kaltota legend of the
Neelamaha Yodaya, notes Jayasuriya,
is only a dramatic version of history.
The failure of the irrigation system
brought about a failure of water-
sources, and with that a decline in
fertility. As a result there grew a
legend that the women of Kaltota
were barren.

22 Ibid., p. 3.

23 See Edmund Burke's thesis in
The Sublime and the Beautiful, that the
'sublime' is invariably tinged with
'terror'.

24 Cf. Drabble, *Writer's Britain,*
p. 162.

25 Percy Bysshe Shelley, 'Alastor, or
The Spirit of Solitude', in Thomas
Hutchinson (ed.), *The Complete
Poetical Works of Percy Bysshe Shelley*
(Oxford 1917), p. 26.

26 Woolf, *Letters*, p. 131.

27 See Ch. 5.

28 Cf. Machiavelli, *The Prince,*
pp. 112–13.

29 Jayasuriya, 'Ratnapura Diaries',
p. 4.

30 R.S. Thomas, 'Reservoirs', in
Selected Poems 1946–1968. (London
1973), p. 117.

31 Leonard Woolf, *Growing: An
Autobiography of the Years 1904–1911*
(London 1961), pp. 180, 225.

32 Ibid., pp. 246–52.

GLOSSARY

Adigar, Adikaram (Sinhala) chief officer of state, chief minister in the Kingdom of Kandy. The First Adigar took precedence over all others in the chiefly hierarchy

alankara (Sinhala) bright

appuhamy (Sinhala) gentleman-in-waiting

bhikku (Sinhala) Buddhist monk; a member of the Buddhist order

chatties Anglicized version of *chutty*, or *hutty* (Sinhala), clay cooking-pots

Dalada (Sinhala) relic of the Buddha's tooth; **Dalada Maligava**: the temple or palace in which the sacred relic of the Buddha's tooth is enshrined

devale (Sinhala) a shrine of the gods of the Buddhist/Hindu pantheon

Dhamma (Sinhala) Buddhist scriptures

disave (Sinhala) a chief who has been appointed governor of a province or *disavani* in the Kingdom of Kandy

kachcheri (South Indian) local government office

maha (Sinhala) great

mahanayake (Sinhala) chief priest (of a Buddhist temple)

mohandiram (Sinhala) a title of rank; a senior official of the low country (Maritime Provinces)

mudaliyar (Sinhala) an official appointed to administer a province or korale in the low country, higher in rank than a *mohandiram*

ola (Sinhala) treated palm-leaf on which writing is inscribed with a stylus, used as writing-paper

Pali Indian language, in which the Buddhist scriptures have been recorded

perahera (Sinhala) procession or pageant, the most ancient and important of which in Sri Lanka was, and is, the *Esala Perahera* of Kandy

raja (Sinhala) royal, a king; hence *Rajasinha*, 'Lion King'

rajakariya (Sinhala) work performed in the service of the king (or, by extension, of a lord or a temple)

sangha (Sinhala) Buddhist clergy

sinha (Sinhala) lion, hence Sinhala or Sinhalese (English), the people or language of the Lion Race

vihara (Sinhala) a Buddhist temple

walauwa (Sinhala) manor house; a chief's residence

276

BIBLIOGRAPHY

Primary Sources

Unpublished Records

Public Record Office

Methodist Missionary Society Muniments. Ceylon Papers: Letters and journals of Methodist missionaries in Ceylon, correspondence between missionaries and government officials and other persons.

1. Box Ceylon IA:	Files	1814–1817
		1816–1818
		1817–1819
		1817–1820
2. Box Ceylon IIA:	Files	1818–1821
		1818–1822
		1820–1822
		1819–1820
		1817–1836
3. Box Ceylon III:	Files	1822–1823
		1823
		1824
4. Box Ceylon IV:	Files	1827–1829
		1825–1826

Private Papers

Correspondence and papers of the D'Oyly and the Thomas families 1711–1928. East Sussex Record Office: AMS 6185

Published Works 1600–1900

Anderson, Philip, *The English in Western India*, 2nd edn, rev., London 1856

Arnold, William Delafield, *Oakfield, or, Fellowship in the East. By Punjabee*, 2 vols, London 1853

Baker, Sir Samuel White, *Eight Years' Wanderings in Ceylon,* London 1855.
——*With Rifle and Hound in Ceylon.* London 1854

Bennett, J.W., *Ceylon and its Capabilities. An Account of its Natural Resources, Indigenous Productions, and Commercial Facilities*, London 1843

Bertolacci, A., *A View of the Agricultural, Commercial and Financial Interests of Ceylon*, London 1817

Boyd, Hugh, *The Miscellaneous Works of Hugh Boyd. With an Account of His Life and Writings by Lawrence Dundas Campbell*, London 1800

British Parliamentary Papers (as quoted or cited in various modern secondary works)

Burke, Edmund, *A Philosophical Enquiry into the Origin of our Ideas of the Sublime and Beautiful* (1756), ed. James T. Boulton. London 1958

——*Reflections on the Revolution in France,* 1790

Burke's Extinct and Dormant Baronetcies of England, Ireland and Scotland, 1841

Calladine, George, *The Diary of Colour-Sergeant George Calladine 19th Foot, 1793–1837;* ed. M.L. Ferrar, London 1922

Campbell, James, *Excursions, Adventures and Field-Sports in Ceylon: Its Commercial and Military Importance, and Numerous Advantages to the British Emigrant,* 2 vols, London 1843

Caunter, Herbert, *The Oriental Annual, or, Scenes in India. Comprising 25 Engravings from Original Drawings by William Daniell, RA, and a descriptive account by the Rev. Hobart Caunter, BD,* London 1834

Cobbett, William, *Rural Rides: In Surrey, Kent, and Other Counties* (1822), Penguin edn, Harmondsworth 1967

Coleridge, Samuel Taylor, *Lectures (1795) on Politics and Religion,* in Lewis Patton and Peter Mann (eds), *The Collected Works of Samuel Taylor Coleridge,* Princeton 1971

Cook, James, *The Journals of Captain Cook,* ed. J.C. Beaglehole, 4 vols, 1955–1967

Cordiner, James, *A Description of Ceylon,* 2 vols, London 1807

Davy, John, *An Account of the Interior of Ceylon* (London 1821), 2nd edn, Dehiwela 1969

de Alwis, James, *The Sidat Sangarava: A Grammar of the Sinhalese Language. Translated into English, with Introduction, Notes and Appendices,*

Colombo 1852; 2nd edn, Colombo 1966

de Bussche, Captain L., *Letters on Ceylon,* London 1826

de Joinville, Joseph, 'On the Religion and Manners of the People of Ceylon', *Asiatic Researches* 7 (1803), pp. 307–444

Dilke, Charles Wentworth, *Greater Britain: A Record of Travel in English-Speaking Countries during 1866 and 1867,* 2 vols (London 1868), 6th edn, London 1872

Dona Isabella Perumal (Gajaman Nona), 'Poems of Gajaman Nona', *The Sinhalese Friend* 1/10 (March 1913), pp. 208–10

——*Poems by Dona Isabel Cornelia Perumal (Gajaman Nona),* ed. J.D. Fernando, 'with an account of the poet's life by G.H. Perera (24 pp., of which pp. 3–5 are missing), Colombo 1917

Downs, E.V, and Davies, G.L. (eds) *Selections from Macaulay: Letters, Prose, Speeches and Poetry,* London 1932

Doyley, Charles, *The European in India. From a collection of drawings, Engraved by J.H. Clark and C. Dubourg; with a Preface and Copious Descriptions, by Captain Thomas Williamson; Accompanied with a brief history of ancient and modern India ... by F.W. Blagdon, Esq.,* London 1813 (20 coloured plates)

D'Oyly, John, 'Commercii Laus', Latin ode, awarded the Sir William Browne's Medal at Cambridge University in 1795. Published as Appendix A (pp. 136–8) of P.E. Pieris (ed.), *Letters to Ceylon 1814–1824, being correspondence addressed to Sir John D'Oyly,* Cambridge 1938. Published as Appendix 2 of this book, with a translation by Professor J. Nicholls

——'The Elephant Kraal of 1809', A letter written by John D'Oyly to Thomas D'Oyly dated Colombo 18 June 1809, printed in *JRASCB* 34/91 (1938), pp. 240–63

——*Diary of Mr John D'Oyly, (Afterwards SIR JOHN D'OYLY, BART.), Resident, Principal Accredited Agent, and First Commissioner of the British Government in the Kandyan Provinces (1810–1815).* With Introduction and Notes by H.W. Codrington, Ceylon Civil Service. Special publication issued by the Ceylon Branch of the Royal Asiatic Society, 25/69, Colombo 1917, 2nd edn, New Delhi 1995

——'Official Declaration of the Settlement of the Kandyan Provinces', dated Kandy, 3 March 1815, contained in an Official Bulletin issued from British Headquarters, Kandy, 2 March 1815 signed by James Sutherland, Deputy Secretary 'By His Excellency (Robert Brownrigg)'s command, published as Appendix 1 in John Davy, *Account of the Interior of Ceylon* (1821), 1969, pp. 369–375

——*A Sketch of the Constitution of the Kandyan Kingdom (1832) and other Relevant Papers.* Collated under the Orders of Government, ed. L.J.B. Turner, Colombo 1929; 2nd edn, ed. and with an introduction by S.D. Saparamadu, Dehiwela 1975

D'Oyly Family, *Letters to Ceylon 1814–1824. Being Correspondence Addressed to Sir John D'Oyly*, ed. Sir Paul E. Pieris, Cambridge 1938

Ehelepola Maha Nilame, *Representations to His Majesty's Commissioners of Enquiry* (1829). Reprinted *Ceylon Literary Register*, Vol. 2, nos. 8, 9, 10 (1932)

Ellis, Sara, *The Wives of England, Their Relative Duties, Domestic Influence, and Social Obligations*, London 1843

——*The Women of England, Their Social Duties and Domestic Habits*, London 1838

Fasson, Stewart M., and Hamilton, Vereker M., *Scenes in Ceylon. Illustrated*, London 1882

Ferguson, John, *Ceylon in 1883. The Leading Crown Colony of the British Empire, with an Account of the Progress Made since 1803*, London 1883,

——*Ceylon in the 'Jubilee Year'*, London 1887

Forbes, Major, *Eleven Years in Ceylon. Comprising Sketches of the Field-Sports, and Natural History of that Colony, and an Account of its History and Antiquities*, 2 vols, London 1840

Froude, J.A., *Oceana, or, England and her Colonies*, London 1886

Gilpin, William, *Three Essays on Picturesque Beauty*, London 1792

——*Remarks on Forest Scenery (Relating Chiefly to Picturesque Beauty)*, London 1791

Gunasekare, Bandusena (ed.), *Gajaman Nona's Verse Compositions (Gajaman Nonage Kavi-Seepada)*, Maradana 1991

Hardy, R.S., *Eastern Monachism*, London 1850

Harvard, William M., *A Narrative of the Establishment and Progress of the Mission to Ceylon and India Founded by the Late Rev. Thomas Coke under the Direction of the Wesleyan Methodist Conference*, London 1823

Heber, Reginald, *Narrative of a Journey Through the Upper Provinces of India, 1824–1825 (with Notes upon Ceylon)*, 2 vols, London 1828

Hume, David, *A Treatise of Human Nature: An Attempt to Introduce the Experimental Method of Reasoning into Moral Subjects*, 1738

Johnston, Captain Arthur, *Expedition to Candy*, London 1810

Jones, Sir William, *A Discourse on the Institution of a Society for Enquiring into the History, Civil and Natural, the Antiquities, Arts, Sciences and Literature of Asia. Delivered at Calcutta, 15 January 1784.* London 1784

Kames, Lord, *Elements of Criticism* (1762), 2 vols. 6th edn, Edinburgh 1785

Knighton, William, *Forest-Life in Ceylon*, 2 vols, 1854

——The History of Ceylon from the Earliest Period to the Present Time. With an Appendix, Containing an Account of its Present Condition, London 1845

Knox, Robert, An Account of the Island of Ceylon . . ., London 1681

Laurie, W.F.B., Sketches of Some Distinguished Anglo-Indians. With an Account of Anglo-Indian Periodical Literature, London 1857

——Sketches of Some Distinguished Anglo-Indians (Second Series). Including Lord Macaulay's 'Great Minute on Education in India', with Anglo-Indian Anecdotes and Incidents, London 1888

Liesching, L.F., A Brief Account of Ceylon, Jaffna 1861

Locke, John, An Essay Concerning Human Understanding, ed. A.S. Pringle-Patterson, Oxford 1934

Lord, W.F., Sir Thomas Maitland: The Mastery of the Mediterranean, London 1897

Lyttleton, Lt. William, A Set of Views in the Island of Ceylon, London 1819

Mackintosh, R.J. (ed.), Memoirs of the Life of the Rt. Honourable Sir James Mackintosh, 2 vols, London 1835

MacVicar, John Gibson, On the Beautiful, the Picturesque, the Sublime, London 1837

Marshall, Henry, Ceylon: A General Description of the Island and its Inhabitants, London 1846; reprinted Dehiwela 1969

Mill, James, The History of British India, 3 vols, London 1817

——The Oriental Annual, or, Scenes in India. Comprising Twenty-five Engravings from Original Drawings by William Daniell, RA, and a Descriptive Account by the Rev. Hobart Caunter, BD, London 1834

Parks, Fanny, The Wanderings of a Pilgrim in Search of the Picturesque during Four-and-Twenty Years in the East (1850), reprinted Lahore 1975

Percival, Robert, An Account of the Island of Ceylon, London 1803, 1805; reprinted Dehiwela 1975

Philalethes, The History of Ceylon from the Earliest Period to the Year MDCCCXV. With Characteristic Details of the Religion, Laws, and Manners of the People and a Collection of their Moral Maxims and Ancient Proverbs. To which is subjoined Robert Knox's 'Historical Relation', London 1817

Price, Sir Uvedale, An Essay on the Picturesque, as Compared with the Sublime, and the Beautiful; and on the Use of Studying Pictures, for the Purpose of Improving Real Landscape, London 1794

Purchas, Samuel, Purchas His Pilgrimage, or Relations of the World and the Religions Observed in All Ages and Places Discovered, from the Creation unto This Present. In Foure Partes, London 1613

Roe, Thomas, The Embassy of Sir Thomas Roe to the Court of the Great Mogul 1615–1619 (London 1899), ed. William Foster, Delhi 1990

Skinner, Thomas, Fifty Years in Ceylon: An Autobiography, ed. Annie Skinner (London 1891); containing Major Skinner's 'Memorandum with reference to the Past and Present Social Condition of the Native Population of Ceylon . . . referred to in . . . Evidence, before a Select Committee of the House of Commons', July 1849, pp. 214–36

Southey, Robert (with illustrations by Thomas Rowlandson), Mr Rowlandson's England (1807), ed. John Steel, Woodbridge 1985

Tennent, Sir James Emerson, Ceylon. An Account of the Island Physical, Historical and Topographical, with Notices of its Natural History, Antiquities, and Productions. Illustrated by Maps, Plans and Drawings, 2 vols, London 1859

Turnour, George, An Epitome of the History of Ceylon. Compiled from Native Annals; and the First Twenty Chapters of the 'Mahawanso', Translated by the Hon. George Turnour, Esq., Cotta 1836

Valentia, G., *Voyages and Travels to India, Ceylon, the Red Sea, Abyssinia & Egypt in the Years 1802, 1803, 1804, 1805 & 1806*. 3 vols, London 1809

Secondary Materials

Bibliographical Works

Goonetileke, H.A.I., *A Bibliography of Ceylon. A Systematic Guide to the Literature on the Land, People, History and Culture published in the Western Languages from the Sixteenth Century to the Present Day*, Zug, Switzerland 1970–

Histories

Arasaratnam, S., *Ceylon*, New Jersey 1964

Carrington, C.E., *The British Overseas: Exploits of a Nation of Shopkeepers*, Cambridge 1950

Codrington, H.W., *A Short History of Ceylon*, rev. edn, London 1947

de Silva, K.M., *A History of Sri Lanka*, Oxford 1981

Dewaraja, L., *The Kandyan Kingdom of Sri Lanka, 1707–1782*, Colombo 1972, 1988

Durand Appuhamy, M.A., *The Kandyans' Last Stand against the British*, Colombo 1995

Gooneratne, B., *From Governor's Residence to President's House. Being an Account of the Building Formerly Known as 'Queen's House', Colombo, and of Some of the Personalities Associated with It*, Colombo 1981

——'*The Epic Struggle of the Kingdom of Kandy and its Relevance to Modern Indo-Sri Lankan relations'. The 1990 Sally Sage and David McAlpin Lecture*, London 1995

Halevy, Elie, *A History of the English People in the Nineteenth Century* (1924), 6 vols, London 1961

Hulugalle, H.A.J., *British Governers of Ceylon*, Colombo 1963

——*Ceylon of the Early Travellers*. Colombo 1965, 1969

Kannangara, P.D., *The History of the Ceylon Civil Service 1802–1833: A Study of Administrative Change in Ceylon*, Colombo 1966

Ludowyk, E.F.C., *The Modern History of Ceylon*, Colombo 1966

——*The Story of Ceylon*, London 1962

Mendis, G.C., *Ceylon Under the British*, 3rd edn, Colombo 1952

Pieris, Sir Paul E., *Sinhale and the Patriots 1815–1818*, Colombo 1950

——*Tri-Sinhala: The Last Phase 1796–1815*, Colombo 1939

Powell, G., *The Kandyan Wars: The British Army in Ceylon 1803–1818*, London 1973

Vimalananda, Tennekoon, *The Great Rebellion of 1818: The Story of the First War of Independence and Betrayal of the Nation*, Gunasena Historical Series, vol. V, part I, Colombo 1970

——(ed.), *The British Intrigue in the Kingdom of Ceylon*, Colombo 1973

——(ed.), *Sri Wickrema, Brownrigg and Ehelepola. Being letters addressed to the Home Government from 1811–1815 by Major General John Wilson and Lieut. General Robert Brownrigg, Governor of Ceylon*, Colombo 1984

Principal Journals and Newspapers Consulted

Asiatic Researches

Bulletin of the History of Medicine

Ceylon Daily News

Ceylon Government Gazette

Ceylon Literary Register

Ceylon News

Hemisphere

Island

Island International

Journal of Commonwealth Literature

Journal of the Royal Asiatic Society (Ceylon Branch) (JRASCB)

The Oriental Annual

Rubicon

Sensibilities

The Sinhalese Friend

South Asia

Sri Lanka News

Sunday Island

Sunday Observer

Sunday Observer Magazine

Sunday Times

Sydney Morning Herald

Times of Ceylon Annual

Weekend

Westerly

Modern Secondary Works

AA Illustrated Guide to Britain, London 1971

Rajpal Abeynayake, '"Gajaman Tales" Survive the Translation', in *Sunday Observer*, 9 February 1992

Abrams, M.H., *A Glossary of Literary Terms* (1993), 6th edn, New York 1985

Appuhamy, Durand, 'The Crown must bow', *Sunday Leader,* 11 January 1998

Autobiography of a Periya Durai (n.d.) quoted by J.P. Lewis, in *Tombstones and Monuments*, 1913, p. 295

Ayling, Stanley, *A Portrait of Sheridan*, London 1985

Ballhatchet, Kenneth, *Race, Sex and Class under the Raj: Imperial Attitudes and Politics and their Critics*, London 1980

——*Social Policy and Social Change in Western India 1817–1830,* London 1957

Bax, B. Anthony, *The English Parsonage*, London 1964

Beach, Milo Cleveland and Koch, Ebba (eds), *King of the World: The Padshahnama. An Imperial Mughal Manuscript from the Royal Library, Windsor Castle. With New Translations by Wheeler Thackston*, Washington 1997

Bearce, G.D., *British Attitudes Towards India, 1784–1858*, London, 1961

Bence-Jones, M., *Clive of India*, London 1974

Benterrak, K., Muecke, Stephen, Roe, and Roe, Paddy, *Reading the Country: Introduction to Nomadology*, Fremantle Arts Centre Press 1984

Berry, Chris, 'Dead or Alive: Reflections on Translating Non-Western Literature', in W. Ommundsen and M. Boreland (eds), *Refractions: Asian/Australian Writing* (special issue), *Rubicon* 1/2 (May 1995), pp. 3–6

Beveridge, Lord, *India Called Them*, London 1947

Bodelsen, C.A., *Studies in Mid-Victorian Imperialism*, Kjoberhavn 1924

Boyle, Richard, 'Of Pearls and Pearl Fisheries', in 3 parts, *Sunday Times*, 11, 18, 25 May 1997

Broadus, Edmund K., *The Laureateship*, Oxford 1921

Brougham, Lord, *Historical Sketches of Statesmen who Flourished in the Time of George III*, 2 vols, London 1839

Brown, C.K. Francis, *A History of the English Clergy 1800–1900*, London 1953

Brown, Ford K., *Fathers of the Victorians*, Cambridge 1961

Brown, Hilton (ed), *The Sahibs*, London 1948

Coleman, Deirdre, 'Conspicuous Consumption: White Abolitionism and English Women's Protest Writing in the 1790s'. Unpublished conference paper

Conrad, Joseph, *Youth*, 1902

Coomaraswamy, Ananda, *Christian and Oriental Philosophy of Art*, New York 1956

Coward, Noel, *The Cream of Noel Coward*, ed. Michael Cox, London 1996

Cruse, Amy *The Englishman and his Books in the Early Nineteenth Century*, London 1930

Daniel, Mohan, 'Ode to Ola', *Sunday Times,* 3 September 1995, p. 10

Dassanayake, M.B., 'When the Kandyan Convention was Signed', *Ceylon Daily News,* 28 February 1987

——'The Day 2539 Years of Freedom Ended', *Weekend,* 1 March 1987

Davies, R.G., 'Leonard Woolf: The Making of a Feminist'. Thesis presented to the University of Western Australia for a Master of Arts degree in History, February 1996

de Alwis, Lt.-Col. A.A., 'Island Exile', *Sunday Observer Magazine,* 13 August 1995, p. 21

——'The Secret Pass of One Thousand Steps: How the British Forces Entered the Kandyan Kingdom'. *Sunday Observer,* 1 June 1997, p. 47

de Silva, Lakshmi, 'Cornelia Perumal (Gajaman Nona): Her Life and Writings'. Unpublished essay, 1997

de Silva, R.K., *Early Prints of Ceylon 1800–1900,* London 1985

de Soysa, G.H., '"Queen of Candy" – Painted in Colombo!', *Ceylon Daily News,* 26 January 1983

Denwood, Philip, 'Introduction', in Brian Houghton Hodgson: *Essays on the Languages, Literature and Religion of Nepal and Tibet,* New Delhi 1972

Devy, G.N., *After Amnesia: Tradition and Change in Indian Literary Criticism,* Orient Longman, 1992

Dictionary of National Biography, entries on William, Thomas and Samuel Daniell; John Hobart Caunter

Dissanayaka, J.B., 'The Romantic Life of a Beautiful Poetess', *Island,* 25 February 1992

Drabble, Margaret, *A Writer's Britain: Landscape in Literature,* London 1979

Edirisinghe, Padma, 'Was it Imperialist Hauteur at its Worst?', *Sunday Observer,* 9 July 1995, p. 48

——'The Missing Chapter in Kandyan History', *Sunday Observer,* 15 June 1997, p. 36

Ellis, Royston, 'Buried History', *Sunday Times,* 24 April 1994, p. 13

Fanon, Frantz, *The Wretched of the Earth,* 1965

Fernando, Vijitha, 'A Delightful Translation', *Ceylon Daily News,* February 1992

Fitzherbert, M., 'A Parti-Coloured Pedigree', review of Barbara Strachey, *The Strachey Line: An English Family in America, India and at Home from 1570–1902* (1986), *Times Literary Supplement,* 7 February 1986, p. 135

Fitzpatrick, David, Macquarie University essay, 1994

Fletcher, Brian H., 'The Prince Regent and the World of Jane Austen', *Sensibilities* 12 (June 1996), pp. 14–30

Forster, E.M., *A Passage to India* (1924), Harmondsworth 1960.

Fullerton, Ian, 'Trade, Finance and Tax in Jane Austen's Time', *Sensibilities* 12 (June 1996), pp. 31–44

Gathorne-Hardy, Jonathan, *The Public School Phenomenon,* London 1977

Godakumbure, C.E., *The Literature of Ceylon,* 1963

Gooneratne, Brendon, 'Elephants for Want of Towns', *Hemisphere* 17/3 (March 1973), pp. 34–39

——*The Epic Struggle of the Kingdom of Kandy and its Relevance to Modern Indo-Sri Lankan Relations,* London 1995

Gooneratne, Yasmine, *English Literature in Ceylon 1815–1878,* Dehiwela 1968

——'Introduction', in John Davy, *An Account of the Interior of Ceylon* (1821), reprinted Colombo 1969, pp. v–xv

——'Historical "Truths" and Literary "Fictions": Some Alternative and Interacting Viewpoints in English and Commonwealth Literature Studies'. Paper delivered at the Triennial Conference of the International Association of University Professors of English, University of York, September 1986

——'Australia and her Postcolonial World', *Australian–Canadian Studies* 10/2 (1992), pp. 118–26

——'Misreadings', *24 Hours*, November 1992, pp. 60–4

——'Desire, Death and the Jewels of the Orient: Rear-Admiral Charles Austen and Sir John D'Oyly, Baronet', *Sensibilities* 12 (June 1996), pp. 1–13

Goonetilleke, D.C.R.A., 'Forgotten Nineteenth-Century Fiction: William Arnold's *Oakfield* and William Knighton's *Forest Life in Ceylon*', *Journal of Commonwealth Literature* 7/1 (June 1972), pp. 14–21

Hettigoda, Arthur, 'Fall of Kandy as a London Timesman saw it', *Sri Lanka News*, 28 November 1985

Greenberger, A.J., *The British Image of India: A Study in the Literature of Imperialism 1880–1960*, Oxford 1969

Gunawardena, Dayananda, *The Gajaman Story (Gajaman Puwatha)*, trans. Lakshmi de Silva, 1991

Harris, Elizabeth J., *The Gaze of the Coloniser: British views on Local Women in 19th Century Sri Lanka*, Social Scientists Association, Colombo, 1994 (illustrated)

Hopkins, Kenneth, *The Poets Laureate*, London 1954

Houghton, Walter E., *The Victorian Frame of Mind*, 1830–1870, London 1957

Hudson, Roger, *The Grand Tour 1592–1796*, London 1993

Hulugalle, H.A.J., *British Governors of Ceylon*, Colombo 1963

Hyam, Ronald, *Empire and Sexuality: The British Experience* (1990), Manchester 1992

James, Lawrence, *The Rise and Fall of the British Empire*, London 1994

Jayasuriya, Wilfrid, 'The Ratnapura Diaries' (4 pp.). A research paper, part of a larger work later published. In his research paper Dr Jayasuriya presents material from the diaries kept by government agents of the Ratnapura District which until the early 1960s were kept in the Record Room of the Ratnapura Kachcheri, and are presently in the Sri Lanka National Archives, Colombo

Jayawardena, Kumari, 'Liberalism and the Women's Movement', in *Feminism in Europe: Liberal and Socialist Strategies 1789–1919*, The Hague 1982

——*Feminism and Nationalism in the Third World* (1986), 2nd edn, Colombo 1986

Jayawardene, Elmo, 'In Search of Ehelepola's Tomb', *Daily News*, 2 April 1994

——Vilbave *alias* Kirti Sri – Was He Our Last Crowned King?', *Daily News*, 24 April 1995

——Ihagama: A Forgotten Hero of Sinhale', *Island*, 26 April 1998

Jennings, Sir William Ivor, *The Kandy Road*, edited and introduced by H.A.I. Goonetileke, University of Peradeniya Library 1993

Johnson, Paul, *The Birth of the Modern: World Society 1815–1830*, 1991

Kappagoda, D.B., 'Gajaman Nona: The Songstress of Ruhuna', *Island* (n.d.)

——'How the Last King of Kandy was Captured', *Monthly Literary Register* (n.d.), extracted in *Sunday Island*, 8 May 1994

Karunaratne, Nihal, *From Governor's Pavilion to President's Pavilion*, Dept. of National Archives, Sri Lanka n.d.

Kehelpannala, T.B. Pohath, *Life of Ehelepola*, quoted in A.A. de Alwis 'Island Exile', *Sunday Observer Magazine*, 13 August 1995, p. 21

Kelegama, J.B., 'The Last Days of the Sinhala Kingdom and the Kandyan Convention of 1815', *Sunday Observer*, 25 January 1998

Kincaid, D., *British Social Life in India 1608–1937*, 2nd edn, London 1973

Kitson Clark, G., *The English Inheritance*, London 1950

Krishnamoorthy, P.V., 'Unfolding Vellore', *Sunday Times*, 3 September 1995

Lasz, Wilfred, 'John D'Oyly 1815: From Suave Civil Servant to Sinhala Recluse', *The Island*, 3 September 1995, p. 2

Lewes Town Guide, Lewes Chamber of Commerce, 1984

Lewis, J.P., *List of Inscriptions on Tombstones and Monuments in Ceylon of Historical and Local Interest with an Obituary of Persons Uncommemorated*, Colombo 1913

Longley, K.O., 'Fabricating Otherness: Demidenko and Exoticism', *Westerly* 42/1 (Autumn 1997), pp. 29–45

Lord, John, *The Maharajas*, London, 1972

Lowell, A.L., *Colonial Civil Service: The Selection and Training of Colonial Officials in England, Holland and France. With an Account of the East India College at Haileybury (1806–1857) by H. Morse Stephens*, New York 1900

Ludowyk, E.F.C. (ed.), *Robert Knox in the Kandyan Kingdom*, London 1948

——'The Eighteenth Century Background of Some Early English Writers on Ceylon', *Ceylon Historical Journal* 3/3 and 3/4 (January and April 1954), pp. 268–74

——*The Footprint of the Buddha*, London 1958

Machiavelli, Niccolo, *The Prince* (1513), trans. Luigi Ricci, Oxford 1961

Mack E.C., *Public Schools and British Opinion, 1780–1860*, London 1938

McGowan, William, *Only Man is Vile: The Tragedy of Sri Lanka*, New York 1992

Mahaarachchi, Leonard R., 'When we Lost our Freedom in 1815', *Sunday Times*, 1 March 1998

Marshall, P.J., 'Lord Macartney, India and China: The Two Faces of the Enlightenment', *South Asia*, 19, special issue (1996), pp. 121–31

Mendis, G.C., *Ceylon under the British*, 3rd edn, Colombo 1952

Mills, Lennox A., *Ceylon under British Rule 1795–1932*, London 1933

Milton, John, *Paradise Lost*. Cf. John Milton, *Paradise Lost, Samson Agonistes, Lycidas*, ed. Edward Le Comte, New York 1981.

Montgomery, J., *Toll for the Brave: The Tragedy of Major-General Sir Hector Macdonald*, London 1963

Morris, James, *The Pax Britannica Trilogy*, 3 vols: I: *Heaven's Command*; II: *Pax Britannica*; III: *Farewell the Trumpets*, London 1992

Muller, Carl, 'Reopening of Kandy's Garrison Cemetery', *Sunday Times*, 4 October 1998

Nanayakkara, S.M., 'Martyrdom of Keppetipola and Madugalle: Heroes of the 1817–1818 Uva Rebellion', *Sunday Observer*, 27 March 1994

Nanayakkara, Vesak, *A Return to Kandy*, Colombo, 1971

O'Brien, Geraldine, 'Collars of Colonialism', *Sydney Morning Herald Good Weekend*, 22 May 1993

Oliver, Roger W., *Dreams of Passion: The Theater of Luigi Pirandello*, New York 1979

Panawatte, Senarath, 'The Medamahanuwara Episode and its Aftermath', *Sunday Observer*, 2 July 1995, p. 48

Parsons, Nicholas T., *The Joy of Bad Verse*, Cambridge 1988

Pieris, Anoma, 'Gender, Representation and Photography', *Pravada* 3, 8, 9 (November/December 1994), pp. 29–35

Pieris, Sir Paul E. (ed.), *Letters to Ceylon 1814–1824. Being Correspondence Addressed to Sir John D'Oyly*, Cambridge 1938

Pieris, Ralph, *Sinhalese Social Organization: The Kandyan Period*, Colombo 1956

Piggin, Stuart, *Making Evangelical Missionaries 1789–1858*, Sutton Courtenay 1984

Pool, Daniel, *What Jane Austen Ate and Charles Dickens Knew: From Fox-Hunting to Whist – The Facts of Daily Life in 19th-Century England*, New York 1993

Punchihewa, Gamini G., 'Place Names of Gajaman Nona', *Ceylon News*, 9 March 1978

Ratnasinghe, Ariyadasa, 'Destiny of Lanka's Last King', *Sri Lanka News*, 2 February 1984

——'Tyranny Held Sway under Last King of Kandy', *Island,* 9 December 1984

——'Exploring the Gamut of Ayurvedic Cures', *Sunday Observer*, 1 March 1992, p. 39

Raven-Hart, Rowland (trans.), *Heydt's Ceylon. Being the Relevant Sections of the 'Allerneuester Geographisch- und Topographischer Schau-Platz von Africa und Ost-Indien etc. etc.'*, Colombo 1952, pp. 14–15

——*Ceylon: A History in Stone*, 2nd edn, Colombo 1973

——*The Dutch Wars with Kandy, 1746–1766*, Colombo 1966

Reynolds, Christopher, 'British Orientalists and Ceylon', *Ceylon Daily News*, 5 December 1961

'The Riddle of "The Queen of Candy"', unsigned article in *Ceylon Daily News,* 5 January 1983, announcing a symposium on the theme 'Portrait of a Queen' to be held at the Sri Lanka Foundation Institute on Saturday 8 January 1983

Rocher, Rosanne, *Orientalism, Poetry and the Millennium: The Checkered Life of Nathaniel Brassey-Halhed, 1751–1830*, Delhi 1983

Ross, Richard S., 'John Davy', *Bulletin of the History of Medicine* 27/2, (March–April 1953)

Royle, T., *Death Before Dishonour: The True Story of 'Fighting Mac'*, London 1982

Russell, Jane, 'Keeping an Even Keel in Ideologically Choppy Waters', review of Elizabeth J. Harris, *The Gaze of the Coloniser: British Views on Local Women in 19th Century Sri Lanka* (1994), *Sunday Observer,* 29 January 1995, p. 11

Rutnam, James T., 'Kandy Queen's Picture Starts a Debate', *Ceylon Daily News,* 16 February 1982

Ryan, Bryce, *Caste in Modern Ceylon: The Sinhalese System in Transition*, New Brunswick 1953

Said, Edward, *Orientalism*, London 1978

——*The World, the Text and the Critic*, Cambridge, Mass. 1983

——*Culture and Imperialism*, Harmondsworth 1992

Samarajiwa, Carlton, 'Lord Leuke in Sinhala Folk Poetry', *Island*, 11 January 1998

Samat, T.M.G., 'Gajaman Nona: The Well Known Poetess', *Ceylon Daily News*, 6 November 1975

Senaratne, L.B., 'Were the Signatures Forged?' *Island International*, 11 March 1992, p. 7

Seneviratne, Maureen, 'Memorial to an Eccentric Englishman', *Sunday Times*, 23 May 1993

Shelley, Percy Bysshe, *The Complete Works of Percy Bysshe Shelley*, ed. Thomas Hutchinson, Oxford 1917

Shellim, Maurice, *Patchwork to the Great Pagoda: India and British Painters*, Calcutta 1973

Singh, Khushwant, *Delhi*, New Delhi 1989

The Sinhalese Friend 1/10 (Sinhala Mithraya) (March 1913)

Sitwell, Edith, *English Eccentrics*, 1933, 1994

Spence, Keith, *The Companion Guide to Kent and Sussex*, London 1973

Srivastava, Sanjay, 'The Management of Water: Modernity, Technocracy and the Citizen at the Doon School', *South Asia* (n.s.) 16/2 (December 1993), pp. 57–88

Stokes, Eric, *The Political Ideas of English Imperialism*, London 1960

Suraweera, Stanley, 'Who Painted Her?', *Ceylon News*, 15 June 1978

——'The Painter and the Queen: Who painted her?', *Ceylon News* , 22 June 1978

Sweetman, John, *The Oriental Obsession: Islamic Inspiration in British and American Art and Architecture 1500–1920*, Cambridge 1988

Tambiah, H.W., *Sinhala Laws and Customs*, Colombo 1968

Tennent, J.E., 'Notes and Drawings of Ceylon', a manuscript compiled in preparation for writing *Ceylon* (1859), Gooneratne Collection

Thomas, R.S., *Selected Poems 1946–1968*, London 1973

'Valli', 'Gajaman Nona', *Times of Ceylon Annual 1962*

Vimalananda, Tennekoon, 'The Kandyan Convention: Its significance', *Ceylon Daily News*, 2 March 1972; part II: 'D'Oyly, the Crown's Crafty Agent'; Part III: 'Last Days of the Kingdom'

Vyas, Ravi, 'Between Lies and Silences', *Hindu Magazine Literary Review*, Sunday 2 February 1997, p. ix

'Wayfarer', '1815 and the "D'Oyly Aristocrats"', *Times of Ceylon*, 2 March 1965

Weeks, David, and James, Jamie, *Eccentrics*, 1995

Welch, Stuart Cary, *Room for Wonder: Indian Painting during the British Period 1760–1880*, New York 1978

——*India: Art and Culture 1300–1900*, New York 1985

White, R.J., *Life in Regency England*, London 1963

Wickremasinghe, G.T., 'The King Observes Table Manners', *Island*, 27 December 1981

Wijetilaka, Henry, 'Nightingale of Sri Lanka', *Ceylon News*, 30 January 1975

Willan, Anne, *Great Cooks and their Recipes: From Taillevent to Escoffier*, Harmondsworth, 1993

Wimalaratne, K.D.G., 'Gajaman Nona: The Celebrated Poetess', *Ceylon Daily News*, 15 December 1978

——'Did D'Oyly Grant Land to Gajaman Nona?' *Sunday Observer*, 4 December 1983

——'The Day the Last Stronghold Fell: Historic Flashback to March 2 1815', newspaper article, date and source not known

Woolf, Leonard, *Diaries in Ceylon 1908–1911*, *Ceylon Historical Journal* 9/1–4 (July 1959–April 1960)

——*Stories from the East: Three Short Stories on Ceylon*, *Ceylon Historical Journal*, 9/1–4 (July 1959–April 1960)

——*Growing: An Autobiography of the Years 1904–1911*, London 1961

——*Diaries in Ceylon 1908–1911: Records of a Colonial Administrator*, Colombo 1962

——*The Village in the Jungle*, Edward Arnold 1981

——*Letters of Leonard Woolf*, ed. Frederic Spotts, New York 1992

Woolf, Virginia, 'Walter Sickert: A Conversation (1934), new edn, introduced by Richard Shone, London 1992

Worswick, Clark (ed.), *Princely India: Photographs by Raja Deen Dayal 1884–1910*, New York 1980

Wright, Arnold (ed.), *Twentieth Century Impressions of Ceylon: Its History, People, Commerce, Industries and Resources*, London 1907

Young, G.M., (ed.) *Early Victorian England 1830–1865*, 2 vols, London 1951

INDEX

Abhayagunewardena, Don
Janchi Samarajeeva
82–3
Act of Settlement of 1815
see Kandyan
Convention
'Adam's Peak' (Sri Pada)
87, 164, 186, 231
Ainslie, Robert 33, 61–2,
77, 194
Allan, Major A. 38–9
Allen, Baugh 33, 61–2, 194
Andrasy, Count Emanuel
100; see also Ch.5,
n.47
Aravidu, royal house of 114
Asiatic Journal 54, 158–9
Asiatic Society of Bengal
36
Austen, Rear-Admiral
Charles 216
Austen, Jane see Ch.1, n.12,
Ch.6, n.38
Austin, Alfred 28

Baker, Sir Samuel 226
Ballhatchet, Kenneth 76
Barbut, Lieutenant-Colonel
62, 70
Barbut, Mrs 62–3
Barnes, Sir Edward 13, 54,
156–7, 190, 197,
201, 207–15; see also
Ch.5, n.21
Barnes, Lady 156, 207
Barry, Robert 49, 72
Bathurst, Lord 110–11,
188, 208–9
'Bayley' 33
Bellin, M. 79–80
Bene't (Corpus Christi)
College, Cambridge
25–6, 37
Benstead's at Cambridge
77
Berry, Chris 161
Bertolacci, Anthony 49
Blake, William 228
Boswell, James 17, 20, 141
Boyd, Hugh 78
Boyle, Richard 49

British
attitudes to the 'exotic'
40–7, 76–7, 91–2,
111–12, 225–6; see
also Ch.5, n.29
Colonial Civil Service 2,
6–8, 11, 17, 37–9,
42, 50, 155, 161,
164, 224, 226–7,
231; see also Ch.5,
n.24
Colonial Office 8, 70,
208, 231
(English) East India
Company 11, 25,
30, 34–8, 163; see
also Ch.1, n.13
'gentleman', ideal of the
41–2, 48
Houses of Parliament
35–6, 111
in Asia 2, 6, 8, 10, 30, 35,
40, 50–1, 56–8,
60–4, 76–7, 91–3,
111–12, 137, 152–7,
186–7, 189–90, 203,
215–19, 223–5; see
also Ch.7, n.18,
Ch.12, nn.10, 13, 15,
16
laws 162–3, 169–70
missionaries 9, 13, 42,
50, 84, 151–2, 160,
186–7, 203
Museum 38
'nabobs' 30, 35, 60
Poets Laureate 27–9
society of Colombo
47–8, 62, 71–2
sportsmen 81, 100
'West India merchants'
30
Brownrigg, Governor
Robert 3, 8, 13–14,
17, 51, 54, 105–12,
120–7, 133–41, 144,
146–53, 156–7,
162–3, 166, 171–2,
174, 180, 183–6,
188, 190, 192, 197,
202, 205, 215, 224

Brownrigg, Lady 51, 121,
133, 156, 171–2,
183, 185, 190
Buddhism 5, 11, 13, 74,
84–5, 112–14,
119–20, 143, 151,
160, 166, 169,
176–7, 182–3, 186,
202–3, 222–3, 225;
see also Ch.10, n.22
Burgoyne, John
('Gentleman
Johnny') 35
Burke, Edmund 35, 147,
153, 228
Burke, *Extinct and Dormant
Baronetcies of
England, Ireland and
Scotland* 1, 234–5
Burmese court 116–17
Buxted (Sussex) 6, 25, 28,
98, 187, 192–3
Byron, Lord 27–8, 60

'Caffre' soldiers 105
Calladine, Colour-Sergeant
George 4, 42,
132–3, 135, 178–82;
see also Ch.7, n.12,
Ch.10, n.11
Campbell, James 42
Caunter, Rev. Hobart 3,
139–42; see also
Ch.7, nn.20, 21, 25
Ceylon (Sri Lanka)
British administration in
14, 34–5, 41, 49–51,
200
British–Ceylonese
relation in 2, 10–11,
48, 63, 91–2, 100–1,
169, 200–2, 223
British in 2, 21, 38, 221,
225
Burghers 47
Central Province of 113,
159–60, 163–4
Civil Service 2, 7, 10,
20–1, 39, 42, 48–51,
64, 78, 93, 133, 146,
155, 161, 163–4,
187, 195, 200, 203,
205, 219, 221, 227–8
Crown Colony of 7, 10,
38, 47–8, 86

289